RETURN OF THE GOLDEN AGE

"Ed Malkowski's previous books show evidence of Civilization X in a well-researched, enlightening, and entertaining way. In *Return of the Golden Age* he takes readers from the present to pre-cataclysmic times and the Golden Age that existed with Civilization X. He then brings us back to the upcoming Golden Age. A truly wonderful read!"

BRUCE CUNNINGHAM, DIRECTOR OF
ANCIENT MYSTERIES INTERNATIONAL, LLC

RETURN OF THE
GOLDEN AGE

Ancient History and the
Key to Our Collective Future

Edward F. Malkowski

Inner Traditions
Rochester, Vermont • Toronto, Canada

Inner Traditions
One Park Street
Rochester, Vermont 05767
www.InnerTraditions.com

Library of Congress Cataloging-in-Publication Data

Malkowski, Edward F.
  Return of the golden age : ancient history and the key to our collective future /
Edward F. Malkowski.
     pages cm
  Summary: "The truth behind ancient myths and the return of the celestial
conditions for a Golden Age of peace and abundance"—Provided by publisher.
  Includes bibliographical references and index.
  ISBN 978-1-62055-197-4 (paperback) — ISBN 978-1-62055-198-1 (e-book)
  1. Golden age (Mythology) 2. Civilization, Ancient. 3. Civilization, Western—
Forecasting. 4. Social change. I. Title.
  BL325.G55M35 2013
  200.9—dc23

                                                                    2013018293

Printed and bound in the United States by McNaughton and Gunn

10 9 8 7 6 5 4 3 2 1

Text design by Brian Boynton and layout by Priscilla Baker
This book was typeset in Garamond Premier Pro with Trajan Pro and Legacy Sans
used as display typefaces

To send correspondence to the author of this book, mail a first-class letter to the
author c/o Inner Traditions • Bear & Company, One Park Street, Rochester, VT
05767, and we will forward the communication, or contact the author directly at
wiseowl427@gmail.com.

CONTENTS

ACKNOWLEDGMENTS

Many influences over many years have helped form the thesis of this book, including the insights of Graham Hancock, John Anthony West, Robert Schoch, Thomas Brophy, Christopher Dunn, and John Burke, to whom I am grateful. I extend a very special thank you to Barbara Hand Clow, not only for her critical analysis of an early version of the manuscript, but also for the inspiration she has provided to me in seeing history as a flowing human experience.

PREFACE

Although the political, social, and economic issues of our time are pertinent to this book's thesis, this book is not exclusively about those concerns. Neither is this book an investigation into some grand conspiracy of the power elite to control nations and the world, although what appears to be a conspiracy is also addressed.

This book is about the human species and the experience of being human during the past twelve thousand years. The discussion includes why we exist as we do somewhere between the realms of the objective and the subjective, why we believe the things we do, and why we behave the way we do as social groups, with our need to control and dominate resources and people. This book addresses where we've been as a species and where we are going, tying our mythical past to today's events and a future Golden Age of humanity.

FOREWORD

Barbara Hand Clow

As we move into the early stages of a Golden Age, Ed Malkowski offers this wonderful book that integrates today's life with our mythical past. He has a vision of our coming great future, a message based on sound values and profound intelligence. In my 2011 book, *Awakening the Planetary Mind,* I suggest we were once a very advanced species that regressed during a great cataclysm 11,500 years ago, yet now we are reaching for those ancient attainments again. I believe this is happening because we are recovering skills and abilities that we lost thousands of years ago. Malkowski has already delved into high spiritual levels and advanced stone technology in ancient Egypt. In *Return of the Golden Age,* he explores how what we imagine is possible determines what we create. Co-creation with divine potential was mastered by the ancient Egyptians, and his deep research in Egyptology is probably the reason he so adeptly shows us how we can do it again. Realizing the miracles of the past is important, but what matters more is using that knowledge to create a better world now; that is this book's genius.

Since the 1970s, a new assessment of ancient cultures has been unfolding in humanity's collective mind, especially in Egyptology, and now we are poised at a critical juncture, the *paradigm shift* that has been anticipated. Much evidence has been convincingly presented showing that some ancient cultures were technologically advanced, possibly far beyond or at least more broadly than our own. For conventional archaeologists, anthropologists, and historians, such a suggestion is outrageous blasphemy, so for forty years they have greeted these exciting findings with a cruel silence. Regardless, the public has been deeply considering new paradigm writing. At this point, a brilliant past has become visible because advanced scientific discoveries, such as quantum physics and string theory, make it possible to see what the ancients knew. *We couldn't comprehend their images, languages, and symbols—their mythology—until we approached their level.* Like the icebergs relentlessly melting at the poles, the conspiracy of silence melts away as the sun shines on convincing evidence for cultural advancement long ago. We have crossed the line that blocks the past, and this book envisions future pathways.

During the 1980s and 1990s, I was the copublisher of Bear & Company when I sought the new paradigm researchers. For example, we published Chris Dunn, a veteran machinist and manufacturing expert, who hypothesized that the Great Pyramid of Giza was once a power plant. Many people laughed at Dunn's exposition, which was based on a careful analysis of five-thousand-year-old stones that were cut and polished with machines. When I retired from my job in 2000, thankfully Bear & Company continued to aggressively pursue new paradigm research. Ed Malkowski explored Dunn's findings, and in 2010 he offered new evidence for advanced ancient engineering. He names the culture with this technology *Civilization X,* which goes back more than forty thousand years, and he offers very exciting and convincing evidence for how it all worked and what its purpose might have been. In 2007, Laird Scranton engaged in a deep analysis of Egyptian hieroglyphs and Dogon symbols; he found in them the full range of the scientific components of matter. That is, *quantum physics and string theory were known at least five thousand years ago!*

Putting this all together and adding my own ideas, I've come to the conclusion that Civilization X developed extremely advanced technologies based upon their understanding of quantum physics and string theory as well as other sciences, and that the remnants from five thousand years ago are the legacy from that deep past! Furthermore, in 2005 John Burke and Kaj Halberg discovered how our ancient ancestors used this understanding of physics to improve crop growth. Technically, they used slow-moving electrons to invigorate the seed's immune system. In layman's terms, it is simply the enhancement of the seed's life force. I have spent a lot of time studying megalithic sites wondering why anybody would expend so much effort building them. These authors have found the biological basis of ancient cultures.

Regarding my own writings, I have always known that cultures existing more than twelve thousand years ago were very advanced because that is what I was taught as a child. My grandfather, who was a Cherokee wisdom keeper, told me the story of a great cataclysm 13,000 to 11,500 years ago that caused a regression in human cultures. I researched this sacred legacy deeply because he insisted we are doomed unless we remember our ancient story. Thankfully, as a result of books like this one, we are not doomed. Malkowski and I believe that when enough people realize they are the descendants of an advanced global civilization, they will embrace creativity, peace, and brilliance, our true heritage. We will transform within a short space of time once we remember how to create reality with our *imaginations,* not just with our limited logical brains. During the 1980s and 1990s, I studied in Egypt with my great teacher Abd'El Hakim Awyan of Giza, and he told the same story of the great cataclysm and regression. Fortunately, researcher Steve Mehler has recorded much of Hakim's knowledge and has saved his living keys that unlock the doors to ancient wisdom. Now we are reaching the critical leap as the dots between the findings of the new paradigm writers are being connected; the false story of the ancient world is crumbling. We are discovering the correct timeline for a culture that reaches back *one hundred thousand years*!

The key point of the book you hold in your hands is that it investigates ancient knowledge to see how it informs us about what we are experiencing today. Malkowski was deeply moved by my 2011 book, *Awakening the Planetary Mind,* because it explores how our current state of mind and emotions are deeply affected by the lost past. As my grandfather insisted, our species was multitraumatized during the great cataclysm, and our inability to remember it blocks us from attaining peaceful, scientific, artistic, and happy lives.

Malkowski says, "I cannot help but connect in an experiential way the mythical Golden Age of antiquity to our future in a global civilization." This is absolutely true because the ancient ones thoroughly understood the Earth's powers. They did not *use* Earth as we do today; they worked *with* Earth. Now that the new paradigm movement has demonstrated that the ancient civilization mastered the sciences that we value so highly today, we must gain a grasp of ancient Earth science. We must connect with the planet *experientially* as the ancient ones did. Malkowski notes that the physicist Wallace Thornhill and the comparative mythologist David Talbott have demonstrated that plasma forms found in modern laboratories mysteriously match up with ancient iconography. Also, ancient myths describe plasma discharges, which could not be understood until modern scientists found these odd shapes. Thornhill and Talbott have shown that the ancients understood plasma's effects on the planets, including Earth. And they were quite concerned about it for some reason, which could be critical information for us today: Current solar activity is producing dramatic plasma activity, and scientists are studying how it affects Earth and the whole solar system. As I write this foreword, I wonder if pyramid technology and megalithic structures were built to handle these influences, possibly even to utilize their powers?

As of 2013, the case for ancient advanced technology has been made, and scientists are finally detecting evidence for the Higgs boson, the basis for string theory. Surely, only a fool (or a dying civilization) would ignore what the ancients already knew? Will orthodoxy say "so what"? We need the ancient wisdom to survive now. Malkowski not only believes the same, he also thinks we must seek their spiritual direction. Judging by the quality of the world we live in today, we should take this idea seriously. This book is the ideal tool because Malkowski shows that we are living a virtual existence by the power of our imaginations, but we don't realize it, so we're creating madness and mayhem. What happens to us and what we create comes out of what we imagine. The discovery that we were once very advanced, living lives that were totally different from the current lives, unleashes the powers of our imaginations. Once we come to terms with our past, we will easily bring back a Golden Age of humanity, what I call the *golden world,* an ever-present field *in potentia* in which we are in total symbiosis with nature. All we need to do is intentionally precipitate it into our everyday lives. We have the knowledge and technology to do so.

The finest things about *Return of the Golden Age* are its comprehensiveness and its relevance to people of all ages. Ed Malkowski is much younger than me, and I really like the way this book is user-friendly for the "forty-somethings," the ones who are carrying such a heavy weight in the world right now. I like his idea that we all exist somewhere between the objective and subjective, and amazingly he looks at both of those ways from many points of view. He wanders blithely through ancient myth, such as my favorite Sumerian story of Enkidu and Gilgamesh, and he begins the book by wondering if the over-determined date of 2012 is actually George Orwell's 1984. Malkowski's entertaining mental turnings are wonderful examples of how knowledgeable we all can be if we take seriously humanity's changing existence over long spans of time. It is time to wake up and remember the golden world.

BARBARA HAND CLOW is an internationally acclaimed ceremonial teacher, author, and Mayan Calendar researcher. Her numerous books include *The Pleiadian Agenda, Alchemy of Nine Dimensions, Awakening the Planetary Mind, Astrology and the Rising of Kundalini,* and *The Mayan Code.* She has taught at sacred sites throughout the world and maintains an astrological website, www.HandClow2012.com

INTRODUCTION

Piecing together human history is a difficult passion. Piecing together the *experience* of human history as our ancestors lived it, and as we live it today, is an even more difficult passion. Documented history goes back approximately five thousand years. No written records exist before that time, at least of which historians are aware. Consequently, trying to piece together the earliest of human experiences is a challenge.

The earliest records of human history are stories told as myth. The ancient Greeks and Romans spoke of their gods, and before them, the ancient Egyptians told the story of their first god in the death and resurrection of Osiris. The mysterious Sumerians of Mesopotamia compiled lists of gods and planets. From the Americas to the Far East, every ancient culture passed down myths from generation to generation. Cultures across the world, it seems, experienced a similar chain of events during the same general time period. Trying to make sense of these myths is like reading an alien language that is yet to be deciphered. The "gods" consorted in a pantheon and lived in the sky. They were planets, stars, and star constellations. It makes no sense to us that there were "gods of the sky" carrying out a drama. At least, not the sky we are accustomed to seeing.

So why did our ancient ancestors tell these mythical stories? Were myths symbolic of real events? Or were the stories created in an attempt to explain life? Or, perhaps, both?

Whatever the case may be, myth was the first recorded human experience, and whatever the ancients experienced must have been phenomenal, considering that they inspired such incredible stories. More important—and here we come to the subject matter of this book—does the way they experienced the world so long ago have anything to do with the way we experience it today?

I am convinced that it does and that myths have played a role in society since the beginning of human civilization. Not on a conscious level, but by providing an emotional foundation and a state of mind that have been passed along to succeeding generations for the last twelve thousand years in every culture and every nation.

According to the evidence, human life as we know it—the anatomically modern human—began more than one hundred thousand years ago in South Africa, spread northward throughout Africa and then east along the Indian subcontinent to Australia, then advanced into Europe, Asia, and finally the Americas. All the while, humans hunted animals and gathered any plants, fruits, and nuts they could find. Only in the last ten thousand years did humans invent agriculture and domesticate animals in order to provide for their sustenance.

Despite the evidence, this prehistoric movement of human cultures defies common sense. Why would anyone move into a harsher, colder climate, as some of the evidence suggests? Perhaps the prehistoric climate of Earth was very different in ancient times. Let's consider the magnificent ruins of a sophisticated civilization in Africa's Nile Valley. Since modern interest in Egypt began more than two hundred year ago, explorers and tourists have been drawn to the region's incredible megalithic monuments, temples, and pyramids, particularly the pyramids of Giza; they are majestic and a sight to behold. And since the first scientific investigation of these phenomena in the late 1880s by William Flinders Petrie, they have remained an enigma, a next to insolvable mystery. Such fine work was performed in their design and construction that the imagination runs wild trying to solve the riddle of not only why they were built, but when they were built. Today, even our most skilled of construction companies would have a difficult time building the pyramids of Giza. So, how did they build them and why did they do so?

A project on such a massive scale as the three pyramids of Giza could never have been accomplished with simple copper chisels and stone hammers. Unfortunately, myth is all we have to rely on as history from the period in which Giza's pyramids were supposedly built. Such a wide discrepancy between technical skills and communication skills conjures the notion that we don't know the entire story of human history and also suggests that the human species must have reached a level of sophistication long before the birth of civilization in 3000 BCE. So why is it that the first story ever told is about the "death of the gods"? Add to that the fact that the ancient Egyptians, in two different sources, tell of a time on Earth when "the gods ruled."

Perhaps we are missing something significant within the grand and cumulative human experience. Myths across the world also speak of a Golden Age when human beings prospered and lived in peace. Could the pyramids of Giza possibly belong to a mythical Golden Age civilization in existence long before our history of civilization began? In my previous book, *Ancient Egypt 39,000 BCE: The History, Technology, and Philosophy of Civilization X,* I came to that conclusion. I also observed that history, technology, and philosophy are highly intertwined and must be understood as a single subject in order to paint a more accurate picture of the human experience.

Taking this broader view of the human experience will, I believe, shed light on many of the problems we face today as a global civilization. Perhaps understanding history in a more experiential way will help solve some, if not all, of those problems we face: hate, violence, hunger, and disease. Throughout our history these byproducts of human existence have always led to a struggle for resources and, in the end, death and destruction on a massive scale through war.

In 1987, a few years before the Soviet Union disbanded, Soviet President Mikhail Gorbachev stated in his book *Perestroika: New Thinking for Our Country and the World* that he envisioned for the future "a 'Golden Age' which would benefit the USSR and the USA, all countries, and the whole world community."[1] It was an important moment in world history.

The great divide between East and West was closing, and as one must sense, Gorbachev understood that the world was soon going to change in a profound way. Not long after Gorbachev announced the prospects of a Golden Age, the iron curtain separating East and West came crashing down. A few years later, as the hostilities in the first Gulf War came to a close, President George H. W. Bush announced that a "new world order" had emerged. Capitalism and the free market economy had won. The world was now open for business. China quickly understood that the world had changed in a profound way, and by 2003 abandoned the core concept of its communist state. No longer would they embrace a planned economy. Capitalism won its final victory, and from that victory was born the concept of "globalization"—a world of multinational corporations and economics without borders. Gorbachev's vision of a Golden Age, it seems, is on the verge of being realized.

Yet, this idea of a coming global Golden Age depends upon personal perception, which depends on the person's economic status. For the working poor, the unemployed, and underemployed of the world—the great masses of people—a Golden Age is someone else's dream, and for the homeless and hungry the announcement of a Golden Age is someone's bad idea of a joke.

Traditional history explores political movements, kingdoms, empires, and wars, fashioned around a set of events and dates focusing on the objective, the progression of technology and conquest through the ages, but divorced, however, from the subjective experience of people and cultures, ignoring entirely the broad quest of the human species itself. Rarely does history approach the subjective elements in life—what actually makes life "life." Nor does history traditionally seek to understand the human experience in its entirety. History always puts kings, presidents, and dictators at the cusp of change, but fails to address the driving force of history itself: the human condition, experience, and consciousness as a totality. Is there some grand purpose designed around the human experience that we have failed to identify?

Seeing the full length of the human experience is impossible, for we do not know when the human experience actually began. Neither do we know if the human experience will ever end. We, today, as in every generation, find ourselves in a sliver of time insignificantly small compared to the entirety of human history. It's difficult to grasp the meaning of our lives in the flowing river of the human species. It is a mistake to separate history into periods of time based on empires, kingdoms, or ruling nations, because the human experience flows seamlessly from one generation to the next and from one age to the next. Even though we define life as a physical thing, our lives are experienced in the realm of the subjective, as is the life of every human being who has ever lived. And it is within this realm of the subjective where history finds its ultimate meaning: ideas, concepts, and worldviews passed from parent to child over and over again for many thousands of years.

What our true nature is as humans, where we came from, and where we are going as a conscious, self-aware species emerging from the natural forces of a living planet are mysteries to behold and exciting to engage. Therefore, we should take everything our ancient ancestors passed down to us with all seriousness, mythology in particular, for it has been said history repeats itself time and again.

Knowing that leaders of the world today envision a new age approaching, such as President Gorbachev's vision of a Golden Age, I cannot help but connect in an experiential way the mythical Golden Age of antiquity to our future in a global civilization. I do so not from a political point of view, but rather from the basic individual human desire to experience the joys of living: peace and love with goodwill to all. For it is the people—the masses—who constitute human culture and drive life experiences forward through imagination manifesting as acts of creation, invention, and innovation. As a whole, these things are what constitute the human experience. Not just now, but for all time.

Return of the Golden Age is not just my search for truth in history, but humanity's quest for peace and prosperity in the world today, an investigation into the past to explain why we as a species are "the way we are." By tying these two Golden Ages together—one in the mythical past and the other a vision of the future—our experience in today's world can be effectively explained.

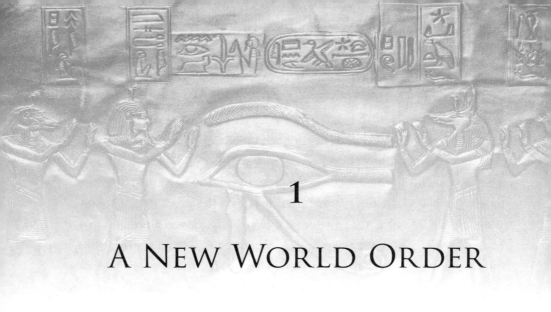

1

A NEW WORLD ORDER

In December 1981, a high school friend invited me to listen to a tape recording of a presentation made to a group of central Illinois farmers. The speaker on the tape was a retired Air Force lieutenant colonel by the name of J. C. Lewis, at the time a farmer near Guymon, Oklahoma. He was with the American Agricultural Movement and had been seeking political answers for the desperate situation farmers were experiencing. A few years before, in 1977, Congress enacted new legislation, called the Food and Agricultural Act, introducing target prices for grain, loan rates, and the use of production costs to escalate target prices. It also removed historic farm acreage allotments and introduced a farmer-held grain reserve. According to the taped presentation, this new act of legislation ensured that farmers received prices for their grain below their production costs. Lewis had wanted to know what was going on in Congress, and he seemed to be quite sure that he had found out.

According to Lewis, a private organization called the Trilateral Commission was serving as a think tank to help direct policy in the congressional and executive branches of government. Created in 1973 by David Rockefeller and Zbigniew Brzezinski, the Trilateral Commission was formed to foster closer cooperation among the regions of North

America, Western Europe, and Japan. It sought to "improve public understanding of problems common to the three regions and to support proposals for handling them jointly, and to nurture habits and practices of working together among these regions."[1]

Lewis, however, believed that there was more to the story and that this private think tank represented the true power behind the government of the United States. Members of the Trilateral Commission were wealthy bankers and corporate CEOs as well as elected and appointed officials in both houses of Congress, the White House, and the President's Cabinet. They were also members of another organization created in 1921 called the Council on Foreign Relations. By keeping "its members in touch with the international situation and devoting itself to a continuous study of the international aspects of America's political, economic, and financial problems, it would develop a reasoned American foreign policy."[2] Their goal, Lewis believed, was not only to promote relationships between North America, Western Europe, and Japan, but to form, over time, a one-world government.

The retired colonel was convincing and also talked about a computer study performed by the Senate on U.S. corporations, *Interlocking Directorates among the Major U.S. Corporations.* According to this study, performed on 122 major U.S. corporations, a significant number of board directors were directly interlocking and a large number of board directors were indirectly interlocking through intermediary corporations.* As a business student at the University of Illinois, I was fascinated and wrote to my congressman, Edward Madigan, requesting a copy of the study. He cordially obliged, sending me a copy of the study introduction and summary. Lewis's facts were correct, so, as it was in those days, I dialed operator assistance, requested Lewis's phone number, and called him. We talked for several minutes, and as a result I obtained the address of a publisher that had released two books on the subject matter, *Trilaterals over Washington,* published in two volumes.

---

*"Interlocking" is when the same people sit on various corporate boards so they can make decisions across a large number of companies for the same purpose.

A year later I mentioned the Trilateral Commission to my European Economics professor and asked if I might write my term paper on the subject. He chuckled, mentioned something about "the shadow" in reference I am sure to a shadow government, and hinted it probably wasn't a good idea. There were much more interesting topics to write about, he said. That was the last I thought about either the Council on Foreign Relations or the Trilateral Commission. Until now.

After thirty years of experiencing corporate life in the commercial real estate industry and the banking industry, as a software consultant for McDonnell Douglas, and as an employee for a state agency, I began to question why society "is the way it is," and the world too. People, in general, seem to be unhappy with their jobs while at the same time grateful that they have a job. In order to make ends meet, some people today work two or three jobs. Now, our youth are demonstrating "against the system." Not just in the United States, but around the world. With these demonstrations, which have attracted considerable media attention, I am reminded of the protests and demonstrations against the Vietnam War, but without a war.

Why?

The short answer is joblessness, along with a sense that the country's political and economic affairs are tilted in favor of big business. The long answer, however, runs deep into history before the dawn of our civilization into the murky past, an answer that ties all aspects of human society into an inseparable twine of economics, government, and religion.

CHILDREN OF THE MILLENNIUM: CATALYST FOR CHANGE

Every so often a generation is given a label. The most well-known generation is the baby boomers, men and women born between 1946 and 1964, of which I am one. They are the children of those who sacrificed greatly and fought a world war to defeat fascism. Before them came the depression children, who struggled to eke out a living amid an economic dark age, and after the baby boomers came Generation X. More recently, those born from the early 1980s through the year 2000 have been labeled the millennial generation, or generation Y. These young people, currently between the ages of thirteen and thirty-three, are our future, and there are a lot of them. Fifty million of them are eighteen years of age or older, and in less than ten years, seventy million more will join their ranks as adults.

This generation is unlike any previous generation. Their top three priorities are being a good parent, having a successful marriage, and helping others in need. Owning a home and living a religious life are fourth and fifth, respectively. Only then is a high-paying career important, their sixth priority.[3] Today's youth are so civic minded that some social commentators have dubbed them the "civic generation." For them, it seems the American Dream has taken on a whole new meaning: it's all about the people. "Community service is part of their DNA. It's part of this generation to care about something larger than themselves," according to CEO Michael Brown of City Year, a nonprofit organization dedicated to keeping students in school and on track to graduate.[4]

On September 17, 2011, the millennials, as they have been dubbed by the press, began occupying Wall Street to demonstrate their dissatisfaction with the state of U.S. politico-economic affairs. Within a few weeks the demonstrations grew to thousands and spread to twenty-five cities across the United States. Within a month like-minded people across the world showed their support by staging their own "occupy" demonstrations, from Chicago to Los Angeles, and from London to Hong Kong. By the end of October 2011, the movement had spread to nearly one thousand cities across the world.[5]

Their purpose is to fight back "against the corrosive power major banks and unaccountable multinational corporations wield against democracy, and the role of Wall Street in creating the economic collapse that has caused the greatest recession in nearly a century." They aim to "expose how the richest 1% of people are writing the rules of a dangerous neoliberal economic agenda that is stealing our future."[6] According to Mark Bray, a media spokesman for Occupy Wall Street, "Fundamentally what we are looking for is economic justice. We want to create a society where the needs of the vast majority of people are prioritized over the profits of a small number of corporations which have an undue influence on the organization of our society. Moreover, we are looking for a more democratic structure, a way that the people can hold those officials that make these decisions accountable."[7]

Occupy Wall Street wants to end the tyranny of the 1 percent of people who have the greatest influence upon the political and financial system of the United States. They are against corrupt banking systems, war, and foreclosure. Occupy Wall Street, simply, demands economic justice for the 99 percent of the people who have little or no influence on the corporate and governmental forces that shape society. These demands are simple, but at the same time deeply complex.

"Economic justice" sounds like Marxist rhetoric, which prompted television personalities such as Bill O'Reilly of Fox News to refer to the protesters as an "amalgamation of anti-capitalist people, anti-American people."[8] Conservative radio showman Rush Limbaugh believes that the Obama administration concocted Occupy Wall Street to target Republican presidential hopeful Mitt Romney.[9] On a more sinister note, conservative talk show host Glenn Beck warns that Occupy Wall Street is a Marxist revolution that is global in nature.[10] Conservative political commentator Charlie Wolf agrees, stating that the Occupy Wall Street movement is being controlled by "by a bunch of people who have nefarious means and desires on wanting to change the constitution of the United States." They want to turn the United States into "some sort of communist or socialist-Marxist entity."[11]

If the Occupy Movement is indeed a Marxist revolution, why would 43 percent of those polled by CBS News agree with the protestors' so-called anticapitalist views?[12] More important, why would the youth of America, and the world, start a Marxist revolution when it is common knowledge that communism is a failed governmental ideology, that its application in the real world is impractical, particularly now since China has entered the global economy as a capitalist force?

The millennial generation appears to understand that something is wrong with the political and economic forces at the foundation of society, that the United States has become more a republic of the corporations as opposed to a republic of the people. Government is a necessity, and a government that ensures the rights and freedoms of its people will always be successful. Still, any government can be corrupted by people who care more about power and control than the general welfare of the citizens. Consequently, I find it ironic that in an interview with Al Jazeera's Mike Hanna, conservative political commentator Charlie Wolf suggested that "what they all [the Occupy Wall Street demonstrators] need right now is for some rich millionaire or billionaire that they despise to buy a couple hundred thousand copies of *Animal Farm* and to hand them out to the protesters and let them have a good read."[13]

Animal Farm is a satire on the ills of Stalinist communism, and it is understandable why Wolf would suggest such a book. However, what Wolf might not know is that after writing *Animal Farm,* George Orwell immediately wrote *1984,* a chilling and disturbing exposé on the social, economic, and political truths hidden behind the rule and rhetoric of the modern industrial state and its socialistic style of government, a book published in 1949 that to this day, more than sixty years later, still ranks as a bestselling book.

GEORGE ORWELL'S ~~1984~~ 2012

Nineteen Eighty-Four is the story of Winston Smith, a middle-aged member of the Outer Party whose job at the Ministry of Truth is to revise history by editing past editions of newspapers and magazines, removing photographs of and references to people who have been removed from existence (murdered) by the party known as INGSOC, an acronym for English socialism. Their slogan is "Who controls the past, controls the future, and so who controls the present controls the past." The theory is that if everyone accepts the lie that the party imposes, and if all the records tell the same story, then the lie would pass into history, thereby becoming truth. With the current generation having no experiential memory of the past, accomplishing such a seemingly arduous task, Orwell writes, is easier than one might think. Over time, by constantly bombarding the people with their message, they win a never-ending series of victories over people's memories, a policy the Inner Party calls *Reality Control*. Their goal is to build a new language in order to remove the ability to think unfavorably about the party, a language referred to as *Newspeak*.

As a member of the Outer Party, Smith lives in torment, consuming food and drink of inferior quality while under the surveillance of Big Brother, a wall-mounted television that serves as a means of dispensing party propaganda, as well as a spy camera with a view into his personal life. Regularly, Smith and his colleagues are required to participate in Two Minute Hate sessions, in which people gather in front of a "big telescreen" to view the image of the people's enemy, Emmanuel Goldstein, a former Inner Party member who backslid, sought revolution, and somehow escaped the Thought Police. In Two Minute Hate sessions, the Outer Party members hiss and scream at the image of Goldstein. Even Smith, who himself contemplates a better way of life, cannot help but scream at the image of the traitor Goldstein. Hate is infectious, but it is necessary for the Inner Party to maintain support for the perpetual state of war between the countries of Oceania and Eurasia. (Oceania encompasses the Americas, the United Kingdom, and Australia, as well as other locations. England is known as Airstrip One.)

Smith hooks up with a younger Outer Party woman named Julia, who secretly passes him the message "I love you," written on a small piece of paper. When they meet again, in secret, they indulge in sexual intercourse for pure pleasure, an act prohibited by the party. As their sexual meetings continue, Smith sinks deeper into the idea that there is a better way of life outside control of the party. He sees the proles (proletariat), poor people, the masses of people, living a happy, simple life.

He also suspects that a man named O'Brien might be another person who seeks a way of life outside party control. O'Brien is an Inner Party member and the holder of some post so important that Smith has only a dim idea of its nature. One day, O'Brien contacts Smith under the auspices of being a revolutionary and allows Smith to read Goldstein's forbidden book, *The Theory and Practice of Oligarchical Collectivism,* exposing the ideology behind INGSOC. In the end, Smith is arrested and discovers that O'Brien had been watching him and Julia all along through hidden telescreens. For Smith, things are not what they seem, and through psychological torture he succumbs to the party line, a broken man.

When I first read *1984* I was a high school student and lacked life's experience to understand the depth of Orwell's story. At that time, *1984* was little more than dark science fiction of a technology-controlled society. After reading it again, however, more than thirty years later, Orwell's literary genius was apparent. Underneath the seemingly unrealistic Two Minute Hate, Big Brother, Newspeak, O'Brien's cruelty, and the mysterious figure of Emmanuel Goldstein lay the modus operandi of the institutionalized social powers that have existed for thousands of years. Although their names change from century to century, and their empires are replaced by more powerful empires, the pattern of ideological control always reasserts itself, even after revolution in the name of liberty.

In *1984,* Orwell was commenting on the sociopolitical and economic truth that lies at the base of human civilization. He did so in an exaggerated fashion to make his point. The slogans for INGSOC—War Is Peace, Freedom Is Slavery, and Ignorance Is Strength—are in fact the underlying principles for the modern social democratic state. These three principles of social organization and government control exist but not in the extreme way described by Orwell. They are subtle and buried deep within a self-perpetuating system that marries war-oriented nationalism to a network of powerful corporations, a system that is masked from the public by corporate media, a system that President

Jimmy Carter referred to as "a more just and equitable world order" in his letter to the 1977 Trilateral Commission meeting in Tokyo, Japan.[14]

What appears in the United States to be a two-party democratic system is essentially a one-party system divided into two conferences, one group being more conservative and the other more liberal. Both receive campaign funding from wealthy corporations and individuals, reflecting the social and political foundation that the business of America is business. This truth is played out in almost every election and is voiced in the typical campaign question "Are you better off now (financially) that you were four years ago?" The same is true for the election process. The candidates who can acquire more funds in their political campaign are typically voted into office. It's a system based on profits and the accumulation of wealth in which the vast majority of people hang in the balance, needing jobs provided by the system. And as long as the system continues to grow and generate profits, there is ample employment for the masses, which in turn help sustain the system through consumption and the use of debt for housing and other expensive goods. This is capitalism.

Such a capitalistic system based on a free market economy appears to be an equitable, well-conceived system. And it would be if the system's resources and needs (supply and demand) were allowed to freely operate according to the principles of a free market economy. If that were the case, the system would be focused on providing people with affordable goods and services, and the ways and means for people to improve their own lives and communities, such as off-grid solar and geothermal power systems, hydrogen fuel cell automobiles, and reasonable health care through a holistic system in which diet and medicine are combined. The system, however, does not do this because corporations are loyal to their shareholders (their owners), and that loyalty is dedicated to increasing the value of corporate stock through growth in profits. Thus, costs must be kept as low as possible in order to maximize profits. Such costs include labor, one of the largest factors affecting profit. As a consequence, the majority of jobs are relatively low paying, and the state and federal governments must step in to enforce a minimum wage.

According to the law of supply and demand, the greater the supply of anything in relation to its demand, the lower the price required to acquire it. In the case of labor, unemployment means that the supply of labor exceeds its demand, which in turn requires that the price for labor to drop in order for the supply of labor to reach equilibrium with demand. Because there almost always is an excess supply of labor, meaning that there are more people wanting jobs than there are jobs, corporations in the past took advantage of low labor costs. This led to the organization of laborers into unions and to the creation of the minimum wage, which provides an incentive for large corporations to move some of their operations overseas, where the cost of labor is lower, which, in turn, leads to vital national interests in other countries. This is true for all resources, such as oil.

Oil is an important aspect of the economy, not just in producing gasoline for automobiles but also in generating plastics. As a result, oil-producing countries, even countries that are remote or sparsely populated, are of vital interest to the world economy, and any disruption of the oil flow can be viewed as a threat to national security justifying the need for military force. Such is the case with current U.S. military operations in Iraq, which have their origins and justification in the Carter Doctrine, a policy put in place by President Carter in 1980 stating that the United States would use military force if necessary to protect its national interests in the region of the Persian Gulf.

Every country in the world has a right to protect its vital interests. The more interesting question is *why* do countries (groups of people bound by common interests represented by government) insist upon military action either through preemptive strikes or as a reaction to failed diplomacy?

WAR IS HISTORY

Anyone who has taken a few history classes knows that war has been the main feature of civilization since the beginning. In fact, world history can be defined as a cataloging of war, the redrawing of political boundaries, and the conquering of new territories. In the ancient world there was the Achaemenid Empire, Babylonian Empire, Greek Empire, Macedonian Empire, and the Roman Empire. In Medieval times there was the Mongol Empire, Islamic (Caliphate) Empire, Ming Empire, Chola Empire, and the Sassanid Empire; as long ago as 3000 BCE war has been documented.

In modern times, empires became distinctly Western European with the British, Russian, Spanish, French, and Portuguese imperialism. However, there was also the Ottoman Empire of the Near East that spanned medieval and modern times as well as the short-lived twentieth-century empires of Imperial Japan and Nazi Germany. Fueled by industry and the mechanization of armies, with its two world wars, the twentieth century might very well have been the most violent period in our civilization's history.

In 1914, all the major world powers were drawn into a European war, history records, because of the assassination of Archduke Franz Ferdinand, the heir to the Austro-Hungarian throne. The assassin: a member of the Serbian nationalist movement called the "Black Hand." The true roots of the war, however, lie in the culturally Slavic peoples of the Balkans and their domination by both the Austro-Hungarian Empire and the Ottoman Empire. In simple terms, these Balkan Slavs wanted their independence. With the assassination of the archduke, the Austro-Hungarian Empire took the opportunity to exercise their dominance on Serbian lands by offering the Serbs an ultimatum they would likely reject. Serbia, on the other hand, looked to Russia with which they had close ties to aid in their cause. As a consequence, the Austro-Hungarian Empire looked to the Germans for support, who willingly agreed. So, on July 28, 1914, the Austro-Hungarian Empire declared war on Serbia, which created a chain reaction of war declarations involving France, Britain, Japan, the Ottoman Empire, and eventually the United States, the results of which devastated Germany and sowed the seeds of another world war two decades later.

During the 1930s, the National Socialist German Workers Party rose to power in Germany with the promises of a restored economy and a new empire. At the same time, Italy and Japan began flexing their muscles. All three countries expanded their territories first through intimidation and then by invasion and occupation. The expansionist policies of Germany, Italy, and Japan led to land being taken by force and people being subjugated, which in turn created a threat to the interests of other countries, namely France, the United Kingdom, and the United States. The result was another world war in which tens of millions of people lost their lives. The final act of war was the detonation of two nuclear bombs on the civilian populations of Hiroshima and Nagasaki, Japan, killing more than 75,000 people in less than a day. In the ensuing months another 150,000 people died from burns, radiation poisoning, and other trauma-related illnesses. In the course of six years of war between 1939 and 1945, more than 60 million people lost their lives.

Although there are many reasons why the countries of the world entered into another war in 1939, the underlying reason is greed, along with the quest for the control of resources and peoples through territorial expansion, regardless of the political rhetoric put forth of individual countries acting in their own best interest. This propensity for war is as much the defining quality of civilization as are the institutions of education, science, and religion. History demonstrates that the rise and fall of kingdoms, nations, and empires typically involves death and destruction. And war is waged not necessarily in accordance with the will of the people, but by those with power and influence who find it necessary to protect or expand the system that they manage.

Yet killing is against the nature of the human species. Even cases of self-defense and accidental killing create psychological trauma within the human mind. Killing another human being takes special conditioning, a fact that military forces around the world recognize; therefore, they psychologically condition their recruits to kill in a process called basic training. We further condition recruits, as well as society, by associating the process of killing with national pride, medals for bravery, and civil accolades in defending the "homeland." Yet few combat veterans are willing to talk about their experiences on the battlefield—their honor of defending the homeland—for the horrors of war far exceed anyone's worst nightmare. We have it in our minds to kill or be killed. Why?

The Christian might argue that it's because people are inherently evil.

The Darwinist might argue that it's because only the fit survive.

The socialist might argue that it's because of greed.

The person belonging to an ethnic minority might argue that it's because of prejudice.

The capitalist might not care as long as there is a way to profit, because it's just business, in the sense that war is about protecting a nation's vital interests, which is almost always about resources and commerce.

Major General Smedley Butler (1881–1940), the recipient of two Congressional Medals of Honor and the most decorated Marine prior to the Second World War, would agree that it's just business. After his career in the Marine Corps, and long before the antiwar culture of the 1960s, Butler concluded, "War is a racket. It always has been. It is possibly the oldest, easily the most profitable, surely the most vicious. It is the only one international in scope. It is the only one in which the profits are reckoned in dollars and the losses in lives."[15] Butler's deduction is simple, and one of today's more popular clichés. *Follow the money.* Corporate enterprises that contract with the federal government during times of war increase their profits dramatically, and it's all paid for by the people.

Butler confesses:

> I helped make Mexico, especially Tampico, safe for American oil interests in 1914. I helped make Haiti and Cuba a decent place for the National City Bank boys to collect revenues in. I helped in the raping of half a dozen Central American republics for the benefits of Wall Street. The record of racketeering is long. I helped purify Nicaragua for the international banking house of Brown Brothers in 1909–1912. I brought light to the Dominican Republic for

American sugar interests in 1916. In China I helped to see to it that Standard Oil went its way unmolested.[16]

For the famed author H. G. Wells, World War I was "the war to end all war." On April 2, 1917, President Woodrow Wilson asked Congress for a Declaration of War against Germany so that the world would "be made safe for democracy." Congress obliged, and the United States entered the war. Eighteen months later World War I ended on November 11, 1918. The peace treaty that was signed at Versailles, however, led to a much more devastating war twenty years later. Again, the United States sought to remain out of the conflict and did so for two years. Unlike the First World War, the Second World War ended in unconditional surrender and occupation. Like the war before it, the Second World War also sowed the seeds of war, conducted not on the battlefield, but on the field of international politics and economics. Known as the Cold War, this was a war against the threat of communism. The Cold War quickly turned hot in the Asian country of Korea, where more than two million people lost their lives. A decade later the same scenario repeated itself in the small Southeast Asian country of Vietnam, where more than five million people died.

The Cold War between what Western countries called the "Free World" and the "Communist World"—East and West—lasted another fifteen years and finally ended when the Soviet Union dissolved under its inability to house and feed its own people. In a sense, the West won the Cold War by forcing the Soviet Union to continually use more and more of its resources on military and defense programs, prompting a self-inflicted bankruptcy, discharged on Christmas 1991.

While the Soviet Union was crumbling under its own weight, Iraq annexed the small country of Kuwait on its southern border through military occupation, a country that was a close ally during their war with Iran in the previous decade. International outcry led to immediate economic sanctions by the United Nations, and ultimately a UN coalition of forces was dispatched to liberate Kuwait.

A decade later an Islamic fundamentalist militant group known as Al-Qaeda (meaning *the Base*) flew hijacked jet airliners into New York's World Trade Center and the Pentagon in a suicide mission, which generated great outcry among the people of the United States. Not since the surprise attack on Pearl Harbor by the Japanese Imperial Navy have so many people been killed on U.S. soil in an act of war.

A few years later, U.S. intelligence agencies informed their government that Iraq was involved in training terrorists, had not been cooperating with UN representatives, and was not adhering to seventeen UN resolutions. With the support of Congress, the next President Bush ordered the invasion of Iraq. The intent was to overthrow and occupy the country, with the goal of bringing about democracy to a once-imprisoned people; the justification was that Saddam Hussein owned weapons of mass destruction. A year earlier, U.S. forces invaded Afghanistan to eliminate terrorist bases and to overthrow the existing Taliban extremist government. The "War on Terror" began with both of these countries being former U.S. allies in the Cold War against the Soviet Union. Now they had become enemies, not because of direct actions against the United States, but because of their sympathies to private militant organizations with anti-Western views.

The War on Terror has continued now for more than a decade. Why?

It's a matter of perspective. The viewpoint of the U.S. government is that they have the right to protect their interests abroad. From a very different—and valid—perspective, the United States can be construed as an imperialist force trying to control world politics and commerce; in other words, it wants to control people and resources.

In a 2011 Republican debate in Tampa, Florida, presidential hopeful Ron Paul argued that "We're under great threat [citizens of the United States], because we occupy so many countries. We're in 130 countries. We have 900 bases around the world. We're going broke."[17] According to the Department of Defense *Active Duty Military Personnel Strengths by Regional Area and by Country,* as of September 30, 2010, the United States has 1.1 million troops stationed within its borders and territories;

80,000 in Europe; 44,000 in East Asia and the Pacific; 8,000 in North Africa, the Near East, and South Asia; 2,000 in sub-Saharan Africa; 2,000 in other countries of the western hemisphere; and even 145 in former countries of the Soviet Union. Add to that the 96,200 troops in Iraq and 105,900 in Afghanistan.[18] According to *The Economist*, the ten largest defense budgets in the world add up to more than a trillion dollars, of which the United States accounts for 60 percent, with a 2010 budget of 696 billion dollars.[19]

The important fact is that the United States has been at war, off and on, for one hundred years, and for the past fifty years more on than off, nearly continuous. And with this continual state of war comes the growth of industries specializing in producing the instruments and technologies of war, paid for by taxes.

Growing up during the Cold War, I believed, as did many other people, that the archenemy of the United States, the Soviet Union, was the reason for the world being as it is: a world divided, us and them, two opposing forces that if provoked enough might destroy the planet. The Soviet Union and communism in general were a threat to our principles of government and our way of life. President Reagan's "Evil Empire" was guilty of closing off their borders and enslaving their people.

Through the course of the Cold War, trillions of dollars were spent on weapons, particularly deadly machines bordering on the edge of science fiction, such as the Stealth Bomber and Fighter, aircraft invisible to radar. Missile silos were built throughout the Great Plains. Development ensued on the Trident Nuclear Submarine, which amounts to a missile silo built into the belly of a submarine, enough firepower for destruction not only of the Soviet Union, but of the planet as well.

In 1991, when the Soviet Union dissolved as a political entity, the Cold War ended. One might think that the United States would disarm and focus its resources on domestic products and programs. It didn't because there was a new threat. What if some rogue country got hold of a nuclear bomb? What if Iran developed nuclear weapons and started World War III? A decade after the Cold War came to an end, a new enemy arrived on the political world scene, an invisible enemy without borders with the ability to set up operations in any country, even the United States. The sky-bombing of the World Trade Center and the Pentagon provided proof that they exist. Their message: the intent of the United States government is global commerce and influence backed by a massive military-industrial complex with bases around the world, headquartered at the Pentagon. The United States and its allies are and have been building an economic world empire, and it is this empire that we have declared war against.

U.S. citizens don't see it that way because the media generally report the political and diplomatic goings-on of the U.S. government. By nature, the U.S. media are sympathetic to the government's politics and seek to fashion public opinion around characteristics of the Democratic and Republican parties, essentially a single party divided by the amount of money that should be spent on social programs. Heated arguments between the parties take place, to be sure, but other perspectives are rarely offered. Nor are the people told the whole story behind any national policy or event. It would take too long, given a thirty minute newscast. More important, what should be stated in order to explain the whole story can't be told because the facts, more often than not, involve national security, and therefore are secret.

PRESIDENT EISENHOWER'S WARNING

President Dwight D. Eisenhower was one of the greatest generals in U.S. history, a man well acquainted with public service and the military, the Supreme Commander of the Allied Forces in Europe during World War II, and the first Supreme Commander of NATO. On January 17, 1961, in his presidential farewell address, he warned us of the dangers that a corporate warfare system might generate. Although realizing that a military establishment was necessary, President Eisenhower cautioned us, and the world, that the total influence of such a military-industrial complex on society would be "economic, political, even spiritual" and would be "felt in every city, every Statehouse, every office of the Federal government." Such a system would have "grave implications."[20] Thus, he warned:

> In the councils of government, we must guard against the acquisition of unwarranted influence, whether sought or unsought, by the military-industrial complex. The potential for the disastrous rise of misplaced power exists and will persist. We must never let the weight of this combination endanger our liberties or democratic processes. We should take nothing for granted. Only an alert and knowledgeable citizenry can compel the proper meshing of the huge industrial and military machinery of defense with our peaceful methods and goals, so that security and liberty may prosper together.[21]

President Eisenhower also warned the American people that "we must also be alert to the equal and opposite danger that public policy could itself become the captive of a scientific-technological elite."[22] He also made it known the true meaning of the American Dream:

> We pray that peoples of all faiths, all races, all nations, may have their great human needs satisfied; that those now denied opportunity shall come to enjoy it to the full; that all who yearn for freedom may experience its spiritual blessings; that those who have freedom will understand, also, its heavy responsibilities; that all who are insensitive to the needs of others will learn charity; that the scourges of poverty, disease and ignorance will be made to disappear from the earth, and that, in the goodness of time, all peoples will come to live together in a peace guaranteed by the binding force of mutual respect and love.[23]

Eisenhower's successor, John F. Kennedy, seemed to share his vision. In June of 1963, President Kennedy spoke to the graduating class of American University in Washington about world peace, a topic on which "ignorance too often abounds and the truth is too rarely perceived."[24]

Kennedy believed in the dignity of the human spirit and that all people genuinely wanted peace:

> What kind of peace do I mean? What kind of peace do we seek? Not a Pax Americana [America peace] enforced on the world by American weapons of war. Not the peace of the grave or the security of the slave. I am talking about genuine peace, the kind of peace that makes life on earth worth living, the kind that enables men and nations to grow and to hope and to build a better life for their children—not merely peace for Americans but peace for all men and women—not merely peace in our time but peace for all time.[25]

Kennedy also informed the American University's graduating class that he believed too many people thought peace was impossible, dangerous, and a defeatist belief. He advised that we need not accept this view and that our international problems were solvable because humans created them. For Kennedy, world peace was not to be based on "sudden revolution in human nature but on a gradual evolution in human institutions." There would be no grand formula or magic solution by a few world powers; rather, "Genuine peace must be the product of many nations, the sum of many acts."[26]

Five months after sharing his vision of world peace, he was assassinated, an act that would be speculated on for decades. Why was Kennedy murdered? Some believe that responsibility lies with dark forces within our own government tied to the military-industrial complex and that the motive was to prevent peace-making efforts with the Soviets and to prevent a U.S. withdrawal from South Vietnam. Others believe it was mob related in retaliation for helping "get the vote out." Unfortunately, we may never know if Oswald acted alone—the official story—or if conspiracy truly existed. The debate continues to this day.

Since the early 1960s armed conflict and other U.S. "military actions" have been nearly continuous. One has to contemplate whether the advice of President Eisenhower has fallen on deaf ears, or disinterested minds. Whatever the case may be, the government-based system for funding the research and development of weapons technology, which was born out of World War II, has come of age, producing a society that eerily resembles, although subtly, the dark esoteric truths of George Orwell's *1984*:

War is peace

War must exist—if only as a mentality—for the system to exist, even though there is peace. So, when war is talked about, officials and managers of the system are really talking about peace. Peace is possible only after every enemy has been vanquished.

Freedom is slavery

Freedom exists only in the meaningless choices of which food to purchase, which television program to view, and which consumer goods the amount of money you earn can buy. Freedom is gained only by selecting from the available jobs provided by the system, beginning at minimum wage. For the vast majority of people, life involves paying off mortgages, auto loans, and consumer debts, with the hope that enough money can be saved by the age of sixty-five. In effect, the vast majority of people are labor slaves to a system that owns the resources that must be purchased in order to survive.

It's the ultimate Monopoly game, for if your debt gets too large for you to manage, bankruptcy is available, thereby dismissing all your creditors. You get to return to "Go" and start over instead of leave the game.

Ignorance is strength

Ignorance is not even knowing that the system is a system, camouflaged by the electoral process, mass media, executive directives, and secret projects under the guise of national security. These institutions and policies insulate and strengthen the system.

However, what I refer to as "the system" is not something modern society has created. The system is as old as civilization itself, appearing first in Mesopotamia five thousand years ago. This system, which is best described as ruling by the elite, is simply human nature and has reasserted itself time after time with each new kingdom and empire, century after century and millennium after millennium. It just so happens that the latest incarnation of this system centers on the United States of America, which is in effect a country formed by nearly every culture in the world.

Throughout history there have always been three classes of people based on wealth: the poor, the middle class, and the elite. The perspective and goals of these classes are irreconcilable. The elite want nothing more than to maintain their status, and to do so they fund public projects, give to charity, and support the government, whose role is to manage the people and protect the system. The poor are too tired from constantly struggling to care about anything other than the immediate needs of their lives. Members of the middle class want to join the upper class, of which, really, they know nothing about. And because of their desire to be of the elite class, they will do almost anything to achieve that goal, and with their greed they create a "rat race" for themselves and a "dog-eat-dog" world for everyone else.

Rats don't race, and dogs don't eat dogs. Everyone of the English-speaking language has heard these two phrases and knows deep down what they really mean. It's a human race in which ignoring and running others over is the norm. It's a people-eat-people world, a cannibalistic world where "I will get you before you get me," a world where "there is no free lunch" and everyone has the attitude of "not on my dime." In this, the middle class has created a society of selfishness from which emerges violence. Not in a criminal manner that can be prosecuted, but in thought and in spirit, reflected in wars on just about anything deemed unwanted: war on drugs, war on crime, war on poverty, war on cancer. Most recently, war on terror. All of which result in futility.

Such violence is reflected in the government we have created for ourselves, a violence based on fear. The violence is so ingrained that we have become paranoid, and through our paranoia we have created Big Brother. According to Georgina Prodhan, writing for Reuters, "Internet companies such as Google, Twitter and Facebook are being increasingly co-opted for surveillance work as the information they gather proves irresistible to law enforcement agencies."[27] In the United States, the FDA has approved a radio frequency identification chip the size of a grain of rice to be implanted in the human body.[28] More recently, on January 31, 2011, President Obama signed into federal law the National Defense Authorization Act, which allows the federal government "trial-free, indefinite detention of anyone, including American citizens, so long as the government calls them terrorists."[29]

To hide the reality of our violence, we have created Orwell's Newspeak, a deliberate substitution of words with new words in order to permanently alter our thinking and to make critical thinking anti-American. In the theater of war, civilians killed by mistake or simply because they happened to be in the wrong place at the wrong time are not killed civilians, but *collateral damage*. Bombing missions have become *sorties*. Battles have become *troop surges*. Going off to war has become *deployment*. In a very strange sense, war has lost its meaning and has been redefined. Through language war has become neutralized and normalized.

War has become peace.

THE COMING NEW WORLD ORDER

With the idea of war now substituted for the idea of peace, there is a new order emerging in the world. On September 11, 1990, a year before the dissolution of the Soviet Union, President George H. W. Bush announced live on television and before a joint session of Congress his dream of a new world order:

> We stand today at a unique and extraordinary moment. The crisis in the Persian Gulf, as grave as it is, also offers a rare opportunity to

move toward an historic period of cooperation. Out of these troubled times, our fifth objective—*a new world order*—can emerge: a new era—freer from the threat of terror, stronger in the pursuit of justice, and more secure in the quest for peace. An era in which the nations of the world, East and West, North and South, can prosper and live in harmony. A hundred generations have searched for this elusive path to peace, while a thousand wars raged across the span of human endeavor. Today that new world is struggling to be born, a world quite different from the one we've known; a world where the rule of law supplants the rule of the jungle; a world in which nations recognize the shared responsibility for freedom and justice; a world where the strong respect the rights of the weak. . . .

Once again, Americans have stepped forward to share a tearful goodbye with their families before leaving for a strange and distant shore. At this very moment, they serve together with Arabs, Europeans, Asians, and Africans in defense of principle and the dream of a new world order. That's why they sweat and toil in the sand and the heat and the sun. If they can come together under such adversity, if old adversaries like the Soviet Union and the United States can work in common cause, then surely we who are so fortunate to be in this great Chamber—Democrats, Republicans, liberals, conservatives— can come together to fulfill our responsibilities here. Thank you. Good night. And God bless the United States of America.[30]

Six months later, on March 6, 1991, after the dissolution of the Soviet Union and the successful campaign again Iraqi forces in Kuwait, President Bush announced to a joint session of Congress that a new world order had arrived:

Until now, the world we've known has been a world divided— a world of barbed wire and concrete block, conflict and cold war. Now, we can see a new world coming into view. A world in which there is the very real prospect of a new world order. In the words of

Winston Churchill, a "world order" in which "the principles of justice and fair play . . . protect the weak against the strong . . ." A world where the United Nations, freed from cold war stalemate, is poised to fulfill the historic vision of its founders—a world in which freedom and respect for human rights find a home among all nations.

The Gulf war put this new world to its first test, and, my fellow Americans, we passed that test. For the sake of our principles, for the sake of the Kuwaiti people, we stood our ground. Because the world would not look the other way, Ambassador al-Sabah, tonight, Kuwait is free.

Tonight as our troops begin to come home, let us recognize that the hard work of freedom still calls us forward. We've learned the hard lessons of history. The victory over Iraq was not waged as "a war to end all wars." Even the new world order cannot guarantee an era of perpetual peace. But enduring peace must be our mission.[31]

For some people, mentioning the phrase "new world order" automatically conjures the thought of conspiracy and a one-world government, but trying to govern seven billion people across many different cultures would soon become an exercise in frustration. President Bush's new world order refers to something other than what conspiracy theorists might think. He was clear in his first new world order speech about what it means: "freer from the threat of terror, stronger in the pursuit of justice, and more secure in the quest for peace. An era in which the nations of the world, East and West, North and South, can prosper and live in harmony." In Bush's statement the key words are "prospering and living in harmony," which from the American perspective can only be conducting business abroad under Western principles of justice, an international policy that strikes the same chord as Roosevelt's "making the world safe for democracy."

President Bush is not alone on this either. Four years earlier Soviet President Mikhail Gorbachev stated almost the same thing, but in a slightly different way. He wrote that "great work of historic importance lies in store both for the Soviet Union and the United States."[32] This work of "staving off the threat of humanity's destruction in a nuclear war" could not be accomplished by either the United States or the Soviet Union alone. If they were successful, however, he foresaw "a bloom in Soviet-American relations, a 'Golden Age' which would benefit the USSR and the USA, all countries, and the whole world community."[33]

I am convinced that Gorbachev is referring to a Golden Age of the commercial system, and that he knew while he was president that the communist system was collapsing. He also knew that for the country to survive, the Russians would have to meet the West on their terms through capitalism. Gorbachev was writing about a new world order of global commerce, a Golden Age of capitalism in which multinational corporations across the world are free to engage in business without the threat of their operations being jeopardized by warring countries. For the wealthy corporations and governments that control most of the world's resources, such a goal as a new world order provides purpose, a purpose they believe to be necessary.

According to *The Crisis in Democracy: Report on the Governability of Democracies to the Trilateral Commission,* the people of democratic societies have lost their sense of purpose:

> In the past, people have found their purposes in religion, in nationalism, and in ideology. But neither church, nor state, nor class now commands people's loyalties. . . . Protestantism sanctified the individual conscience; nationalism postulated the equality of citizens; and liberalism provided the rationale for limited government based on consent. But now all three gods have failed. We have witnessed the dissipation of religion, the withering away of nationalism, the decline—if not the end—of class-based ideology.[34]

As a result, the democracy continues to operate but loses its ability to make purposeful decisions as special interests and competing private interests create conflicting wants. Thus, the governing "system becomes one of anomic democracy, in which democratic politics becomes more an arena for the assertion of conflicting interests than a process for the building of common purposes."[35] Purpose, consequently, must come from a "collective perception by the significant groups in society of a major challenge to their well-being and the perception by them that this challenge threatens them all about equally."[36]

In other words, those who have the greatest stake in a country need to provide the course for that country's policies, while managing the government and population. For the United States and Britain, that means ensuring a competent and authoritarian government because the people of the United States and Britain have a strong tradition of being politically active, which reduces the competency and authority of the government by dividing officials' attention between the demands of the people and the demands of business. Japan, on the other hand, which has always had a strong authoritarian and bureaucratic government, requires more democratic participation of its people. In continental Europe, however, both governability and democracy seem to be problematic.[37]

Therefore, from the perspective of a wealthy businessman engaged in international commerce, the new world order is nothing more than those who have great interest in their respective country cooperating with their counterparts in other countries to ensure peace and prosperity for the sake of all, insinuating profitability. Neither the Trilateral Commission nor the Council on Foreign Relations is a secret society, but a group of men and women devoted to maintaining a prosperous course for their respective nations and the world. And if these men and women did not endeavor to promote commerce and cooperation, societies would aimlessly quarrel with one another, at best. At worst, there might be revolution and anarchy.

There are those who believe that the Trilateral Commission is a shadow government dedicated to instituting some type of world government. There are also those who think the Trilateral Commission is a natural and necessary part of U.S. international relations in a world with dissolving borders. Most people probably have never heard of the

Trilateral Commission and don't care. For the biggest players in commerce and politics, the Trilateral Commission is just a means to plan, promote, and cultivate relations between countries, a necessary and proactive approach to preventing another world war and generating commerce. It's a matter of perception.

The average person doesn't live life from the perspective of a multinational corporate executive. Rather, he or she sees the world through the eyes of a laborer. Blue or white collar, it doesn't matter. On the other hand, for multinational corporate executives as well as the political leadership of the country, the appropriate way of viewing average people is as a collective and as a labor force to be dealt with. This relationship between labor and capital is often an uneasy balance of economic affairs, as history demonstrates, particularly during the nineteenth and the early twentieth century, when child labor, employee health, and working conditions were serious issues along with the right for laborers to unionize and bargain with their corporate employers.

A number of economic theories have been put forward over the past few hundred years on how all this works between owners and workers. Mercantilists believe that wealth comes from the accumulation of gold and silver; classical economists believe that land, labor, and capital are the source of national wealth; Marxists believe that labor determines the value of a society because they are the force that actually manufactures products. Today, we live in a Keynesian world of capitalist economics in which the government spends money and levies taxes to stabilize the economy. According to Keynes's model, during a recession the government should spend more and tax less to stimulate growth, while in times of growth, tax more and spend less in order to control inflation. Also coming into play is supply-side economics, based on the idea that people will save and invest when given the incentive to do so and that this stimulates the economy. Monetary theory suggests that the supply of money can be used to stimulate the economy.

Society and civilization—domestic and international—regardless of the time period or age of humanity are all about economics in a very fundamental way. Economics is a systematic, almost mathematical, approach to using natural resources to live life. All the different economic theories are a fine-tuning of the system that Adam Smith described in classical economics. There are land, labor, and capital. Stated more fairly, there are resources, people, and ownership. Today, the general concept of economics is very simple. Large corporate enterprises own vast resources and create products that ordinary people must purchase in order to live, while at the same time providing the labor for those enterprises to turn resources into products. In a sense, the relationship between labor and capital is a card game, a very important card game with very high stakes. Too many unhappy people, as history demonstrates, leads to revolution if an equitable, nonviolent solution between the parties cannot be found. This is why capitalists display such a dislike for Marxists and Marxist ideas. They've observed that where communist experiments have succeeded, business owners lost everything.

You might think that if there are so many workers compared to owners, a ratio of more than 50 to 1,*[38] then why don't workers have more say in the state of economic affairs. Although there are a number of reasons, the primary reason is beliefs.

---

*In the United States, there are 5,767,306 firms, 7,433,465 establishments, and 313,098,826 people.

2

RESOURCES AND BELIEFS

The Social Experience

The law of supply and demand is a naturally occurring economic principle that has always existed. Humans have always traded goods and services, going back to prehistoric times. We are social animals, and we are embodied with the desire to interact with other people, whether for entertainment or obtaining something we want.

At a point in time long ago, someone realized that the personal accumulation of goods created an opportunity to acquire other necessities that also could be accumulated in order to make life easier, and the concept of ownership was born. In the beginning, commercial endeavors were family oriented, but as the human population grew, families living in proximity to each other banded together to form villages, and as villages grew, they became city-states. Along with the birth of the city-state came hierarchy and social status. Whoever owned most of the resources ruled, and to justify that rule, the concept of divine kingship was created. Everyone served the king in some way, depending on their level of wealth and the goods and services they provided. Those who had little to offer the king and city-state became laborers in order to do their part for the betterment of society. Mainstream history refers to this as the birth of civilization, and it occurred simultaneously in Mesopotamia and Egypt around 3000 BCE. It was the birth of capitalism. War followed closely behind, particularly in Mesopotamia.

In economics, supply refers to the natural and manufactured resources available for use and consumption, the simplest of which are food, water, clothing, and shelter. Today, we need to add to that list transportation, building materials, and other usable consumer goods, such as tools and TVs. Demand refers to the number of people who need available resources, and in what amount, in order to sustain life.

Capitalism, which is the opportunity for anyone to produce goods and services and sell those goods and services to whoever chooses to purchase them, is driven by the law of supply and demand. Capitalism thrives on businesses that compete to produce the best goods and services at the lowest price for their buyers. Capitalism is good because it provides the incentive for a society to continually be more productive, to be the best it can possibly be. This is freedom, and it is the underlying concept behind democracy. It's the rhetorical freedom the U.S. military fights for. However, the manipulation of markets, which ultimately is the monopolization of markets, creates the opposite, slavery. Not slavery in the strict sense of the word—a person being owned by another person—but slavery in an indirect sense: slavery to the prevailing economic forces and the powers that ride those forces. Ultimately, the manipulation of markets and competition for natural resources between nations lead to war.

Throughout history, the economic system of turning natural resources into usable goods and providing services for those goods has always existed. So has government, associated with this economic system as a means to manage the system. For Western civilization, in the beginning the system of government was a monarchy, which lasted from 3000 BCE to the ninth century CE and was replaced by feudalism, in which a king distributed large estates to friends and relatives. Everyone else, the peasant class, worked for estate owners. With the rise of industry and the growth of a merchant class at the beginning of the sixteenth century, nation-states gradually replaced kingdoms, and wealthy merchants replaced monarchs, mostly through revolution and violence.

In the New World, a system of government was designed different from all the previous nation-states. In their quest for independence, the thirteen British colonies of North America, understanding the need for revolution when governments no longer represent the needs of the people, built into their national constitution the apparatus for peaceful revolution. Those who make the laws and the director of the government—Congress and the president—were to be periodically elected. Thus, if the people willed a change in government, then revolution through violence was unnecessary. All that citizens had to do was vote out of office those who had misrepresented the people and vote in those who would represent them fairly, taking into account the old adage that "power corrupts and absolute power corrupts absolutely."

A vast continent of resources and a self-checking system based on economic liberty allowed the United States of America to achieve a level of industry and culture never before known in history. Within a hundred years of its founding, the United States became known as "the land of opportunity." Tens of millions of immigrants from all over the world flocked to her shores, and the country's essence became a blend of world cultures seeking to build a better life and a better society through education, invention, industry, and technology—liberty and capitalism being the principles behind the power of success. However, as had taken place with previous empires throughout history, the natural pattern for the wealthy to assert their influence upon government in order to maintain their wealth soon emerged, and by the early twentieth century created a highly refined feudal-like system managed not by land lords, but by immense corporate power.

RESOURCES AND BIOLOGY: THE VISIBLE SYSTEM

There are only three basic roles for women and men in the system we call society. Some are involved in civic affairs, some conduct business, and some educate. Then there are "the people." Everything previously discussed concerning economics is really all about the people, for without people there would be no one for whom to manufacture products, no one to serve, no one to educate, and no one to govern. We've been a world at war for five thousand years, and finally a group of people with significant interests have pulled together enough wealth and resources throughout the world to form an economic alliance to put an end to the bloodshed. Even though bloodshed remains, it is their goal to bring all nation-states into a cooperative relationship based on trade. It is truly a noble goal. However, there would be no goal if it wasn't for "the people."

A symbiotic relationship exists between the people and the three roles within society. Businesses must have consumers, and without the people, there would be few consumers. The same is true for those who govern and educate. Without people, there's no need for governing or educating. We need each other's cooperation, and this is the fundamental philosophical principle behind democracy.

As individuals living a lifetime, which is a small fraction of human existence, we have a difficult time perceiving the importance of our species, and that of the planet from which we grow. The memories of the oldest generation of people alive today began during the late 1920s and 1930s, a time of severe economic hardship, global depression, fascism, and then a world at war. For the generation of people now entering retirement, their earliest memories are of a world rebuilding itself after the bloodiest war in human history. For the middle-aged people of today, their earliest memories are of a social revolution of the '60s and the geopolitical Cold War of East versus West. The youth of today, however, are very different from any generation before. They know nothing of the Cold War, the Cultural Revolution, World War II, or the Great Depression. They know of technology, the Internet, smartphones, and the immediate communication and social networking that technology creates.

Knowledge about the world is passed from generation to generation. The next generation always inherits a world their parents and grandparents shaped, a world that actually exists as opposed to a world that the youth inherits and often perceive in a new and different way. We teach our children to be better and smarter, and to go farther in society than we did. In ancient times, Greek civilization created an institution of thought that we mark as the beginning of Western civilization, even though the Greeks themselves learned from an even more ancient civilization, the Egyptians. The Greek Miracle was not so much a miracle as it was a surge forward away from a mythical understanding of the world to a scientific one. Still today, those Greek philosophers from Thales to Socrates and Plato to Iamblichus are revered as philosophical icons of Western civilization. Consider also the philosophy of Aristotle, the embryo of scientific inquiry that eventually gave birth to the modern scientific method, and the work of Democritus, one of the earliest Greek philosophers, who speculated that everything is composed of atoms that are not geometric, are indivisible, and indestructible. From Democritus's imagination came truths that weren't discovered until more than two thousand years later, an important principle of history to remember. In a strange way, Democritus is the father of nuclear physics.

Another important principle of history to recognize is that knowledge is not only passed on to the next generation through written documents, but also by genetics. DNA not only changes randomly but also changes as a result of life experiences as those experiences affect the person. Recently, DNA has been believed to have emerged from the oceans, where a pool of raw genetic materials served as the platform for life, what scientists call the last universal ancestor. Anything further than that is unknown. So, in an esoteric way we are the consciousness of the planet itself because all life on Earth is genetically related. The Human Genome Project discovered that humans have between 30,000 and 40,000 genes, number that is much lower than expected because a mustard seed has 27,000 genes and a fruit fly, 13,300 genes.

Regardless of whether the principles of biological evolution—mutation, natural selection, and genetic drift—are accurate, evolution itself is evident in nature. What was once an evolution of form, during most epochs in Earth history, has now become an evolution of the human species, which we see as increasing levels of knowledge implemented into society through technology. Over the eons, what was once a barren, oxygen-less world has become a planet teeming not only with plant and animal life, but with human life, whose dominance through intelligence over all other living things has harnessed nature's knowledge and the resources of the planet. As a result, today, we have reached a unique position never before accomplished in world history. A thousand years ago the interactions between peoples were constrained by rudimentary methods of travel. Even a hundred years ago, prior to the invention of the airplane and the development of international flights, travel took a significant amount of time, particularly across the oceans. Today, however, many thousands of people fly to destinations across the world every day. Business and communication that were once geographically restricted now have no restrictions. Business and communication are not only worldwide, but also instantaneous as well as interdependent, as a recent *Time* magazine cover states, "The China Bubble: We're Counting on China's Growth to Save the World."[1]

Since the end of the Second World War, most nations have adopted a socioeconomic system based on capitalism. The former Soviet Union and recently China have given up on their centralized, government-run economies and joined the world market in trade. These are historic events because at no other time has the world economy been so homogenized. Yet, at the same time, every individual is unique is his or her own way.

The visible system (the physical universe) is planetary and biological tucked into the cycle of birth and death. Lurking behind this system, an even deeper system exists, responsible for nearly all of our actions and thoughts. This system, however, has no physical qualities to it.

BELIEFS: THE INVISIBLE SYSTEM

The main difficulty with the visible system in which we live is that it is a perceived reality. Therefore, it is subjective. Everyone has a point of view and an opinion—a belief—and most of the time thinks and acts differently from anyone else. More important, the leaders of our social institutions want to persuade you, to get you to think the way they do. They are there to instruct and indoctrinate a social norm. In essence, our social institutions train people to think in a certain way, believe the unfolding of life in a certain way—even believe history in a certain way. This indoctrination is nothing less than belief management. As a consequence, for the individual the daily experience of living is never quite what it should be amid all the ordered chaos that transpires in the world around him or her. This, in turn, creates tension and stress, and an inner search for who or what is responsible. Everything from alien visitations to the zero-point energy field as an interdimensional corridor to other realities is on the table.

Whether you are a beggar or miser, rich or poor, sinner or saint, down on your luck or the luckiest person in the world, whether American, European, Arab, African, or Asian, you were born into a system of belief management that slowly changes from generation to generation. Chances are, what you think about yourself, what you think about the world, and how you perceive yourself and the world are very different from the reality of you and the world around you.

People across the world believe many different things about life and society. Politically, we have socialism, communism, nationalism, republics, kingdoms, and dictatorships. Religiously, we find Catholicism, Protestant Christianity, Judaism, Hinduism, Islamism, and Buddhism. Science has its theories too, such as materialism, biological evolution, planetary evolution, intelligent design, global warming, and the big bang, each of which has merit yet is disputed. Economically, we have capitalism, Keynesianism, consumerism, monetarism, and globalism. Socially, we find hierarchical class and caste systems in every country.

We human beings created all of these social, scientific, economic, political, and religious concepts and theories in an attempt to understand our existence and conduct our lives as individuals and sociopolitical groups, ultimately as nation-states. None of these concepts and theories, however, is fact. Neither are they fiction. Rather, they are a perception, a point of view, and a way of understanding existence and forming that understanding into a system for conducting personal affairs in order to extract resources from the Earth to maintain the going concern of life. More important, each of these beliefs, whether social, scientific, economic, political, or religious, cannot be separated from any other belief.

You and I, and everyone else, live and work in a planet-wide, multilayered, invisible belief system that is as much social, scientific, economic, and political as it is religious, a belief system of our own creation that does not reflect an ultimate truth or the purpose of our existence, unless that purpose is to do nothing more than consume. This belief system didn't appear in the last hundred years or even the last thousand years, but has developed throughout history, beginning more than five thousand years ago at the dawn of civilization.

Beliefs are also interrelated, almost always. A person who is conservatively religious will most likely support social, economic, and political organizations that benefit and promote his or her conservative religious ideals. The same is true for the opposite. Those who are liberal in their religious views will most likely support liberal organizations in order to promote their liberal views. Life, however, is not so simple, for there are nonreligious persons who are conservative politically while being liberal in other areas of society, and vice versa. Then there is the power of economics, which is also based on beliefs about the nature of the human experience. Corporations, and entire industries, will support political campaigns and lobby elected representatives who support legislation in their favor.

The quest of the ordinary person, however, is tied to the most basic elements of human nature. Children grow up, marry, have children, and then watch their children have children, most likely work some unfulfilling job for fifty years to own a home and a car, and maybe set aside a little money for retirement. At some random point in time, however, whether the result of an accident, disease, or old age, the inevitable occurs: death. Except for a few loved ones, maybe, a few years later no one knows or cares that you or I or any other anonymous person was ever here—as if we were never here at all.

Death is inescapable, despite the fact that we as an advanced scientific society do everything we can to prevent it. The reality, however, is that we cannot prevent death, no matter what medical technology we develop. Death is a certainty, and only a matter of time. Whether rich or poor, famous or anonymous, death is guaranteed. You will die, and knowing this creates fear. Not necessarily a fear of death, but fear of the unknown. What lies after death? Does life continue after death, or is death the finality of being? This is the great question to which humankind has always sought an answer. There are other questions that go along with the great question. Why are we here in the first place? Where did we come from, and where are we going, if anywhere at all?

The answers to these questions are as diverse as the people who ask them. Some believe that we exist solely in a material reality and that death is the annihilation of our being and existence. Others believe that life in some way continues after death. Unfortunately, for those who believe the latter, from the traditionally religious to the self-styled spiritualists, a multitude of philosophical doctrines explain what happens after death and why. So which religious or spiritual philosophy is the correct one, if any? And, how do we know that there is life after death?

There's no scientific proof that we survive death. Therefore, from a purely scientific point of view, the materialists who argue that death is annihilation of personal existence must be correct. However, the same science that is used to defend the materialists' argument also describes material reality as not so much a reality that is permanent or of substance, but rather as a reality that represents what appears to be a virtual existence that we are born into. Upon death we either cease to exist or pass into another form of existence. This is troubling, a conundrum, because as people we experience the world as real and of substance.

Quantum physics, however, tells a very different story of what is substance. Everything that exists in our universe is composed of atoms, which are composed of particles known as electrons, protons, and neutrons, held together by an unbelievably strong force known as the nuclear force. More bizarre, these subatomic particles are not really particles at all, but what physicists call waves of energy that appear to us as particles only when we interact with them.

For example, the light that the Earth basks in is an energy wave we call sunshine. Only when the sun's energy waves impact the eye's retina does the sunshine existing as a wave become a particle called a photon, with velocity and a location in space. Indeed, all we ever truly see are photons that are reflected off of objects, and it is the functioning of our brains that creates a representation of the world around us. Seeing, combined with hearing, touching, smelling, and tasting, is formed somehow into what we call conscious perception, which is accomplished automatically by the brain. Yet, exactly what consciousness is and how it becomes a biological phenomenon is a mystery. There is no central place in the brain where sensory information comes together to become consciousness. In fact, there is no reason why consciousness should emerge from brain activity at all, but it apparently does, because each person knows that he or she is conscious, which is a unique subjectivity that gives each person a unique perspective and identity.

Today, there is no viable theory describing precisely what consciousness is or how it comes about. There is no single part of the brain responsible for consciousness in humans or in any other animal, so there is no consciousness-detecting machine that determines which animals are conscious and which are not, or at what level. Consciousness is a biological mystery, yet it appears to be as fundamental as the three spatial dimensions of our universe. Life as we understand and experience it is based on the concept of consciousness, a life that continually reproduces within the cycle of birth and death. Such a cycle is fundamental, as is our conscious experience of that cycle. It's a fact of our existence that is the basis for nearly everything that we do as individuals. Regardless of intelligence, religious belief, political persuasion, or cultural context, we are sexually driven. In fact, the attraction between people—sex and love—is the foundation of human experience, and is so for a reason. Procreation brings about not only the continuation of our species, but the steady swapping of genetic information.

These three things—the cycle of birth and death, our desire for love and sex, and our conscious experience—are the only facts in life. Whether religious, social, economic, political, or even scientific, everything else is argued except for one thing, the thing that is responsible for art, invention, and innovation. Without it we would still be living in the forests or jungles eating whatever we could find. Without imagination there can be no civilization.

THE POWER OF IMAGINATION

What we call the universe and our lives within this universe are a virtual existence, one that does not reflect the reality that is truly enduring, that which is eternal. Because our perception collectively forces the universe to exist in the single state from which we observe it—from a set of all potential states that the universe can exist in—our universe is applicable only to us. Even physical concepts are free creations of the human mind, and are not, even though it seems so, determined by what we call the external world. This is a very difficult concept for some people to accept because they have been taught that imagination is a fiction within their mind. Although this is certainly true at times, human action upon imagination brings creation into the world in which we live, in all kinds of things, most of which have to do with making life easier, but also for pleasure in the arts and entertainment. One has to wonder what truth is.

Is truth what we experience physically? Or is truth what we experience internally through the mind and emotion? Is truth defined by religion? Is it defined by society? Can science define truth?

The answer depends on what is meant by science. If science is understood to be a systematic study of natural phenomena, then there is some truth there, at least an explanation of natural world processes.

However, scientific truth as an explanation of natural world processes misses the truth of being because it does not take into consideration the state of being and knowing we experience on a daily basis, experience that is defined primarily by our five senses and turned into what we typically call perception through our minds. Exactly how sensory information is formed into our conscious experience remains a scientific mystery despite the fact that science now knows much about the natural world. The state of being we experience cannot be measured, so ultimately science cannot define this truth. Consequently, I am convinced that we are living in a virtual existence.

I am convinced of this because of those three facts of life I previously mentioned: the cycle of birth and death, the desire for love and sex, and the conscious experience of those things. These three things are phenomenological and unexplainable. There is no explanation as to why we must die other than to state that all that lives must die. Neither is our conscious perception explainable, the focal point of what creates the human experience. All that can be said without doubt is that we are born to consciously perceive and must at some point die, all the while enjoying sex in order to reproduce. Sex, however, is just the most intense pleasure from a wide range of pleasures. People take pleasure in art, sports, hobbies, books, movies, plays, and music, to name a few. The second most important pleasure is enjoying life among friends and family.

The most important piece of evidence that our lives are virtual is the power of imagination. I take great pleasure in talking with people. One afternoon a young scientist along with his brother and father visited my coffee shop. We talked for hours. Somehow the chat developed into a discussion on experience. The young scientist commented that if all your senses were removed, all you would have to experience would be your imagination. He is right, but what is imagination?

For most people, imagination refers to something that does not exist in physical reality, a trick of the mind, so to say. Usually, the word imagination is used in disbelief of someone else's statements or experiences, as in the statement "the ghost you thought you saw was your imagination." However, imagination is not always used in the context of disbelief. A novelist, for example, must have an active and vivid imagination, so it can be said that Stephen King and Dean Koontz have great imaginations in order to write the stories they do.

Regardless of how the word is used, imagination refers to something that physically does not exist. The important questions are: Why do we have an imagination at all, and why, like having a physical body, does everyone have an imagination? Where does it come from?

Without imagination, there would be no art or invention. Without imagination, culture and civilization would not exist. Without imagination, science and the quest for knowledge would not exist. Without imagination, there would be no systematic belief, no religion. Without imagination, we would be like the animals, having form without the ability to reason and without conscience to weigh the consequences of our deeds. Thus, our state of existence, our state of being, appears to be dependent upon imagination, for without imagination there would be no creativity, no creation. We would be living in a pristine wilderness as animals.

For imagination to be useful, however, in creating what we have created, individually and collectively, there needs to be memory of the past as well as anticipation of the future. Without memory, the knowledge that is manifest in our lives through imagination would be instantly gone with the wind. Without anticipation of the future, that knowledge could not be put to good use. So it seems that imagination, memory, and the concept of a future life are tied together in some way, for a reason, which is obvious as we have demonstrated over the millennia. It is how we improve our physical state of existence, individually and collectively. Yet by no means is our creation of civilization altruistic. One organization and its ideas conflict with other organizations and their ideas, generating discord and ultimately war. This also works on an individual level, so there is also personal conflict and abuse. Ultimately, abuse becomes murder. As much as we are creative, we are also destructive. Interestingly, this destructive potential that exists in society reflects the natural state of the planet that we live on. Tragedy and suffering arise from hurricanes, tornados, earthquakes, and drought. They wreak havoc and death on our civilization. And for these unsolicited displays of destruction there is no one to blame, except God.

But no, it can't be God's fault. We have done something bad, something to infuriate God. Somewhere along the way we have brought onto ourselves the wrath of God. Haven't we? It has to be our fault. We are to blame because somehow we are not "right with God." The indiscriminant destruction of life and property is the penalty we collectively pay for displeasing God. God wants atonement. Therefore, we must sacrifice a portion of our rewards to God, and that will makes things all right.

Such was the thinking in the sixth millennium BCE of a desperate patriarchal culture that eked out a living in the steppe lands of the Caucasus Mountains. On occasion, this patriarchal culture would sacrifice cattle and horses, the things that provided them with a way of life, to the sky god, an angry god of war and thunder. It was their conception of a vengeful sky god that spread south and west into Mesopotamia and beyond and brought about a way of life that eight thousand years later we now herald as the birth of civilization. Despite the erudite prose of great philosophers from the Egyptians and the Greeks, civilization demanded a sacrifice to God. It is amazing that this concept of atonement and the mentality of sacrifice exist to this day, although the sacrifice itself, the letting of blood, has been replaced conceptually with a belief system of guilt based on fear and punishment. We are their legacy.

IMAGINATION AS TRUTH

Imagination spawns creation. For the individual, from imagination comes curiosity—I wonder. And from curiosity comes contemplation—what if? And from contemplation comes action—I must try this. This process of imagining creates knowledge and understanding. In the external world this process leads to invention and a systematic development of technology designed to improve life. Internally, imagination is what makes us come alive. Everyone daydreams of romance and adventure, which is imagination. Everyone dreams of a future life, which is imagination.

Imagination—our imagination—creates the lives that we live.

Most people would agree that imagination gives us our ability to create as artists, our ability to innovate as scientists, and our ability to structure society as business and civic leaders. In 1963, when Dr. Martin Luther King Jr. announced to the world in front of Washington's Lincoln Memorial, "I have a dream," he wasn't just saying that to make his speech more charismatic. He meant it, and through his dream Dr. King changed a nation, because his dream became the people's dream. Dr. King first imagined racial equality when he led the Montgomery Bus Boycott in 1955 and helped create the Southern Christian Leadership Conference in 1957.

I find it fascinating that in his final speech on April 3, 1968, the day before he was assassinated, Dr. King stated:

I've seen the Promised Land. I may not get there with you. But I want you to know tonight, that we, as a people, will get to the Promised Land. And I'm happy, tonight. I'm not worried about anything. I'm not fearing any man. Mine eyes have seen the glory of the coming of the Lord.[2]

I've seen the Promised Land? I'm happy tonight? I'm not worried about anything? I'm not fearing any man? Who says these things with such conviction? What prompted Dr. King to say these things?

I also find it fascinating that Dr. King viewed life, all life, as being interrelated:

Somehow we're caught in an inescapable network [and are] mutuality tied in a single garment of destiny. Whatever affects one directly affects all indirectly. For some strange reason, I can never be what I ought to be until you are what you ought to be. You can never be what you ought to be until I am what I ought to be.[3]

What is Dr. King's "strange reason" that I cannot be what I should be until you are what you should be? And what does it have to do with imagination?

Dr. King, it seems, viewed everyone as being part of a whole and thought that "this is the interrelated structure of reality."[4] It's why I cannot be what I should be until you are what you should be. In other words, we have to go there together. Dr. King, I believe, also understood the divine principle of Oneness—a principle that states, we have to go there together, as one—which is reminiscent of a concealed esoteric tradition that can be found in all major religions of the world: Judaism, Christianity, Buddhism, Hinduism, and Islam.

This divine principle of Oneness, what does it mean? Certainly, we are all separate beings living separate lives from the perspective of each person's point of view. Does each person, then, live in a separate world of his or her own? Are there many worlds we each experience in and of ourselves, or is there a single world that we share?

The answer, which is an observable fact, is that we physically share a single world. Yet, each of us experiences a world of our own within our minds that is dependent upon the world everyone shares. So, do we share one world physically but exist in many different worlds of the mind?

That would seem to be the case because there are five major world religions and an assortment of various beliefs within those religions; add to that other religions, and what has been labeled as materialism or humanism, and a host of metaphysical concepts lumped into a wide category society calls New Age. Still, every person has differences, even large groups of people whose points of view share commonalities. No two people have the exact same point of view. This creates much of the tension we experience in the world. From the level of the family up through municipalities, countries, and cultures, opposing points of view create disagreements, which lead to frustration, then to anger, and ultimately hate.

Why is life like this? Does life have to be like this?

An observation: life does have to be like this because this is how it is, an unarguable fact. Why? What's the point?

The point is, in some way everyone is on their own personal grand search for Truth, whether it takes the form of religion, science, philosophy, or something else entirely. The problem exists when each of us believe we have found "it"—which is a perceived truth—and by relating to a group of like-minded people, suggest to all others outside the group that their understanding is the correct way to understand the world we experience. With such an approach there can be truth for the individual and the group, but there cannot be truth for all people. Absolute truth, therefore, in that all people are united in mind, this divine principle of Oneness must be imaginary. So, truth exists only in our imagination. Yet it is imagination that inspires the artist, and the inventor, and the great men and women of our past, like Dr. Martin Luther King Jr., even the infamous such as Adolph Hitler, who imagined Germany as a world power and a perfect society, or the biblical Joshua, whose army destroyed every person and animal living in Jericho: "men and women, young and old, cattle, sheep and donkeys."[5]

In the Christian and Jewish traditions, how is it that Adolph Hitler is viewed, and rightfully so, as committing crimes against humanity, yet Joshua acted out his atrocities in accordance with divine will? There is no rationalizing an answer to this question. Both men commanded armies that committed atrocities. The difference exists only in personal perspective. In the case of Nazi Germany, they lost the war and those who survived were prosecuted for their crimes. Joshua, whose story was written by the victors, of course is viewed as a hero.

This is how life's events, current and historical, are perceived. Ultimately, they are a direct result of belief systems regardless of whether the belief system is Hitler's blood religion, Joshua's Judaism, or any other belief system, modern or historical. Belief systems always justify the actions of believers, at least to themselves and their followers. Belief systems therefore are a rationalization, an explanation, as it were, of why everything about us and our life on this planet exists as it does. For me, the important question is: Because there are so many belief systems, how can any single belief system represent absolute truth?

It might sound like I am belittling belief systems. I am not. On the contrary, belief systems are a vital part of the human experience. They create structure within societies and provide a way for people to relate to each other, given the fact that we don't know where we came from, other than our mother's womb; neither do we know where we are going when we die, unless there is some validity to near-death experiences. Nonetheless, belief systems, when viewed pragmatically, are not real. Rather, they are a way in which we humans justify our nature and our actions.

Our true nature has little to do with belief systems. It has to do with imagination. Not in the sense that your imagination is a fantasy, but that imagination is the source of your being. And in that way, belief systems are a product of imagination.

To be sure, it is a perplexing statement: imagination is the source of being, the source of existence. It is counterintuitive, a reversal of thought, a reversal of perspective. The notion that imagination is the source of being goes against everything you and I have ever been taught. It even goes against our naturally occurring perception. Yet, imagination is what has made civilization what it is today. Imagination is the inspiring source behind the artist and the scientist, as well as the theologian and the philosopher. Everyone is endowed with some measure of imagination. We read. We watch movies. We listen to music. We imagine. Then, we turn our imagination toward aspects of the physical world we inhabit. Regardless of age, gender, or occupation, if anything in our experience is true, in a sense that it is real and lasting, it is our imagination. We never stop imagining. We desperately want to live a dream, whether that dream is being an astronaut, a ballet dancer, a soldier, a businessman, a physicist, a writer, a musician, or any other self-rewarding profession or occupation.

So, what is truth? Imagination is truth.

Most people would regard this statement as nonsense and argue that imagination is a byproduct of biology, a brain-related feature nature developed for the purpose of survival, and that imagination has little to do with the physical world around us. Imagination, they would say, is nothing more than an evolutionary edge our species developed, and because humans with our imagination are more inventive, more organized, and better equipped to manipulate the environment, we not only survived but thrived.

It's a good theory. But how do we know if imagination is, in fact, nothing more than a brain-related feature that evolved over thousands or millions of years? We don't, and there is no way to prove that is the case without a time machine. Like everything else we theorize to explain our existence, the evolution-based explanation for imagination is a belief system, and it doesn't matter that it is scientific or that much research and scholarship have been dedicated to evolution's academic acceptance. It is still a belief system.

Suppose that imagination is an evolutionary feature we humans enjoy and leverage over our environment to our benefit. How did life, and later sentient life, emerge in the first place? And for what purpose did life and sentient life appear? It is the same question as "where did we humans come from in the first place, and why?" There is even a deeper question. Doesn't there have to be a concept of life as well as a concept of sentience prior to the emergence of either?

The scientific disciplines cannot explain how imagination emerged (or if it did). Nor can science explain where we came from. These events are beyond science's scope of investigation. Neither can religion, other than to state we are God's creation, which is open to wide and various interpretations. Yet, the indisputable fact remains that we exist. We are conscious, sentient beings experiencing what we call life.

What's more intriguing within our conscious experience is that not only are we aware that we exist, but we are also aware that we must die and that with each passing day every person moves a little closer to his or her death. With such awareness there is great propensity for fear and anxiety regarding the kind of a life after death we might find, even whether such an afterlife exists or, on the other hand, nothing at all. Which is more terrifying?

Consequently, we are left with our imagination—our own avenue of truth—to figure it out, each person for him- or herself. But typically, we don't. Instead, we rely on the experts to tell us the truth, particularly theologians, but scientists and philosophers as well. Here lies the greatest barrier to the important questions about life and death: "What is truth?" is answered only through personal demonstration of one's imagination. In other words, every person must experience truth through his or her own imagination, as opposed to believing what someone else knows or claims to know.

Although it might sound so, I am not declaring that everything religious, scientific, or philosophical is to be disregarded. On the contrary, throughout history there have always been great men and women of science, religion, and philosophy who have experienced truth and have expressed that truth in speech, or in writing, or in actions, whether scientifically, philosophically, or theologically. Their testaments are our street signs, guideposts, symbols; they are individual expressions of truth pointing to a higher order of experience that has always existed. We must go there together, as Dr. King put it, since "this is the inter-related structure of reality"[6]—a statement every genuine scientist, philosopher, and theologian knows to be true.

What is this interrelated structure of reality? Such a question probes deep into the nature of being; what is "real," and how do we know that what we think is real is actually real?

Despite the all-inclusive commonality of the tangible experience we are born into and live out our lives in, we inhabit a world of thoughts, a world of the imagination birthed into the realm of the physical. There is little wonder that at every opportunity to do so we escape from the physical and mental demands society places on us through movies, concerts, and books. On the more sinister side of life there is drug use. We call these actions escapism, but is it really escapism?

What is real is that which is lasting, that which is permanent. We believe our planet and the physical universe is real because it is lasting. Our senses tell us so. Yet, astronomers and cosmologists tell us a different story. Eventually, the sun will exhaust its hydrogen core and will begin burning helium instead. As a result, the size of the sun will increase dramatically, consuming Mercury and Venus, and possibly Earth. Even if Earth is not consumed by the sun's shroud of expanding heat, our planet will be reduced to a cinder. So, that narrow gate of habitability we live in courtesy of the exact distance Earth is from the moon and sun? Its permanence is only an illusion. Thus, we are fooled by our perception, the perception of a short life relative to everything else in the solar system and universe. In truth, our planet is not everlasting. Neither are our lives. Like all of nature, human life is a cycle of birth and death, a cycle of rebirth that one day will simply cease to exist.

So, how is it that we are so sure our physical lives on this planet are real?

HISTORY'S FORBIDDEN ZONE

Because we have been convinced through our senses, we *believe* our lives; what we can touch, see, hear, and taste—that is what's real. And based on this experience of the senses, humans have ventured out into the world of science in order to explain ourselves. Not only have we been convinced by our senses that our terrestrial lives are real, but we also have been convinced by our own mental reasoning that our beliefs are real too. We believe that our position in history is purely a current affair and that we are the first to arrive at this modern, technical, civilized state of humanity. We do not believe this because we know it to be true. Rather, we believe it to be true because we want it to be true and work exceedingly hard at trying to prove that it is true.

In the age of information in which billions of people can share information with each other in an instant, the suppression of alternative and novel thought is impossible. There is truth in history too, plainly visible for all to see. All one has to do is travel a little bit, pay attention to details, and assemble the puzzle piece by piece. In doing so, beliefs become myths, and myths become historical facts. Were our ancient ancestors so lacking in reason that they fabricated stories of a Golden Age just to explain in some way their existence or to provide for them a make-believe history just to have a history? Our ancestors aren't the ones who have concocted stories. We have.

A little more than four and a half miles north by northwest of Egypt's Giza Plateau lies another plateau just off the Cairo-Alexandria highway. Naturally disguised by the surrounding barren, rocky terrain, the plateau of Abu Rawash is not on any tourist map; this is a forbidden site that reminds me of the forbidden zone in *Planet of the Apes*. Just off the highway a beaten trail in the sand curves around the hilly landscape, leading to a forgotten pyramid. For the average tourist there is little to see here: a pit several hundred feet deep cutting into the bedrock, a few courses of limestone forming the foundation of a pyramid, and piles of beautiful, pink, sparkling granite standing at various places around the base of the pyramid, some monstrously large. Whoever began this construction project suddenly stopped for a reason that has been lost to history.

At the southern side of the pyramid, the archaeological team that cleaned up the site and exposed the core blocks of the pyramid found something very unusual. Too heavy to remove from the site, this unusual stone was dragged from a rubble heap and positioned on a number of softball-sized rocks. The morning sun glared off its flat, smooth surface. The quartz crystals at the stone's broken end sparkled in the sunshine. I ran my finger across the edge that separated the broken end from the flat, smooth face of the stone. The cut was clean and even in a long arc. Then I ran my hand across the stone's smooth face. Amazing. Whatever cut this sixty-five ton block of pink granite did so with relative ease. I looked closer and could see minute striations evenly spaced across its face (see page 57, bottom). *My God,* I thought to myself.

Granite stone with machined surface at Abu Rawash, with larger detail

Sunshine reflecting off the stone's smooth surface

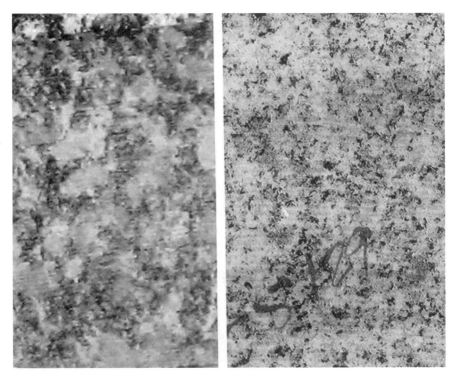

Comparison of machine feed lines from the stone at Abu Rawash to the feed lines on a granite tile purchased at a local home supply store

I had seen photos of this stone the year before and had listened intently to the explanation of its existence by my friend Christopher Dunn, an expert machinist and pioneer researcher of ancient Egyptian machining technologies. Now I was there looking at it, touching it, the peaks of Giza's three pyramids still visible in the distance. Every person who has had wood or metal shop in high school would realize that these minute striations that cover the face of the stone are feed lines or milling marks left from the blade of the saw as it removed material millimeter by millimeter (see page 57, bottom).

The previous day on the Giza Plateau, Chris had pointed out a dozen or more blade marks that could have never been left by handheld tools. Nor were they ever intended to be visible to the public. Over the millennia, a fair portion of the basalt patio on the north side of the Great Pyramid has been scavenged and used for more modern building projects, exposing the mistakes left by whoever built the pyramids. On any construction project, mistakes are made. Still usable, stones that were improperly cut, or waste products from another cut, were recut and placed inside the outer edge of the basalt patio. Millennia ago, no one would have ever seen those mistakes on the finished product. Now they were visible, exposing a technology that we today use sparingly because of the heavy equipment and expense required to make granite countertops and floor tiles.

Basalt patio on the north side of the Great Pyramid

Thousands of men wearing loincloths, pulling sleds of limestone and granite blocks, wielding only a hand chisel and a hammer stone are responsible for these magnificent wonders of the ancient world, structures that we today could build only after inventing special machinery to accomplish the task, costing billions of dollars? How is it possible to turn a hundred-ton block of granite into the most beautiful, perfectly

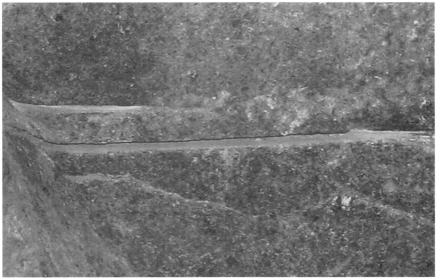

Basalt stone displaying saw marks

shaped oblong box—what Egyptologists refer to as a sarcophagus—with a rounded lid with square corners and a beveled lip?

Things are never what they seem.

Such a beautiful, perfectly shaped granite box could never have been crafted with hand tools. Human civilization is far older than anyone ever imagined. Long ago, forty-one thousand years ago, if you take the ancient Egyptians at their word, a technical human civilization existed. Yet, we want to believe that we are the first people to achieve such a technical, sophisticated civilization.

We are all born into belief systems that have existed for time immemorial. Religion fares no better than our scholarly attempts to explain the past. The philosophy, the understanding of life, from which modern

Granite boxes in situ *at the pyramid temple complex of Abu Sir*

Christianity arose two thousand years ago is as old as humankind itself. History, philosophy, and religion are one giant ball of string intertwined from the core.

Human history is not a segmented set of cultures and civilizations with distinct beginnings and abrupt endings. Humanity, society, is a continuous flow of thought and being since the beginning of time itself, since everything we do is predicated by thought. From one generation to the next, since the very beginning, knowledge of truth has been handed down first in myth and legend and then as sacred writing. The Greek philosophers knew this, and their affiliation with the Egyptian priests was their inspiration. Regardless of whether Plato's specific story of Atlantis is fact or fiction, his inspiration came from the Egyptian priests of Sais by way of a statesman, his uncle Solon.

The physical evidence still existing from ancient Egypt's civilization, examined by qualified individuals with the proper credentials, demonstrates that our level of advancement is not purely a current affair and we are not the first to arrive at this technical, civilized state of humanity. Our social institutions do not want us to believe this because in this understanding of history there is power, power that demonstrates to us that the institutions that are supposed to serve as our educators are wrong in their judgment of the past. That being the case, they might also be wrong in their assumptions of life today.

The individual experience of reality as a conscious perception is denied by our institutions. And they do so not without reason. The individual experience of reality as a biological machine addicted to pharmaceutical potions creates good consumers and taxpayers, and society needs "consumers" and "taxpayers," not people. It's an emotionally dysfunctional society we live in, because the reality that individual human experience is a perception is denied.

To appreciate our subjective experience—what we really mean when we say "life"—and to regain that individual perception of happiness, we must take a lesson from our ancient ancestors and their approach to the journey within.

3

ANCIENT SYMBOLISM
AND THE JOURNEY
WITHIN

Today, that inward journey has been formalized in five major religions: Judaism, Christianity, Islam, Hinduism, and Buddhism. In the earliest of times, however, this inward journey was expressed through myth, a symbolic way of conveying truths through story and art. The earliest human societies, some thirty-five thousand years ago, viewed the giver of life as feminine, because it is through the feminine that all animal life reproduces. Our earliest ideas were not of a god, but of a goddess.

According to Lithuanian-born archaeologist Dr. Marija Gimbutas (1921–1994), the concept of the Goddess was nearly universal in prehistoric cultures.[1] Parts of the female body, particularly the life-giving parts, are typical in Paleolithic art. The vulva was one of the earliest symbols to be engraved, a representation of growth and the seed. In some Paleolithic art, next to the image of a vulva is an image of a branch or other plant design, or within it, a seed or plant. Thus, for prehistoric people the Great Mother Goddess represented the creative power of the Earth that serves as the life force for both plants and animals. Gimbutas notes, however, that although the concept of divinity in these prehistoric cultures was focused on the feminine, their society was not dominated by women. Society was balanced. Women and men had their own power and position, and performed their own duties for the benefit of the family and the clan.

During Paleolithic times (35,000–10,000 BCE) and even Neolithic times (after 10,000 BCE), cultures across Europe and the Mediterranean carved figurines known today as "Venuses," females typically with large stomachs, breasts, and buttocks. According to Gimbutas, these Venus figurines were the epitome of the Mother Goddess, depicting the cycle of life: birth, death, and the process of regeneration. Although there were many types of goddess figurines, they all symbolized the same essence of the Mother Goddess. Divinity itself was embedded in nature, and echoes of this concept are still found today in the term *Mother Nature.*

For example, in Goddess cosmology, the world began when the "water bird" brought the egg. When the egg split, one part became the Earth and the other part became the sky. Figurines with accented breasts were typically carved with a bird's head. The vulture, owl, crow, and raven were common symbols—symbols of death. Figurines carved as a stiff, white goddess also depicted death. Some "death" figurines were also carved as if the creature being carved was wearing a mask. Carvings such as these were often associated with the vulture. According to Gimbutas, this style of symbolism was very long lasting and continued up to historical times.

One of the final vestiges of the goddess culture was lived on the Island of Crete, whose occupants were famous for their jubilant artistic style in ceramics, weaving, metallurgy, engraving, and architecture. They are also known for their art, particularly with their "bull-leaping" frescos. Crete came under Achaean rule during the second millennium BCE, creating a mixed society known as the Minoan-Mycenaean culture. Despite Mycenaean influence, the Goddess and the way of life she symbolized continued. Crete's Minoan-Mycenaean religion was one of realism and sensual celebration. Their values were represented in art by the snake-handling Minoan goddess of nature. Minoans depicted her with bare, full breasts handling a golden snake, which represented the symbol of the soul of the deceased.

Gimbutas also believed that the people of the Goddess culture used hallucinogenic mushrooms or other consciousness-altering plants in their rituals. Particularly in the annual Eleusis initiation ceremonies for the cult of Demeter and Persephone, mushrooms were portrayed as sacred.

During the final centuries of the second millennium BCE, European and Mediterranean cultures become progressively more patriarchal and egocentric, and with the invention of the phonetic alphabet, the general consciousness of the people shifted toward written languages, which led up to the Greek philosophers and the birth of Western civilization. Logic and reason replaced the ancient symbolic awareness. However, this ancient renaissance was short-lived. By the fourth century AD, Western civilization had adopted the politics of guilt and salvation with Christianity and a social rule defined by its priesthood.

Christianity evolved from a mix of Egyptian philosophy and the ancient Mesopotamian "gods of heaven," a new twist on two ancient religions, both of which viewed the serpent as a symbol of divinity. In Christianity, however, the serpent became the embodiment of evil.

Even today, the symbol of the serpent that was prevalent across many ancient cultures remains in our consciousness as the caduceus medical symbol, twin serpents appearing as a helix winding around a pole. Modeled after Hermes's badge of office, the caduceus depicts serpents as messengers of Hermes who escorted souls to the underworld. A wooden staff with a single snake coiled around it symbolizes Asclepius, the Greek physician who was deified after death. However, the origin of the caduceus most likely cannot be traced to ancient Greece. The oldest available evidence suggests the caduceus comes from ancient Sumer during the late third millennium BCE. A cylinder seal from 2200 BCE known as the Serpent Lord Enthroned depicts a deity in human form sitting on a throne before a smoldering altar bordered by entwined serpents. Another seal from the late third millennium reveals a male figure sitting on a throne opposite a female figure and between them, a tree heavily laden with fruit. Next to the female figure in the familiar "S" pattern writhes the serpent Nabu, the god of intellectual activity, wisdom, and writing.

The serpent was also common symbolism in ancient Sumer. In the oldest recorded story known to humankind, *The Epic of Gilgamesh,* the serpent springs from a well, eats the "plant of youth," sloughs off its skin, then disappears, robbing the hero of his opportunity for immortality. Although no editorial provides meaning for the snake's theft of the plant, it is clear from the story the serpent became immortal by doing so, and Gilgamesh did not.

In Sumerian mythology, the primeval sea, Abzu, existed before anything, and from that sea, An (heaven) and Ki (Earth) were formed. Ki is likely to be the original name of the Earth goddess, whose name more often appears as Ninhursag, the queen of the mountains; Ninmah, the exalted lady; or Nintu, the lady who gave birth. Between them was the solid vault of the atmosphere, Lil'. The brighter portions formed the stars, planets, sun, and moon.[2]

In the beginning, as told in *The Epic of Gilgamesh,* all things needed were created. Heaven and Earth were separated. An took heaven, Enlil took the Earth, while Ereshkigal was carried off to the netherworld as a prize, and Enki sailed off after her. Enki consumed the plants (Ninhursag's children) and so was cursed and wounded once for each plant consumed.[3]

In the prologue to *The Epic of Gilgamesh*, a *huluppu* tree was transplanted from the banks of the Euphrates into a garden in the city of Uruk by Inanna, the goddess of love and fertility.[4] There she finds that "a serpent who could not be charmed made its nest in the roots of the tree. The Anzu bird (a lesser divinity) set his young in the branches of the tree, and the dark maid Lilith (the biblical Adam's alleged first wife) built her home in the trunk."[5] At Gilgamesh's death, family and friends weighed out their offering to the gods and among them was Ningizzida, the god of the serpent, the Lord of the Tree of Life, to whom they offered bread.

In another Mesopotamian myth, the large female dragon Tiamat personified the saltwater ocean—the water of chaos—and the primordial mother of all that exists, including the gods themselves. Her consort, Apsu, personified the freshwater abyss that lies beneath the Earth. From the union of saltwater and freshwater, the first pair of gods was born, Lachmu and Lachamu, who were parents to Ansar and Kisar and grandparents to Anu and Ea.

In the Babylonian creation epic the *Enûma Eliš,* written around 2000 BCE, the descendants of Tiamat and Apsu began to aggravate them, so they decided to kill their offspring. Ea discovered their plans and managed to kill Apsu while he slept. Tiamat flew into a rage when she learned of Apsu's death, and wanting to avenge her husband, she created an army of monstrous creatures, which was to be led by her new consort, Kingu, who was also her son. Marduk, born in the deep freshwater sea, killed Tiamat and cleaved her body in half. From the upper portion he created the sky, and from the lower half, he made the Earth. From her water came forth the clouds, and her tears became the source of the Tigris and the Euphrates. Kingu also perished, and from his blood Marduk created the first humans.

Marduk, the patron god of Babylon, was represented in symbol as a pointed hoe placed on a stand and the serpent-dragon who guards the underworld of the gods. The same serpent-dragon carries the scribe's stylet (a slender pointed instrument), which is the emblem of Nabu, Marduk's son.

The symbol of the serpent is the oldest of ancient symbols and was a recurring motif in the prehistoric art of Europe along with the bird. Both were symbols of the Mother Goddess culture. The abstract serpent, a simple spiral, was a central pattern and commonly used as ornamentation going back twenty-five thousand years, possibly even forty thousand. From ancient Greece to India and from China to Europe, central Asia, and Siberia, as well as spanning the Americas, the symbol of the serpent crosses every path in myth, culture, and history.

The serpent symbolized immortality and the water of chaos from which all life sprang—the primordial mother of all that exists, conceptually and physically. The serpent associated with the god Nabu also represented the human ability of writing and thereby was associated with knowledge and wisdom. All these "gods," particularly the serpent, were important symbols for the ancient description of the world our ancestors were experiencing. Ancient symbolism provided a language for their journey within.

THE ROLE OF SYMBOL

Whether ancient or not, symbol is important in anyone's inward journey because *everything is symbol.* All human languages are symbolic. In fact, everything we experience, whether it is by sight, sound, smell, taste, or touch, is symbolic. We don't realize this because just as the Wizard of Oz hid behind a curtain, there is also a veil separating our physical experience and perception from "what really is." That veil is the brain and its connection to the physical senses.

Our brains serve as translators for a multiplicity of waves. What we see, hear, smell, taste, and touch are the naturally occurring elements and diverse combination of those elements that have become our ecosphere of life. It is our perception of waves as particles that is sight, sound, smell, taste, and touch. In truth, there are only waves. We perceive these experiences as particles because that is what our brains do, and they do so at a fundamental level innate not only to our species, but to many other species inhabiting the Earth. The world we live in and experience is therefore symbolized and re-created in our minds through our brains. Electromagnetic energy waves are transformed through a highly complex structure that to us appears real, and it is all accomplished through symbol.

Our origins are unknown and therefore abstract. Yet, our lives are concrete, material in nature. Consider also the experience that our lives bring forth within our being as feelings, thoughts, and emotions. Once again abstract. So, the material world somehow symbolizes a hidden, illusive *cause* that we experience as *effect*. It's the role of science to understand and catalog, essentially, the cause and effect of all things. Because people are limited in their knowledge—we don't know where we came from or why we are here—the question must be posed: Are our conscious lives cause or effect?

FUNCTIONAL THINKING

When cause and effect are applied to the conundrum that to explain the universe, human life also must explained, humankind becomes more of an abstraction rather than a physical form. We experience life between two abstractions, cause and effect. The effect is our perception, and the cause exists outside the physical laws of our universe; thus, between these two abstractions lies the world we experience. This is the mystery on which all religions are based. It is also the mystery where truth lies, which must be discovered exclusively by the individual. However, in order to understand this mystery, rational thinking must be discarded in favor of a more functional approach not limited to the physical world. For an abstraction to appear physical, portions within that abstraction must contrast in order to represent something other than the abstractions that they are. Thus, the abstract, through the application of contrast, creates within itself a large variety of symbols, which is what we perceive as the physical world.

So, reality as it relates to our experience is defined by the life of the symbol (its esotericism, meaning our intuitive and innate understanding) in its identification with the physical life we live (the symbol's exotericism). Therefore, symbols are the experience of our consciousness, which is the effect and at the same time the cause, because cause can be described only as an experience not bound by the material world. The full effect of the symbolism being experienced is a nature that results in awareness of its own consciousness with an ability to self-perceive and self-reflect.

In its simplest definition, a symbol is an object or sign used to represent something else. The use of symbols to express meaning is symbolism, which has a physical existence, whereas the symbolic is a form of communication used to describe an object or phenomenon and occurs in the mind. Symbolism, for instance, was used by ancient cultures to describe the world around them. The symbol already existed in nature as a pattern or archetype to be referenced.

Esoteric symbolism is different from exoteric symbolism (or what we refer to simply as symbolism) in that esoteric symbolism preexists in our nature. Facial expressions, for example, are constant and real regardless of culture. Constricted muscles around the mouth accompanied by glaring eyes always symbolize anger. Likewise, an upturned mouth with a sparkle in the eyes always symbolizes joy. Esoteric symbolism is also auditory. Disharmonious sounds always symbolize unpleasantries. Likewise, soft melodious chords lull us into a state of inner bliss. Within us, these esoteric symbols elicit a response that is expressed physically, mentally, or emotionally and as a consequence can be understood as a relationship to our cause of existence.

We perceive esoteric symbols as harmony, order, and beauty, creating within us a sense of unity, which is the basis for understanding our causality. This cause exists in everything and in effect is that which makes us alive, a point that cannot be argued, because we are obviously here. Consider the concepts of quantity and quality. Everything that we perceive quantifiably also contains quality, which is an aspect of *a priori* knowledge and serves as our experience. In other words, experiencing the world around us is embedded in our physical form. As such, the knowledge of how to experience the physical world does not need to be learned. It already exists in us. How our experience of quantity and quality relate to cause can be reduced to simple chemistry.

We know that matter is energy. However, as long as life is assumed to be purely biological, or material, the natural world is viewed simply as a quantitative sequence of events. With our waking consciousness we see polarized energy as matter and object, and nothing more. This is obvious, but what is not so obvious is the energy that serves as the building blocks for the structure of the atom, and within the structure of the atom, quality is derived according to the periodic chart of elements. Each element is defined by its number of electrons, protons, and neutrons. Therefore, quality, as an abstraction, has no physical substance, but with its movement into a configuration of matter it takes on a substance that can be experienced. This movement or vibration—what we call energy—is by definition our causality, and without cause there can be no effect. The energy that makes up all phenomena is also the cause. As a result, the essence of life, our conscious awareness, exists through the cause, and its materialization into the physical produces the same cause in us. However, it must be noted that from our physical point of view, cause and effect are inseparable. The cause and effect relationship we experience in nature is our perception, and with this mind it can be argued that "things just are" where we are those things in a holistic way.

We are cause and effect, abstract and physical at the same time. This makes cause and effect inseparable, and we observe this in nature. Chemical reactions are instantaneous and permanent. Conception is instantaneous. So is the germination of a seed as it moves from nut to seedling. Nature is constant and exists exclusively in the present moment, which through memory creates an ongoing image we perceive as continuous. In truth, there is no past or future. These are concepts we have devised for referencing knowledge and information. With our ability to remember and anticipate the next moment, we have a sense of time; in truth, however, there is an eternity of the present moment. And this eternity is the esoteric reality we are physically born into to experience subjectively. Conceptualizing this is difficult because of our memory of the past, which creates an anticipation of the future; our memory is bound primarily by physical awareness. This is by design, though, because through our consciousness we attribute an exoteric character to this esoteric reality, which makes our physical world real. This is nature, and it is the symbolic that exists in a transitory state, moving from the abstract world to the concrete world and back again to the abstract. We talk about these as two realities for the purpose of discussion, but in truth the abstract and the concrete are a single reality. Here is an example from the twentieth-century French mathematician philosopher René Schwaller de Lubicz.

Consider a celestial body that rotates on an axis, such as our planet. The tangential projection of a diameter from the plane in which it exists, at right angles to this axis, moves in opposite directions. At the celestial body's center, directly on the axis, the tangential projection is canceled, resulting in no movement at the body's center; such movement is not possible. To compensate for this impossibility, the axial pole is displaced and moves in the direction opposite to the body's rotation. This sounds ridiculous, but it is true. Have you ever watched a vehicle alongside you while driving on an interstate highway? Although you know the wheels of the car are rotating forward, the hubcaps appear to be rotating in the opposite direction. This movement of the celestial body creates precessional motion—the gyroscopic motion of a spinning object, in which the axis of spin itself rotates around a central axis. It's the same principle as a spinning top.

If the axial center were to stop while the celestial body continued rotating, the celestial body would break apart after reaching a certain velocity. This creates a mystery because the axis is not the abstraction of a concrete surface, nor is it possible to define the axis as cause or effect. The axis is an *imaginary* line. Nonetheless, it is a fact of the rotating body's character. However, the axis is not truly abstract, because it plays

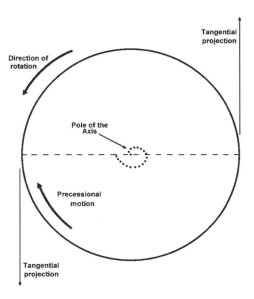

Tangential projections on a celestial body

a large part in the mathematics and the behavior of the system (the rotating body). Nor is it truly concrete, because an axis is a line that is one-dimensional and cannot exist within a physical system. *In effect, the axis is symbolic and is an inherent part of physical reality.*[6]

Herein lies an apparent contradiction between the symbolic and the historical (physical). The symbol exists, yet remains physically incomprehensible. If we view the symbolic as a transitory state, however, from the abstract to the physical, unifying the discontinuity of appearance in the continuity of the present, then the symbolic no longer contradicts the physical fact. As a result, the physical fact appears as the exoteric character of an esoteric reality.

From our physical perspective, the cause outside our universe can never be demonstrated, which, in a duality, always leaves one pole as a matter of faith. From an esoteric perspective, through the symbolic, the poles' divided parts are unified, thereby demonstrating causality. The cause, which is apparently outside the physical system, is actually within it forever, united in the present. The deduction and conclusion is that the abstract world is not only real, but an integral and operating part of the physical world.

In the human experience there are two ways to view the world: the immediate world we observe is experienced through sensation, and the abstract world of the esoteric is experienced through the symbolic. While the experience of the immediate world we observe is objective, creating our sense of detachment from everything else in the world, the esoteric experience of symbol is subjective and timeless. Both perspectives exist simultaneously to create what we call perception.

The three dimensions of height, width, and length do not exist, esoterically. However, observation emanates from the esoteric, the abstract. Spatial vision stems from the center and extends in all directions at once into what we call the volume of space, and within this space the abstract (quality) naturally forms itself into matter (quantity).

Scientifically, form (the atom) is self-configured energy. This spatial "becoming" can be viewed as esoteric and a function of what Schwaller de Lubicz calls innate consciousness, or, to put it another way, as our consciousness of the continuous. Once spatial perception exists, we develop the concept of time based on our awareness of the discontinuous. Substance (what constitutes electromagnetic waves in quantum physics) produces matter through action, and through the principle of bonding, the abstract becomes form. Scientifically, this becoming of form occurs through three principles: repulsion, attraction, and complementarity, which we find in the three charges of subatomic particles: negative (electron), positive (proton), and neutral (neutron).

All three principles must exist to manifest the abstract as the physical, and to derive a quantity of objects where those objects are characterized as quality. This process of quantifying quality is best described as symbolic. As such, all nature, including the human body, is symbolic of the qualities that make us who we really are. Sight, sound, odor, taste, and touch are all symbolic in the translation from the immediate world of biology to the abstract world of the observer, where mind and perception are the only reality; thus, the symbolic is the doorway for the inward journey to truth.

SYMBOLISM AND ANCIENT KNOWLEDGE

Our ancient ancestors understood that the symbolic is the doorway for the inward journey to truth; they knew that the texts they created for their rites and for their posterity were designed to be understood symbolically. To gain such an understanding, however, the rational mind must be put aside in favor of a deeper sense of thought, one that involves a less limiting approach, a functional approach not confined to the material world. Today, we might call this a spiritual approach, but being far removed from the culture and times of the people who wrote ancient texts, we lack their understanding of imagery and are forced by our own modern practices to approach imagery with the rational mind, an approach that will always produce failure to understand, thereby creating a belief based on literalism rather than on the experiential, or what is real.

In order for an abstraction to appear physical, an abstraction within that abstraction must somehow contrast to become something other than abstraction. Thus, as mentioned before, the abstract through contrast creates within itself a large variety of symbols, which we perceive as the physical world. And within those symbols lies the path to permanence that transcends the rational mind. It is just as powerful today as it was many thousands of years ago because those symbols create experiential knowledge within, but do so only in the realm of imagination.

Because there are volumes of ancient texts spread across many cultures, I will focus on what is most pertinent to Western society, Judaism and Christianity, with the core texts being the Old and New Testaments of the Bible. The first eleven chapters of Genesis, up to the call of Abram, are mythical. They are symbolic, which does not mean that these stories are fiction. Rather, the stories are histories told in a manner to effectively explain what we today call irrational truths, discussed in an experiential style (as the story re-creates the experience for the audience) that has been lost to modern societies as a result of our highly materialistic approach to science.

The serpent discussed in the previous chapter was not worshipped as a deity but understood as the primary active principle of nature as humans experience it, an understanding of nature that reaches far back into prehistoric times. Similar ancient motifs include chevrons, X's, zigzags, meanders, streams, and aquatic forms. These depictions were symbolic references to a concept, visible in images of horned snakes and ram-headed snakes. Ram horns and snake coils have similar spiral forms.[7]

The serpent as a symbol, an image, represents the energy responsible for life, energy that embodies the concept of movement and was artistically displayed as such in spirals and coils. This concept of movement links the biblical Genesis to a highly symbolic yet very descriptive explanation of the human experience. In the opening lines of Genesis, we read that "darkness was on the face of the deep." The word *deep* in Hebrew is *tehom,* and *tehom* is a cognate of *Tiamat,* the primordial dragon in Mesopotamian mythology.[8] Tiamat was the serpent mother of the world, just as the talking serpent guarding the Tree of Knowledge was the embodiment of temptation in the mythical Garden of Eden.

The roots of Hebrew serpent imagery can be traced to Mesopotamian and Egyptian symbolism. The serpent was seminal in ancient Egypt, a civilization spanning three thousand years. The pharaoh's golden diadem was fashioned with two symbols at its center, which rested on the forehead, the cobra and the vulture, a snake and a bird—indicative of Gimbutas's prehistoric culture of the Goddess.

Ancient Egypt has been greatly misunderstood since its systematic study began in the mid-nineteenth century. Modern scholars have attempted to investigate through an Aristotelian, reductionary lens a society that viewed life functionally, or holistically. As a result, what actually was a sophisticated egalitarian culture is thought to have been a primitive society. For the ancient Egyptians, there was no separation between art, religion, philosophy, and science. Life was viewed holistically, and that view was reflected in their art and culture. What is believed by scholars to be animism, the worship of animals, is really a means of describing and explaining life and the human experience through *symbol*.

In a sense, this symbolic explanation of life was their philosophy of science, because in their art, architecture, and writing, animals were representative of certain natural principles. By closely observing particular animals, the ancient Egyptians were able to identify specific qualities that symbolized divine principles in a pure and simple way. In other words, an animal symbolized a particular principle of divinity and could be thought of as a part of God, and effectively could be considered a "god" in the sense that all gods equate to God. These "gods" however were not "God" in our modern Judeo-Christian concept of an omnipotent, omniscience God. In ancient Egypt, they were written as NTR, known as *neters* or *neteru* (singular *neter*), and are best understood as principles of nature.

Symbolism allows the mind to intuitively see what is not directly visible in the material world. Each symbol embodies not only a single object or concept, but also a host of invisible qualities. Symbols engage a different part of the brain than does ordinary writing or language.

They engage the intuitive, nonverbal, visually based right hemisphere of the brain, which deals with spatial and abstract relationships. This part of the brain is not bound by rational and linear thought. Symbolism serves as a bridge between the two types of human intelligence, rational and intuitive, objective and subjective, and it promotes unification of the brain's two hemispheres.

From the Egyptian symbolic perspective, Anubis, the jackal, represents the principle of digestion that all life forms display because the jackal is able to digest anything regardless of its state of decay. Hapi, the baboon, represents respiration because of its cry that can be heard for many miles. And, Thoth, the ibis, a crane-like bird that lives along the Nile River alongside the crocodiles, represents the intellect and wisdom, as well as writing ability, because to live among the crocodiles any animal has to be wise. When an animal god was depicted as a head on a human body, it represented the principle associated with that god as it applied to the human being.

The soul, known as the *ba,* was symbolized by a human-headed bird, which is the opposite of the normal depiction of neteru as animal-headed humans, and represents the divine aspect of the terrestrial. The ba was depicted as a stork, which was known for its migrating and homing instinct. And because the stork consistently returns to its own nest, it is the perfect choice to represent the soul.

In *Egyptian Ideas of the Future Life* (1900), E. A. Wallis Budge writes that the Egyptians "believed in One God, who was self-existent, immortal, invisible, eternal, omniscient, almighty, and inscrutable; the maker of the heavens, earth, and underworld; the creator of the sky and the sea, men and women, animals and birds, fish and creeping-things, trees and plants, and the incorporeal beings who were the messengers that fulfilled his wish and word."[9] Even so, at the core of Egyptian symbolism and philosophy is the idea that humans are the ultimate representation of the created universe, yet inseparable from all of nature.

For the ancient Egyptians, there was "the One," called Atum, whose name means "all" and "nothing," representing the creative potential. Atum existed as an indefinable cosmic ocean called Nun, and from within Nun, Atum emerged as the primordial hill, thereby creating the principle of space, called Shu, and the principle of fire, called Tefnut.

In another telling of creation, Atum creates by projecting his heart, thereby bringing forth eight primary principles, which including himself, compose the Great Ennead of Heliopolis, the nine great Osirian gods: Atum, Shu, Tefnut, Geb, Nut, Osiris, Isis, Seth, and Nephthys. These gods represent the cyclical nature of life, death, and rebirth, none of which is apart from Atum, according to the Pyramid Texts. So, from an unknowable cause everything is created. From Atum all other principles of the universe emanate. From Atum is born Shu (air/wind) and Tefnut (water/moisture), the most important elements for life. Shu puts forth the principle of life and Tefnut, the principle of order. From Shu and Tefnut, Geb and Nut, the Earth and sky, were created, and then from Geb, the sun, was born. When Nut and Geb meet Tefnut, darkness occurs. Nut and Geb then give birth to Osiris, Isis, Seth, and Nephthys. Finally, Osiris and Isis give birth to Horus, the child king, representing the human experience in mind and body.

Osiris represents the cyclical nature of life; Isis, the feminine aspect of Osiris. Seth represents the principle of opposition, and Nephthys, the feminine aspect of Seth. These creation events take place outside of terrestrial time, beyond the realm of temporal. They occur in heaven, not on Earth. Horus, the child king, represents creation of terrestrial time and the temporal realm, humans and the cosmos.

The story told is conceptual: the mystery of God's creation, Atum, the One who becomes two, and then eight. But in the end, still, *all is One*.

I am One that transforms into Two
I am Two that transforms into Four
I am Four that transforms into Eight
After this I am One
—COFFIN OF PETAMON, CAIRO MUSEUM, ARTIFACT NO. 116023[10]

Conceptually, to create all existing things, whether invisible or visible, the omnipotent and omniscient Source of Life first transformed itself from a single state of existence into two. Here we uncover the philosophical significance behind serpent symbolism. The serpent, which is a singular animal with no appendages, but has a forked tongue and penis, represents the movement from one to two, the primal first act of creation. This is why the cobra was widespread in ancient Egyptian iconography and appeared alongside the vulture on the pharaoh's diadem. The vulture represents the physical return to the natural elements from which one came. The spirit of the flesh, eaten by the vulture, ascends into the heavens, representing the physical returning to the abstract. The serpent represents the mysterious act of the abstract becoming physical. Thus, it represents energy, the power of creation, and the ability to create.

ANCIENT INSIGHTS INTO STATES OF CONSCIOUSNESS

The serpent plays the central role in the mythical story of the Garden of Eden, the tempter of the first man and women to eat from the Tree of Knowledge, thereby endowing them with the ability to distinguish between good and evil. The story itself is mythology, beginning with a woman and man in a garden paradise, unaware of their state of existence. Until, that is, they eat fruit from the Tree of Knowledge and become self-aware. The serpent represents not a source of evil, but the creative energy of all life. With regard to the human experience, the serpent represents the achievement of transcendence and self-reflection, shifting the mind's focus away from the purely physical toward the abstract, possibly through altered states of consciousness. Perhaps the fruit borne by the Tree of Knowledge was a hallucinogenic plant such as the psilocybin mushroom or the sacred blue lily of the Nile. Perhaps this shift of perception through the consumption of hallucinogens was our ancient ancestors' first glimpse into the invisible world, a world they often referred to as the underworld or the netherworld. The psilocybin mushroom and the blue lily, as well as other hallucinogenic plants, were deemed sacred in ancient cultures and displayed as such in their art.

According to Gimbutas, the prehistoric Goddess culture of Europe and the Mediterranean—what she refers to as Old Europe—used mushrooms or other hallucinogenic plants in their rituals, particularly in the Greek initiation ceremonies of the cult of Demeter and Persephone. In southern Algeria, at Tassili n'Ajjer, pictorial evidence is even more convincing. Rock paintings depict people dancing with fists of mushrooms and mushrooms sprouting from their bodies. One instance shows them running joyfully, surrounded by the geometric structures typical in hallucinations. These earliest known shamans, often accompanied by large numbers of grazing cattle in the paintings, were priests of the Round Head Period, which existed from 7000 to 5000 BCE. A painting from the late Round Head Period shows images of the dancing Horned Goddess, typical of prehistoric Europe some ten thousand years prior.[11]

In *Food of the Gods: The Search for the Original Tree of Knowledge*, Terence McKenna (1947–2000) puts forth evidence for the use of hallucinogens in prehistoric cultures. According to McKenna, while early societies tested all different types of plants for consumption, they came across a particular dung-loving mushroom, *Stropharia cubensis* (renamed *Psilocybe cubensis*). Free from nausea-producing compounds, this mushroom is rich in psilocybin and grows throughout tropical regions, wherever the zebu cattle graze. At an archaeological site in Non Nok Tha, Thailand, fifteen-thousand-year-old bones of zebu cattle have been unearthed near human graves.[12]

McKenna believes the hallucinogenic mushroom is the "Ur plant"— the true tree of knowledge—and the human connection to the feminine, nurturing consciousness of our planet. He argues that when the prehistoric cult of the Great Horned Goddess was predominant, the knowledge of self and nature enabled them to live in equilibrium with nature.[13] Based on pictorial and circumstantial evidence, McKenna also argues that psilocybin mushrooms were used in prehistoric Africa and Asia Minor and sets forth the idea that cognition emerged in the grasslands of Africa, which is possibly the setting for the original, generic religion of human-kind. Like Gimbutas, McKenna believes that all religions in the ancient Near East can be traced to a Goddess cult involving cattle worship, whose roots go back to an ancient rite of eating psilocybin mushrooms. This rite induced ecstasy, dissolved the boundaries of ego, and allowed communion with the ancient "world soul" of plants—the earliest nature of earthly life.[14] McKenna also believes it is impossible not to see the tradition of the Mother Goddess within the cattle cult of the late Neolithic. There, he argues, the mushroom is the third and hidden member of a "Shamanic Trinity." The sacred cow was viewed as the provider of sustenance, the giver of life. However, along with her life-giving essence of meat and milk, we find manure and mushrooms rich in psilocybin. In the ancients' point of view, mushrooms were as much a cattle product as milk, meat, and manure, and they offered a profound, ecstatic connection to Earth itself, symbolized by the Mother Goddess.[15] Perhaps this is the prehistoric source of the Egyptian goddess Hathor, one of the most ancient of Egyptian neters, who in art was depicted as a cosmic cow.

Despite the evidence, such a view of history is not welcomed by modern civilization. Except for alcohol, the use of intoxicants is considered unacceptable, viewed as a scourge leading to an unproductive life that burdens society. Ironically, alcohol, perhaps the most violent, desensitizing, and deadly form of intoxication, is not only acceptable but a rite of passage for young adults.

Why we are like this lies deep in our Indo-European past. In a comprehensive study of archaic techniques of shamanism, Mircea Eliade notes that early on in Indo-European religious traditions, trance and ecstasy resulting from intoxication were viewed as decadent. In commenting on ancient Iranian Zoroastrian texts, Eliade states that shamanic intoxication was viewed with complete hostility, and in the Videvdat, it was demonized.[16]

Although not identical to Christianity, and a thousand years older, Zoroastrianism espouses some of the basic tenets underpinning the Christian worldview. For the Zoroastrian, God is the infinite being and the Almighty Lord. There are heavenly forces of good—angels and archangels—that are opposed to evil and demonic forces that prey upon the minds of humans. For the Zoroastrian, "the history of the world is the history of God's conflict with the devil." And in the end, "on the day of resurrection all may be raised by the savior to face the final judgment."[17]

Long before the ancient civilizations of Egypt and Sumer, prehistoric peoples symbolized the serpent as an integral part of life. Snakes were depicted within the eyes of the owl goddess as well as the sun, as in the winged Egyptian sun disk. It was believed that when the snake's powers were combined with magical plants, the snake was potent in healing and creating life.[18] The serpent had enormous power, and the serpent goddess was considered all-knowing and able to see the future, like her sister, the bird goddess. The serpent goddess "was the owner and the guardian of life water and life milk."[19] Such a view of life and nature did not suddenly disappear as historical times supplanted mythical times. Even as late as the Greek and Roman cultures, snakes were viewed as household gods. These snakes were guardians of the family as well as domestic animals, particularly cows. Each family and each animal had as a patron divinity a snake, whose life energy was the same as that of a human or other animals.[20]

Why was the serpent's "energy" viewed as being inseparable from that of humans or other animals?

Anthropology has an answer.

DNA, THE VOICE OF LIFE

Through research into indigenous cultures of the Amazon rainforest, anthropologists have discovered that the consumption of a potion made from hallucinogenic plants leads to a deep altered state of consciousness, and in that altered state, serpents take form and often speak of knowledge concerning life in the rainforest. The hallucinogenic potion is *aya-huasca,* a brew made from the *Banisteriopsis caapi* vine along with one or more other plant leaves rich in N,N-dimethyltryptamine, a psychedelic compound known as DMT. For those brave anthropologists who have experienced altered states of consciousness under the influence of ayahuasca, the serpent appears as an important visual and archetypal symbol, a terrifying creature but at the same time one offering wisdom and even an explanation of life itself.

In 1985, Stanford anthropologist Dr. Jeremy Narby, then a twenty-five-year-old doctoral student, while living with the Asháninca people of the Peruvian Amazon, underwent such an experience. Shortly after drinking ayahuasca, images began pouring into his head, "unusual or scary: an agouti [forest rodent] with bared teeth and a bloody mouth; very brilliant, shiny, and multicolored snakes; a policeman giving me problems; my father looking worried."[21] Narby suddenly found himself surrounded by two gigantic boa constrictors that seemed to be fifty feet long:

> I was terrified. These enormous snakes are there, my eyes are closed and I see a spectacular world of brilliant lights, and in the middle of these hazy thoughts, the snakes start talking to me without words. They explain that I am just a human being. I feel my mind crack, and in the fissures, I see the bottomless arrogance of my presuppositions. It is profoundly true that I am just a human being, and, most of the time, I have the impression of understanding everything, whereas here I find myself in a more powerful reality that I do not understand at all and that, in my arrogance, I did not even suspect existed. I feel like crying in view of the enormity of my revelations. Then it dawns on me that this self-pity is a part of my arrogance.[22]

According to Narby's indigenous consultant, Carlos Perez Shuma, plant hallucinogens are how nature talks. It is how God, who is in nature, speaks to us in our visions. After people drink ayahuasca, the spirits present themselves and explain everything,[23] an experience Narby found out to be true. Encountering the fluorescent snakes changed his way of looking at reality. In his own hallucinations, Narby learned—

experienced—important things. He found that being human was insignificant and that humans are intimately linked to other life-forms. Reality, he learned, is more complex than our eyes lead us to believe.[24]

Years later, Narby set out to explain his ayahuasca experience and discovered that a few other anthropologists experienced what he had experienced. Searching though anthropology journals, he learned that in the early 1960s another anthropologist named Michael Harner underwent a similar experience with the Conibo Indians of the Peruvian Amazon. After living with the Conibo for a year, Harner had made little headway in understanding their religion. That's when he was told that in order to understand he had to drink ayahuasca. So he did and found himself swept into a hallucination with a celestial cavern where "a carnival of demons was in full swing." Two strange-looking boats floated by with dragon-headed prows. There was a crowd of people on board with the heads of birds—blue jays—and they appeared to be similar to the "bird-headed gods of ancient Egyptian tomb paintings."[25]

In one of his last ayahuasca experiences, Harner believed he was dying and called out to his friends for an antidote without uttering a word. Then he saw that his vision was born from "giant reptilian creatures" from the lowest region of his brain. These giant reptilian creatures told him what he was about to see was knowledge reserved for the dying and the dead:

First they showed me the planet Earth as it was eons ago, before there was any life on it. I saw an ocean, barren land, and a bright blue sky. Then black specks dropped from the sky by the hundreds and landed in front of me on the barren landscape. I could see the "specks" were actually large, shiny, black creatures with stubby pterodactyl-like wings and huge whale bodies. . . . They explained to me in a kind of thought language that they were fleeing from something out in space. They had come to the planet Earth to escape their enemy. The creatures then showed me how they had created life on the planet in order to hide within the multitudinous forms and thus disguise their presence. Before me, the magnificence of plant and animal creation and speciation—hundreds of millions of years of activity—took place on a scale and with a vividness impossible to describe. I learned that the dragon-like creatures were thus inside all forms of life, including man.[26]

Narby read on in Harner's account of his life with the Conibo and discovered a footnote about these creatures, "in retrospect one could say they were almost like DNA, although at the time, in 1961, I knew nothing of DNA."[27] This is an amazing vision because, twenty years later, astronomer Sir Fred Hoyle and Nobel Laureate Francis Crick, one of the discoverers of DNA, both wrote books explaining their views that DNA is extraterrestrial: *Evolution from Space: A Theory of Cosmic Creationism* and *Life Itself: Its Origin and Nature*. Crick put forth the idea that microorganisms might have been sent here by a highly advanced civilization on another planet.

Then Narby considered what one of the Asháninca shamans had told him: "In truth, Ayahuasca is the television of the forest. You see images and learn things."[28] DNA exists in all living tissue plant and animal, and this molecule is a source of information. DNA is internal, but under the influence of ayahuasca, it can be accessed an entity that is external to the human mind. Narby believed that through the use of ayahuasca, the indigenous population of the Amazon learned about nature and medicinal plants, a fact that has made the pharmaceutical industry today what it is. Seventy-four percent of the modern pharmacopeia's plant-based remedies were first discovered by traditional societies.[29] For Narby, what he learned created a dilemma. On one hand, the knowledge derived from hallucinations had been confirmed through laboratory experience, yet on the other, the way the indigenous peoples learned of this knowledge is contradictory to what we Westerners believe to be true. Hallucinations, it is believed, have nothing to do with reality and are nothing more than a drug-induced imagination.

However, if imagination is what's real and lasting behind all that exists, then the Amazonian shamans are correct, and the visions produced by ayahuasca are more than a trip. They are a way of seeing reality for what it is through symbols and images, with no fundamental contradiction between everyday reality and the invisible and irrational world.

Narby considered what he had been told by the Asháninca, that "nature speaks in signs and that the secret to understanding its language consists in noticing similarities in shape or in form."[30] For Narby, this was the key, and he asked himself why the hallucinatory experiences of peoples across the Amazon were similar. In his experiences with the Asháninca and in Harner's experiences with the Conibo, "there were reptiles in the brain and serpent-shaped boats of cosmic origin that were the vessels of life at the beginning of time."[31] Was this pure coincidence?

Part of his answer came from French anthropologist Jean-Pierre Chaumeil in *Vision, Knowledge, Power: Shamanism among the Yagua in the North-East of Peru,* one of the most rigorous texts on the subject, according to Narby. In depicting their cosmology, the Yagua include a celestial serpent as part of their understanding of the universe. They also believe that "at the very beginning before the birth of the earth, this earth here, our most distant ancestors lived on another planet." Narby adds that according to Chaumeil, the Yagua believe that all living beings were created by twins, who are "the two central characters in Yagua cosmological thought."[32]

Another part of his answer came from the work of anthropologist Gerardo Reichel-Dolmatoff (1912–1994). The Desana people of the Amazon's Rio Negro symbolize the fissure of the brain that separates the left and right hemispheres as a deep riverbed, a depression that was formed in the beginning of time—mythical as well as embryological time—by the cosmic serpent. They view the interhemispheric fissure as a stream, a great current of cosmic energy:

> The shaman makes one realize that the river, after all, is the body of the serpent and that the stepping stones are the dark circular markings on the snake skin. Furthermore, since the huge serpent is moving,

it is difficult to gain a firm footing on one spot and to accomplish the crossing by a series of well-coordinated steps or jumps. It is important to never attempt a straight crossing, perpendicular to the river's current; the shortest distance is not the most desirable, and a crossing must be pondered in detail, each move being thought out beforehand.[33]

Such a proposal of "human beginnings"—that our DNA is an entity in itself, and extraterrestrial, as Harner and the Yagua people suggest—contradicted Narby's understanding of reality. Harner, a Western anthropologist, after taking ayahuasca multiple times, gained access to the world of mythological concepts of another culture. This methodology allows people to communicate with life-creating spirits of cosmic origin, possibly linked to DNA. Narby also tried this technique, and he began to consider his encounter with "DNA snakes" as a meaningful experience.[34]

Narby looked further into the work of other anthropologists for clues linking the form of DNA, the double helix, to mythologies of various cultures. DNA is made up of two vertical pairs of sugar phosphate connected by a large number of base pairs. In Mircea Eliade's *Shamanism: Archaic Techniques of Ecstasy,* Narby discovered another form that links DNA to ancient cosmological beliefs, the ladder. The shaman's ladders are "symbols of the shamanic profession" and are present in archaic cosmologies around the world, according to Eliade. Examples of the ladder form exist on all five continents. "Here a spiral ladder, there a stairway or braided ropes. In Australia, Tibet, Nepal, Ancient Egypt, Africa, North and South America, the symbolism of the rope, like that of the ladder, necessarily implies communication between sky and earth. It is by means of a rope or ladder that the gods descend to earth and men go up to the sky."[35] There was even an account of a cosmological ladder in the Bible. In the twenty-eighth chapter of Genesis, the patriarch Jacob falls asleep and dreams of a ladder set up on Earth, its top touching the heavens, with messengers of God moving up and down it.[36]

What can be made of this incredible connection between symbolism and biology, specifically DNA?

Although anthropologist Jeremy Narby, in his book *The Cosmic Serpent,* chooses not to disclose the impact of his work on his own spirituality, neither does he tell his audience what to think about the connections he establishes between mythology, altered states of consciousness, biology, and the symbolism of the serpent. What he does offer is advice and wisdom for those of us living today. Inspiration rests not on doctrine, but on experience,[37] and a reductionist approach to reality does not answer the important questions we all seek. For Narby, it is time to turn the fragmenting approach of science to human culture and the human experience on its head. He asks,

> In the name of what does one mask fundamental similarities in human symbolism—if not out of stubborn loyalty to rationalist fragmentation? How can one explain these similarities [between various cultures] with a concept other than chance—which is more an absence of concept than anything? Why insist on taking reality apart, but never try putting it back together again?[38]

According to Narby, the ingestion of DMT through the ayahuasca drink allows one's mind to be "defocalized" from the senses, attuned to the purely physical, everyday world, and thereby experience the world in an intimate and subjective way that naturally is understood as symbol, leading to a deep knowledge of the web of life in which we exist. It is the same principle as the stereogram. When we look intently at a stereogram, all we see are colorful dots. Only when our eyes are relaxed, defocalized, do we see the true picture hidden within the dots. Narby warns us that we are missing something in our "scientific" obligation to consider the animate reality of DNA, with its proteins and enzymes, as if it were inanimate. "By ignoring this obligation," he writes, "and by considering shamanism and biology as the same time, stereoscopically, I saw DNA snakes. They were alive."[39]

4

SKY GOD

Origins of the Western Belief System

The wisdom of the serpent was widespread during prehistoric times. For many thousands of years this philosophy defined a way of life in which the human experience was understood as an integral part of planetary ecology. Soon after the beginning of the Common Era, however, serpent philosophy and its cultural base all but disappeared, and for last sixteen centuries the serpent has been shunned and demonized by a pervasive, dominant theology in which a deity resides and rules from above, in the heavens. Throughout the history of Indo-European and European peoples, we find the notion that God is "up there somewhere," and he is known as the "man upstairs" and the "man in the sky." The Greek Zeus (Roman Jupiter) was a god of the sky and ruled over all the Olympian gods. The Norse god Thor also ruled from the sky. In Hebrew writings, God is a God of heaven, enthroned in heaven, who reigns down fire from heaven and stoops down to look upon the heavens and the Earth.[1] In Christian texts we find the same concept when Luke reports that according to the stories he had heard, Jesus ascended into the clouds of heaven and that someday he would return in the same way, *from the sky.*[2] The God of Christendom, the God of Western tradition *is a sky god.*

With prehistoric cultures around the world expressing their spirituality through serpent symbolism and passing down their tradition even into historical times, how did the concept of "God in the sky" become so widespread? Why did ancient cultures begin to embrace a sky god rather than the Earth-based tradition of the serpent?

The answer lies in the origin of European cultures and languages.

In 1813, while reviewing Johann Christoff Adelung's *Mithridates*—a massive study of the world's languages though a comparison of the Lord's Prayer—the extraordinary scholar Thomas Young noticed that many European languages were related and hypothesized that there had to be a single prehistoric language from which the European languages developed. Young called this prehistoric theoretical language *Indo-European.*

Take, for example, the modern English word *acre,* which in Latin is *ager,* in Greek, *agros,* in Gothic, *akrs,* and in Sanskrit, *ajras.* Although today the English word *acre* is part of a system of land measurement, its ancient root means *field.* August Schleicher (1821–1868) noticed that the people who spoke the Indo-European Gothic language were consistently replacing a *g* with a *k*. By following these changes in the use of words, one might create the hypothetical original word and language, which were changed through cultural offshoots over time. In the case of the word *acre,* Schleicher believed *agras* was the original word.

With this methodology, linguistic researchers have determined that half of the world's languages are derived from a single prehistoric language called *Proto-Indo-European,* although there is no record of that original language. Still, all of the European languages from Iran in the east to Britain in the west are derived from Greek, Armenian, Indo-Iranian, Balto-Slavic, Germanic, Italic, Celtic, Tocharian, and Anatolian. And these ancient languages are derived from Aryo-Graeco-Armenian, Balto-Slavo-Germanic, Italo-Celtic, Tocharian, and Anatolian, which in turn are derived from Anatolain, Tocharian-Italo-Celtic, and an unknown "B" language from which the Germanic-Balto-Slavic languages and the Aryo-Graeco-Armenian languages developed.[3]

Experts believe that prior to 5000 BCE there must have been a single Proto-Indo-European language. Although there is no consensus regarding the geographical homeland of the Indo-Europeans, there is a general agreement that Indo-Europeans existed broadly through western Asia and Europe between 4500 and 2500 BCE. The Indo-European homeland has been theorized to lie within Central Europe, Turkey, Iran, and Southern Russia. Which homeland is their true homeland, we may never know. However, according to the archaeological and historical evidence, the horse was an important part of Indo-European cultures. So, with this understanding, the center of horse domestication in the ancient world would be the best candidate for an Indo-European homeland.

During the fourth millennium BCE, horse domestication expanded westward into the northwest Pontic, the Balkans, and the Carpathian basin. Assuming that the Proto-Indo-European word for domestic horse is *ekwos,* then the western border of the Indo-European homeland is likely in the area of the Black Sea or just to the east thereof. (The origin of the English word *equestrian* comes from the Latin *equestr,* from *eques* meaning horseman.) Such is the conclusion of archaeologist Marija Gimbutas, whose influential work on Indo-European origins, known as the Kurgan Solution, has been accepted by many archaeologists and linguists.[4] This model has also been adopted by the *Encyclopedia Britannica* as well as the *Grand Dictionnaire Encyclopedique Larousse.*

OLD EUROPE

Gimbutas spent a lifetime searching for prehistoric truth in mythology, folklore, and archaeology, piecing together the history of a great culture that existed from 40,000 to 3000 BCE and formulating ideas about how they slowly vanished while a new and more powerful culture emerged.

Growing up in Lithuania, Gimbutas was familiar with the traditions of the goddess Laima, the spinner or weaver of life, a deity of fate. Women offered her gifts of woven articles. At night, the goddess would often check on her believers by peering through a window. Although Christianized during the fourteenth century, Lithuania remained predominantly pagan for the next several hundred years as a result of Christian missionaries' poor language skills. As late as the twentieth century, in some areas of Eastern Europe some aspect of the Great Goddess remained a part of culture.

Born during a time when Lithuania was as much pagan as it was Christian, Gimbutas held a unique perspective on European history. Fascinated by the culture of her youth, her early work focused on linguistics, ethnology, and folklore, and in 1942 she received her master's degree in archaeology from the University of Vilnius in Nazi-occupied Lithuania. Four years later, concentrating on ancient religions, symbolism, burial rites, and beliefs in the afterlife, Gimbutas received her doctorate, also in archaeology, from Germany's University of Tübingen.

For years, she worked in excavations in southeastern Europe and the Mediterranean region. While doing so she developed the theory that there was once a prevalent culture very different from that of the Indo-Europeans of Neolithic and historical times. When excavation teams she worked with began unearthing small sculptures of women, prevalent throughout Europe, she had an easy time grasping their significance. Gimbutas alone unearthed at least five hundred sculptures, and as her work continued in Yugoslavia, Greece, and Italy, the evidence mounted. So did her confidence in the theory she was considering.[5]

In 1955, Gimbutas was named Research Fellow of Harvard's Peabody Museum. A year later, in Philadelphia, she presented her Kurgan theory to the world for the first time. In 1956, she published *Prehistory of Eastern Europe* and in 1958, *Ancient Symbolism of Lithuanian Folk Art*—the first of many books. In 1963, she accepted a position at UCLA and continued to direct excavation at various European sites. In 1974, with the evidence she needed, she published

Gods and Goddesses, although the original title was *Goddesses and Gods of Old Europe*, changed for marketing reasons by the publisher. Eight years later, *Gods and Goddesses* was published in a second edition under her original title. In 1991, the culmination of her life's work was published as *Civilization of the Goddess*. On February 2, 1994, Marija Gimbutas passed away at her home near Los Angeles.[6]

Her research of prehistoric European peoples tells a tale of a clash of cultures, specifically, the defeated culture of the serpentine Mother Goddess and the powerful invasive cultures of the Indo-Europeans. According to Gimbutas, the earliest prehistoric civilizations were egalitarian, and they focused on the maternal as a cosmological foundation. "In China, the Near East, Europe, and the Americas; from the very beginning the Earth Goddess as a basis for cosmology not only existed, but was common."[7] She adds that the "the sovereignty of motherhood has decided the earliest development of social structures and religion."[8]

According to Gimbutas, the Mother Goddess culture was communal, not communistic. Goddesses were actually creatrixes and in fact were creating from themselves, whether items for the household or a child. She also believes the Mother Goddess culture held a completely different worldview and that their natural artistic expression had nothing to do with pornography. For example, the vulva was one of the earliest symbols engraved by prehistoric peoples, a symbolic expression in that the vulva was related to growth and the seed of life. In some Paleolithic art, as previously mentioned, next to the image of a vulva is an image of a branch or other plant design, or within it, a seed or plant. They understood that life was not divorced from nature, and they symbolized that idea in figurines, which Gimbutas views as the epitome of the Mother Goddess, depicting birth, regeneration, and death. Many types of goddess figurines appeared throughout history during the Paleolithic as well as the Neolithic, but they did not form a pantheon. In essence, they represented different functions of the same goddess, the deity itself being the unseen spiritual forces or principles of nature—the natural cycle of life.

According to Gimbutas, based on the archaeological remains combined with what can be deduced from mythology—mythology being a reflection of social structure—political life for the Mother Goddess culture was regulated by an avuncular system (derived from the word *uncle*). The ruler was the queen, who was also the high priestess, and either her brother or uncle shared in her authority. Such a social structure, Gimbutas explains, is expressed in classical mythology in which sister-brother couples of female goddesses and male gods are common. In Europe (Germanic, Celtic, and Baltic), we find the Earth Mother (or Earth Goddess) accompanied by her male companion. Consider for example the goddess of nature, the regenerator, who appears in the springtime and gives life to all animals and plants. In Greek mythology she is Artemis and is called the Mistress of Animals. She has her male counterpart, called the Master of Animals.[9]

This Mother Goddess culture of "Old Europe"—a term Gimbutas uses to distinguish the European culture of the Mother Goddess from later European cultures—was not without a written form of communication. This peaceful, agrarian civilization developed a near-uniform language of symbols that stretched from Ireland to Turkey. Elements of a "sacred script" have even been discovered in Eastern and Central Europe. Attempts have been made to decipher it, but sentence structure and phrases have not yet been ascertainable. During the Bronze Age (3300–1200 BCE) in Cyprus and Crete, the script persisted in a similar form to what existed in the fifth millennium BCE. Evidence of the script has been preserved, but there are no clear links to any subsequent culture.

Gimbutas believes their language could have been a syllable-based script and would have developed into something more structured if it were not for the culture's destruction. Today, scholars continue to research this script with hopes that it will someday be deciphered. The difficulty is that this prehistoric, Old European language is studied very little. Substrates of the languages are studied in Greece and Italy, but most of the words that have been reconstructed are place names like Knossos, which is, in fact, an Old European name. Little by little, linguists are discovering which words are not Indo-European. Names for seeds, various trees, plants, and animals are easily deciphered. *Apple,* for example, is Old European. There are also several pre-Indo-European names for the same thing, such as *pig.* Some languages use Old European names; others use Indo-European names, or both.[10]

During the fifth millennium BCE, the culture of the Mother Goddess began to urbanize, especially in the southeast regions of Europe—modern-day Romania and the western part of the Ukraine. The Cucuteni culture, by 4000 BCE, was building cities accommodating populations of ten thousand to fifteen thousand people. However, that culture was consumed as a new expanding group imposed their way of life throughout Europe. Gimbutas defines this expanding culture as a race of Indo-Europeans known as Kurgans or Aryans. And it is this culture that sowed the seeds for Western civilization as we know it today.

INVENTING WAR:
HORSEMEN OF THE APOCALYPSE

Around 7000 BCE, east of the Black Sea and north of the Caucasus Mountains, a nomadic culture emerged in Europe based on animal husbandry. By 6000 BCE, this prehistoric culture had domesticated horse and cattle. Life was harsh on the grassy steppe, and men gained a prominent social role as a result of the physically demanding life they led, controlling large herds of cattle and horses. These animals were their main source of food as well as their means of mobility.

According to the archaeological record, during the sixth millennium BCE knives and long daggers were also developed in the same areas. Wars too were evident with neighboring tribes over cattle. For this nomadic culture, it is apparent that the concept of ownership was born. During the next two thousand years, their expanding presence was felt in most parts of Europe. By 4000 BCE, artistic expression in Europe changed dramatically. New gods were introduced, and a new style in social administration developed.[11] Settlements were now built on hilltops, sometimes with grave sites known as *kurgans*—a word of Turkic origin from the Mongolic *kurgan* (or *korgon*), meaning a refuge or "for the dead," from the Mongolic verb *korgodok*. As the Kurgan culture spread everything changed across Europe.

The Kurgan culture was distinctly patriarchal. Only the men were buried, and they were buried alongside their weapons and other symbols of power, such as the horse-headed scepter. Dominance was an intrinsic part of the culture. These nomadic people had weapons and horses. In the Goddess culture of Old Europe, there were no weapons for warfare, only for hunting. In Old Europe, the culture was agrarian, and people lived a settled, domestic life. The new dominating culture, however, was the opposite. These armed, mounted nomads dominated wherever they migrated. When the invading Kurgans arrived, they established themselves high in the hills, sometimes in places with difficult access. But the extent to which the members of the older culture defended themselves is difficult to determine. It is clear that the indigenous cultures were defeated, assimilated, and also at times murdered. There is also evidence of confusion, immigration, flight from war, and shifts of population. They fled to islands, forests, and hilly areas. By 4000 BCE, the patriarchal culture was well on its way to being the established culture, and it introduced the first Kurgan god, the spear, which eventually evolved into the mythical thunderbolt of Zeus.[12]

The new Indo-European gods appeared around 3000 BCE. There were three primary deities: the god of the shining sky, symbolized by the dagger; the thunder god, symbolized by the ax; and the god of the underworld, symbolized by the spear. Their religious beliefs were very different from those of the Mother Goddess, whose cultural icons revolved around nature, such as the serpent and the bird. The Indo-European Kurgan culture was patriarchal, and the psyche of the warrior was predominant. Every god was a warrior, and their goddesses were brides, wives, or maidens, without any power or creativity, beauties like the sun maiden.

These two diverse societies, and their mythologies, formed a hybrid culture in Europe. Indo-European ideas reached the Mesopotamian plain and were seen in Sumerian and Semite stories. Gilgamesh dethroned Lilith in one of the earliest works of literature, symbolic of the defeat of the Mother Goddess culture. In a similar vein, Eve took the blame for paradise lost. Athena of Greek mythology became militarized, but still kept some of her former qualities. Behind her was an owl, and on her shield was a snake, in the tradition of Old Europe. The ideology of separation between body and soul developed from this patriarchal culture. A spiritual connection to the "here and now" world was discarded in favor of the blessings of an afterlife. Life became transcendent, as opposed to immanent, as in the culture of the Mother Goddess.[13]

During the middle of the fourth millennium BCE, bands of Kurgans entered Mesopotamia from the Zagros Mountains. With them came social stratification, war, and the establishment of what we today recognize as civilization.

Two thousand years prior, however, two cultures lived side by side in Mesopotamia. One occupied the northern region and the other, the southernmost areas between the Tigris and Euphrates rivers. The northern culture created various types of ceramic art, including a fine and distinctive style of pottery. These earliest Mesopotamians living in the north were known as the Halaf culture. They were farmers and artists, and relied on natural rainfall for their crops of emmer wheat, barley, and flax. They also herded cattle, sheep, and goats. The Halaf culture was a complex society whose trade contacts with other communities allowed them to amass considerable wealth that included exceptionally decorated pottery, jewelry, sculptures, and obsidian tools.[14] They also baked small clay female figurines in the tradition of the Mother Goddess. With large thighs, buttocks, and breasts, these distinctive figurines, featuring a long braid over the top of the head and large and slanted eyes, were found throughout their shrines. Two particular figurines from 5000 BCE, found in the Upper Tigris Basin, display the exaggerated female characteristics found throughout Old Europe. One figurine in particular contains traces of paint on its arms and legs, possibly the remnants of painted-on jewelry or tattoos.

During the 1980s, in one of the largest Halaf settlements, archaeologists discovered that the Halaf culture developed out of an older, existing culture known as the Samarran. And around 5200 BCE, the Samarrans refined a technique of creating finely textured, highly artistic ceramics painted with designs in black, red, and white. Excavations revealed that they lived in multiroom and multistory rectangular buildings with stone foundations, accessed from the roof. Other circular structures, called *tholoi,* surround these buildings, and were made from blocks of loam and pisé (mud bricks).[15]

THE CONCEPTION OF WESTERN CIVILIZATION

During the middle of the fourth millennium BCE, a different culture, known as the Ubaid, expanded its influence northward at about the same time the Halaf society disappeared from the archaeological record. Whether they were assimilated or conquered by the Ubaid remains unknown. Either way, the Halaf culture faded into obscurity, and their characteristics were never seen again in the region. The Ubaid people lived in small settlements, typically along rivers, and built platform temples from mud bricks with a village at their center.

According to archaeologists, the Hajji Muhammad provided the foundation of the Ubaid culture, which was fully developed by 4350 BCE, occupying most of southern Mesopotamia. British archaeologist James Mellaart maintains that cultural evidence (mainly ceramic) suggests that the Hajji Muhammad descended from modern day Iran's Zagros Mountains onto the Mesopotamian plain. By 4500 BCE, the Hajji Muhammad expanded northward, with its people living in small settlements, typically along rivers, building platform temples from mud bricks, located at the center of a village.[16]

By the end of the fourth millennium BCE, a shift in social organization occurred in lower Mesopotamia that archaeologists and anthropologists refer to as the emergence of the Uruk culture. Society became distinctly stratified. Ranks or classes were created, with certain groups of people having a different function and level of social power. It appears the elite demanded tribute from their subjects, not only to meet their own needs but also to support craftsmen and laborers engaged in constructing temples and fortifications. By 4000 BCE, Uruk had become the largest city in lower Mesopotamia and covered nearly 250 acres. By 3000 BCE, Uruk had entered its early dynastic period, with a majority of the population living within the city.[17] A household-based economy developed in which people belonged to large extended families. Temples themselves constituted a household, although many others were dominated by leading families who actually lived in the temples. No longer self-sufficient, the common people contributed their labor in exchange for the necessities of life. As a result of this structured society, the elite now controlled the production, as well as the distribution, of goods. The first Mesopotamian kingdom was born, and according to Sumerian cosmology, its authority was handed down from the heavens above, from the sky gods.

By 2500 BCE, the Uruk city-state covered one thousand acres and boasted a population of forty thousand people. The first ziggurats were built as temples to their sky gods. Artisans supplied the elite with luxury goods, while the common people used crude, mass-produced earthenware. A diversity of grave goods epitomized the growing chasm between the privileged few and the masses. Judging from the 4,400-year-old Royal Tombs of Ur, those privileges included the right of kings to have their servants sacrificed and buried with them.[18]

This radical change in prehistoric culture on the Mesopotamian plain was not a simple function of wars and conquest. The process was quite slow and far more complex, requiring the establishment of a new social order and a long process of assimilation for those who were subjugated. However, from the very beginning, warfare had been an important method of replacing old cultures, a trend that continued well into the Common Era. What developed over the next thousand years was the blending of an agrarian culture with the hierarchical administration of a kingdom. The Kingdom of Sumer was born, and with it, history and civilization.

According to Gimbutas's Kurgan hypothesis, there was no copper in the Indo-European homeland regions north of the Caucasus Mountains. She theorizes that the Kurgans eventually became aware of metals existing to the south. Consequently, during the fifth and fourth millennia BCE, they migrated into those areas and seized control of those resources. It would have been an obvious choice of expansion. Along with that expansion they undertook the subjugation of indigenous peoples and their agrarian lifestyle. Although there is no library of tablets or scrolls recording the acts and deeds of these Indo-Europeans, their mythology does tell of a "war of functions," describing the conquest of settled agriculturalists by a more mobile society.[19]

THE CRADLE OF WESTERN CIVILIZATION

When Sumerian city-states emerged, kingships were established, but these kingships were not a family-based monarchy. They were a succession of city dynasties ruled by kings based on politics and war. Various titles for rulers were used: *ensi* (governor), *lugal* (king), or *en* (lord). As time passed, lugal became a common title for rulers who controlled more than one city-state, and ensi for those who ruled a single city. En became a common title for high priest. The oldest historical king proven to have existed is Enmebaragesi of the city-state Kish,[20] believed to have rebuilt the house of Enlil at Nippur around 2700 BCE. The Sumerian King List refers to him as he who smote the weapons of the land of Elam. His son, Agga, unsuccessfully laid siege to Uruk around 2680 BCE. Uruk then succeeded Kish as Sumer's ruling city, and it is in the ruins of Uruk that the oldest known writings were found, dating to 3300 BCE.[21]

According to the Sumerian King List, Uruk's King Meskiaggasher "entered the seas and ascended the mountains," meaning that he attempted to conquer foreign lands and explore sea lanes for trade routes.[22] Meskiaggasher's son, Enmerkar, turned Uruk into a great city, and according to legend conquered the land of Aratta—their mythologized homeland in the Zagros Mountains by the Caspian Sea. Lugalbanda succeeded Enmerkar, followed by the kings Dumuzi, and Gilgamesh, who conquered Nippur, and Gilgamesh's son, Urnunga. Lugalkidul (2560 BCE) was the final king of Sumer's first (Uruk) dynasty, which was overthrown by Mesilim of Kish. Over the next two hundred years, eight different kings ruled Sumer, with the son inheriting the throne from his father, their kingships all characterized by war. Then, in 2375 BCE, the last great ruler of Lagash, Entemena, brought peace and prosperity to the land.[23]

During the last quarter of the third millennium BCE, the greatest of all Mesopotamian rulers rose to power, Sargon the Great (2334–2279 BCE).[24] An Akkadian (Semitic-speaking people of central Mesopotamia), Sargon was appointed as the royal cupbearer to the king of the city-state of Kish, and through just or unscrupulous means soon became king and established his capital at Agade, the biblical city of Akkad. He was the first great empire builder and ushered in a new spirit of calligraphy. Such was his fame that two Assyrian kings were later named in his honor.

According to a legend, Sargon was a self-made man of humble origins. A gardener found him, the story goes, as a baby floating in a basket on the river and raised him in his own calling. His mother is said to have been a priestess in a town on the middle Euphrates, and his father, unknown. In defeating King Lugalzagesi of Uruk, who had previously united all the city-states of southern Mesopotamia,[25] Sargon became king and the first great Akkadian ruler. With a desire to secure trade throughout the world, Sargon conquered cities from the middle Euphrates to northern Syria and the mountains of southern Anatolia. He also controlled Susa, the capital of Elam. Commercial connections flourished with the Indus Valley, the coast of Oman, the islands and shores of the Persian Gulf, the mines of Badakhshan, the silver-rich

Taurus Mountains, Lebanon, Cappadocia, Crete, and perhaps even Greece. Such was his fame that merchants in an Anatolian city begged him to intervene in a local quarrel. According to legend, Sargon and a band of his warriors made an amazing journey to the city of Burushanda to settle the dispute.[26]

Because of the logistics involved in governing a vast empire, the latter part of Sargon's reign was troubled with rebellions. Sargon's son Rimush succeeded him and quelled rebellions in Ur, Umma, Adab, Der, Lagash, and Kazallu in Sumer and Elam and Barakhshi in Iran. When he was murdered, his older brother Manishtushu became king and founded the temple of Ishtar in Nineveh. Rebellions persisted, and the strength of the empire continued to wane. Manishtushu managed to keep control of Assyria and Sumer while expanding into the Oman region.[27] Manishtushu's son, Naram-Sin, self-titled as "King of the Four Quarters" and "God of Agade," succeeded him. A natural leader and warrior, Naram-Sin reestablished Akkadian power by defeating another rebel coalition, retaking Syria and Lebanon, and pushing the control of the empire east to the Zagros Mountains. During the twilight years of Naram-Sin's reign, Gutians began their conquest of Sumer. According to legend, it was divine judgment exacted in response to Naram-Sin's destruction of Enlil's temple at Nippur.[28] He was the last great Akkadian king.

With the end of the Akkadian empire, anarchy followed, with city-states struggling for independence while fighting the Gutians. Lagash fell and became the dominant Gutian city. At times the Gutians also controlled Ur, Umma, and Uruk. However, most of their kings reigned for only a year or so, with the longest being seven. Around 2120 BCE, Utuhegal of Uruk led a successful rebellion against the Gutians and restored stability, preparing the way for the resurgence of Sumerian civilization.[29]

Under the kings Ur-Nammu and Shulgi, Sumerian culture and civilization experienced resurgence and renaissance.[30] Peace and prosperity existed throughout the land. The legal system was strengthened, the calendar revised, and towns and temples rebuilt, the most notable being the ziggurat at Ur, which still exists to this day. A conscious effort was made to reestablish Sumerian as the official language and to promote Sumerian culture. However, stability was difficult to maintain. During the hundred-year period of Ur's third dynasty, many resources were directed toward defense. Despite all efforts, Sumerian unity gradually dissolved, and with famine and economic hardship further weakening Sumerian resolve, nomadic Elamites finally, in 2004 BCE, ended Sumerian civilization forever.[31] The Sumerian language, although kept as a tongue of the elite, gradually faded into obscurity and was replaced with the Semitic language of Akkad.

ESTABLISHING THE WESTERN RELIGIOUS TRADITION

War in the Tigris and Euphrates river valleys brought famine and disease. As a consequence, people fled the region, heading west and south. Many were destined for Egypt, particularly the northeast region of the Nile Delta. Over the next several hundred years, Egypt's newcomers became a part of Egyptian society, typically as laborers, but also as merchants and political leaders. As the immigrant population grew in the Nile Delta, the Egyptian government felt politically threatened. Tensions mounted, and between 2345 and 2181 BCE, immigrants streamed out of Egypt to the fabled "Promised Land" on the eastern shores of the Mediterranean Sea, according to University of Lecci archaeologist Emmanuel Anati.[32] Although sensationalized with miraculous signs and wonders, the biblical Book of Exodus tells the story of these Mesopotamian immigrants.

The Egyptian word for the incoming population was *Hiberu* (or *Apiru*), meaning "nomad," "immigrant," or "transitory." The name stuck, and the Hiberu, or Hebrew, cultural identity was born. According to Anati, an emigration of Hiberu people from Egypt did occur, but not necessarily as described in its mythic biblical telling. The archaeological evidence indicates that the Exodus occurred much earlier, and in a lengthy fashion. After 2000 BCE, there is little evidence for habitation sites in the regions of Sinai and Negev, and the few that exist were military and mining operations. During the second millennium BCE, the Sinai Peninsula was arid and essentially uninhabitable. However, before 2000 BCE, the Sinai was not only more hospitable, it was inhabited. The evidence of an exodus has been discovered, as well as of war.

According to the Book of Exodus, these immigrants departed Egypt and lived for a time as nomads in the Sinai Desert; then they became conquerors of the Midianites, Edomites, Moabites, and Ammonites, as their culture passed from a nomadic lifestyle into agriculture and pastoralism. This biblical narrative can be matched with the archaeological evidence and climate change data for the region. Evidence of the ten plagues can be found in the Ipuwer Admonitions, an Egyptian text from the sixth dynasty, between 2345 and 2181 BCE. The text contains numerous hints of invaders or immigrants, stating that "the delta marshes carry shields (meaning they are in turmoil)" and that "foreigners have become landlords" and that "poor men have become possessors of treasures. He who could not make a pair of sandals is the possessor of riches."[33] The text also states that "barbarians from outside have come into Egypt. . . . Foreigners are skilled in the work of the Delta." According to Anati, these are clear reference to the biblical story of the Hebrews, albeit from another perspective, that of the Egyptians.

There are also interesting parallels between the story of Moses and the Mesopotamian myth of Sargon the Great, who, like Moses, led his people from arid lands to the conquest of lands. Like Moses, Sargon's mother bore him in secret then set him in a basket of rushes in the river. According to Anati, the myths of Sargon and Moses are at the roots of the Semitic world and appear to have been inspired by a common narrative, both of which occurred no later than the twenty-third century BCE.

Anati's proof is that he discovered the biblical Mount Sinai halfway between the ancient cities of Kadesh Barnea and Petra, in the Negev

Desert. The biblical Mount Sinai is now called Mount Karkom, and nearly forty Bronze Age villages encircle the mountain. "Plaza" sites also exist, structures enclosing a large circular court. Plazas were situated around the mountain along main pathways and no more than a mile or so from one another. Here, cattle were kept, butchered, and worked. These sites were for men only, shepherds, evident by an abundance of tools necessary for slaughtering and cleaning animals. Amazingly, a stone carved to look like two tablets lies at the foot of Mount Karkom, divided into ten sections.

Biblical text also tells the story of the Hebrew conquest of the Promised Land, Canaan, and the establishment of the Kingdom of Israel with its accompanying monotheistic, sacrificial religion known today as Judaism. According to their history, they were ordered by God to "take vengeance on the Midianites."[34] They did, killing every man and taking the women and cattle as plunder.[35] Their approach was simple: surrender or die. They were told by God to first make a peace offering to the city's inhabitants, and if they acquiesced, to subject them to forced labor. If not, they were to leave no man alive and take everything else in the city.[36] But, according to the Bible, in the cities of the Promised Land, they were told "do not leave alive anything that breathes. Completely destroy them—the Hittites, Amorites, Canaanites, Perizzites, Hivites and Jebusites—as the LORD your God has commanded you."[37]

Their worldview was based on the premise that God was an angry God, and a God of wrath:

> The LORD your God, who is among you, is a jealous God and his anger will burn against you, and he will destroy you from the face of the land. Do not put the LORD your God to the test as you did at Massah. Be sure to keep the commands of the LORD your God and the stipulations and decrees he has given you. Do what is right and good in the LORD's sight, so that it may go well with you and you may go in and take over the good land the LORD promised on

oath to your ancestors, thrusting out all your enemies before you, as the LORD said.[38]

This belief gave them the justification to invade and conquer. It mattered not that other people had built the cities and planted vineyards and olive groves. God's promise was that the land was theirs—for the taking.[39]

More than a thousand years later, during the eighth century BCE, the northern half of the Kingdom of Israel was conquered by the Assyrians. In the seventh century BCE, the Babylonians conquered the region, then the Persians during the sixth century, and the Greeks in the fourth. Rome, then, conquered Europe and the Mediterranean during the last century before the Common Era. Three hundred years into the Common Era, a new theology emerged throughout Europe and the Mediterranean, combining pagan (meaning country) traditions with a new type of redemptive and prophetic faith based on ancient Hebrew beliefs. Christianity was adopted for the sake of empire unity. Despite this religious unity, the power of the Roman Empire slowly dwindled while the power of the religious institution it created grew. As the empire disintegrated, Europe was thrust into darkness with no other institution to provide civil rule except the Roman Catholic Church. During the eleventh century, the eastern half of the empire rejected Roman Catholic rule and formed the Greek Orthodox Church. During the sixteenth century, the Roman Catholic Church split again, a result of the Protestant Reformation, inspired by the teachings of Martin Luther. In the five hundred years since Luther, the Christian religion has been splitting in exponential fashion. All the while, political boundaries have been drawn and redrawn over and over again through a state of near continuous war.

This history is not so much religious as it is cultural, for the same beliefs have existed throughout the ages, and those beliefs are ours today. Our history of civilization is a history of war, with technology and industry the products and precipitators of war. This cultural tradition began nine thousand years ago with the invention of the dagger, the sword, and the ax. Between the sixth and third millennium BCE, it spread regionally south and west, then across the Atlantic Ocean during the fifteenth century CE to decimate the native cultures of the Americas. As a result, half of the world's languages are Indo-European based.

We are the descendants of that cattle-herding culture who worshipped the "sky god" nine thousand years ago. We are their legacy, and we romanticize the conquests of our past in the tradition of the cavalry and cattle-driving of the American West and the taking of land from indigenous American cultures.

Despite the vast changes in language over many thousands of years and the occasional call by inspired priests, ministers, pastors, and devoted laymen to love one another as the Christian gospels state, Western European culture has maintained its basic beliefs and cultural identity: the domination of resources and people through politics and war, justified through a fundamental belief in the biblical "God"—*the angry and indignant sky god.*

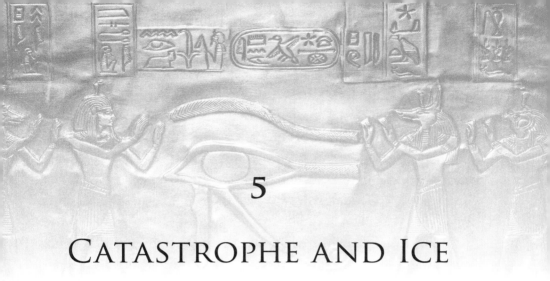

5

CATASTROPHE AND ICE

The Great Historic and Geologic Divide

For tens of thousands of years, the Mother Goddess culture of prehistory lived and celebrated life in a harmonious way, producing even in historical times a society sophisticated in art and innovation, such as the Minoans of Crete. So, *why* did the concept emerge that life needed to be lived through the control of people and resources? And, *why* is the Western religious tradition founded on a belief that God is an angry sky god and that Earth's inhabitants are in need of redemption?

Answering these two questions is of great importance if civilization is ever to become truly "civilized" and if governments are ever to care for their people with fairness and dignity. For many thousands of years, it has been believed—specifically in Hebrew and Christian traditions— that people are inherently selfish, corrupt, and in need of authority and redemption. A reason for why this might be the case has never been offered. Now there are reasons and answers, simply because it is human nature to ask why and search for those reasons and answers in a scientific way.

"Who controls the past, controls the future, and so who controls the present controls the past," George Orwell wrote in *1984*, meaning that the belief system we live in and call civilization is not based on truth. Rather, it is based on thought control, or truth perceived through the lenses of religion and politics. Our Western history, as we know it, as it has been taught to us, begins with agriculture and animal domestication as a means of providing sustenance. Herein lies the mysterious great historic and geologic divide from which all human societies today were born.

Academic disciplines create historical divisions to categorize trends and patterns. In Archaeology there is the Paleolithic, or "Old" Stone Age; and the Neolithic, or "New" Stone Age; the Bronze Age; the Iron Age; and the Dark Ages. In geology and history there is a division between our current age and the previous age. After the Paleolithic Era, people began cultivating grain and domesticating animals as opposed to existing solely as hunter-gathers. Geologists refer to these epochs as the Pleistocene and the Holocene. Historians refer to these epochs as the mythical age and the historical age. In the Bible, these two ages are referred to as the antediluvian and postdiluvian worlds, and up until 1870 the Great Flood was the accepted explanation for Earth's geologic stratification. Today, based on a scientific approach, it is believed that the Earth cools and warms over long periods of time and that this division of history is a consequence of an end to the most recent ice age.

ICE AGE THEORIES

The first ice age theory was created by Bernard Kuhn in the late eighteenth century and further developed by James Hutton, German-born geologist Jean de Charpentier, and Louis Agassiz, who forged forward with glaciation studies and put forth a theory, published in 1840 and entitled *Étude sur les glaciers,* suggesting that a great ice age had once gripped the Earth. In a later book, *Système glaciare* (1847), Agassiz presented further evidence gathered from across Europe that supported his theory. A year later, he accepted a position at Harvard and moved to America, where he discovered even more evidence of glaciation. By 1870, the theory of ancient periods of extensive ice was generally accepted by the scientific community.

One of the first theories of ice ages focused on the Earth's axis and its tilt, which moves between 20.4 degrees and 26.2 degrees over a twenty-six-thousand-year period. According to Joseph Adhémar, every eleven thousand years an ice age would occur in whichever hemisphere had a longer winter. James Croll, a self-taught scholar and one-time janitor at the Andersonian College and Museum in Scotland, objected to Adhémar's theory and wrote that the most likely forces behind climate change were variations in the solar radiation that reaches Earth. Because the Earth's orbit around the sun is elliptical, the amount of solar radiation Earth receives varies up to 5 percent over time.

According to Croll's theory, called insolation, a decrease in the amount of solar radiation during the winter favors the accumulation of snow, resulting in the additional loss of heat by the reflection of sunlight back into space. If winter occurs when the Earth is close to the sun, temperatures would be warmer than usual. But if winter occurs when the sun is farther away, temperatures would be colder than usual. If the polar area of a hemisphere becomes colder, trade winds would be stronger in that hemisphere, and warm equatorial ocean currents would shift toward the opposite hemisphere, further augmenting the heat loss. If Earth's orbit were circular, the slow wobble would have no effect at all on climate. Each season would occur at the same distance from the sun. However, because insolation in the Northern Hemisphere is out of phase with that of the Southern Hemisphere, Croll believed that the ice ages would alternate from the northern to southern hemispheres.

Early in the twentieth century, Milutin Milankovitch, a professor of physics, mathematics, and astronomy at the University of Belgrade, revived Croll's insolation theory and set out on the task of detailing insolation based on Ludwig Pilgrim's latest calculations of Earth's orbit. He showed that insolation was dominated by a twenty-three-thousand-year cycle and concluded that ice ages would be most intense when the solar radiation dropped below a certain threshold. Because the insolation curve has an approximate hundred-thousand-year cycle, he believed that such a cycle might be seen in Earth's past. He also believed that the northern hemisphere would dominate because it contains two-thirds of the Earth's land mass. Driven by the amount of solar radiation in the north, ice ages in both the hemispheres would be synchronized.

When age estimates were made possible by radiocarbon dating, showing that the timing of Milankovitch's ice age calculations were incorrect, his insolation theory was abandoned. In the 1960s and '70s, however, insolation theory was revived when experts began isotope studies of seafloor sediments. Deep-sea sediments containing the shells of small plankton-like organisms, called foraminifers, hold a history of climate change. When alive, they fix themselves to two types of oxygen atoms, the abundant and more common oxygen-16 as well as oxygen-18. Oxygen-18, the heavier atom, is enriched in ocean water; the lighter atom is found in higher concentrations of snow and ice. Whenever water is extracted from the ocean to make more ice, it leaves its calling card in the oxygen. This enrichment, from oxygen-16 to oxygen-18, is seen in the carbonate shells of the foraminifers (made of $CaCO_3$). The carbonate precipitates from seawater, so the oxygen that builds the carbonate crystals reflects the composition of the seawater. By analyzing oxygen isotopes in foraminifers, scientists can determine when the Earth produced more glaciers and the time periods when ice ages occurred.

In seafloor sediments, the presence of one-hundred-thousand-year as well as forty-one-thousand-year and twenty-three-thousand-year cycles in climate have been discovered, although there are still unresolved questions. In glacial data, the one-hundred-thousand-year cycle seems to dominate, with the forty-one-thousand-year cycle weaker, and the twenty-three-thousand-year weakest of all. However, in insolation theory, it is the reverse.[1] The twenty-three-thousand-year cycle dominates, and the weakest appears to be the one-hundred-thousand-year cycle.

A more recent theory explaining Earth's ice ages links global climate change to one of the Earth's most impressive geological features: the Himalayas. According to the theory proposed by Maureen Raymo at Boston University, as the Himalayas grew, massive amounts of rock were exposed to the elements. As monsoon rains soaked the land and combined with carbon dioxide, the face of the exposed rock eroded. This process of chemical weathering extracted so much carbon dioxide from the atmosphere that global temperatures dropped, thus triggering an ice age.[2] To show that this was the case, Raymo turned to the study of seafloor sediments and strontium.

There are several types (isotopes) of strontium, each with a different atomic mass. Strontium-87, a heavier variety, is washed into the sea by the chemical weathering of rock. The lighter variety, strontium-86, is released by the spreading seafloor and comes from deep inside the Earth. By comparing the amount of the isotopes in different layers, Raymo believes that she would learn which process was more active at any point in time. Thirty-five million years ago, strontium-87 increased dramatically, coinciding with the Himalayan uplift. With the strontium evidence, Maureen Raymo believes she solved the ice age mystery. First, the uplift of the Tibetan region intensified the Indian monsoon. Then the monsoon rains eroded the mountains, stripping carbon dioxide from the air. Finally, with less carbon dioxide, the atmosphere gradually cooled.

Although distinct and regular ocean currents have been observed for some time, scientists have only recently determined that ocean currents play a crucial role in climate and weather. New research has shown that shallow, warm water currents from the Pacific flow westward, around Africa, and then northward along the African coast. These warm waters keep Europe balmy in contrast to their counterpart, Labrador, across the Atlantic. These currents provide Western Europe with a third as much warmth as the sun, and they are part of a global oceanic system that maintains the climatic status quo. In the North Atlantic, the Gulf Stream carries heat in the form of warm water to the north and east. And as it moves north, it evaporates and transfers its heat to the coastal areas.

The warm water becomes saltier with evaporation, and when it reaches the latitude of Iceland, its density reaches a point that it sinks to the bottom. Then it becomes part of the cold-water return cycle and flows southward in the Atlantic, around Africa and back to the Pacific.

If the warm waters ceased moving northward, Europe would enter a mini-ice age. Studies suggest that this is a possibility and that the current conveyor belt in the North Atlantic is unpredictable. Since the end of the last ice age, around twelve thousand years ago, the Arctic ice cap has continued to melt, allowing freshwater into the North Atlantic. If too much freshwater enters the ocean, thereby diluting the existing ocean's salt content, keeping it less dense, it would not sink and join the return currents at the bottom of the ocean. The cold freshwater would remain where it is, blocking the warm currents from entering, and altering the climate of Europe.

This same type of ocean current exists in the South Atlantic near Antarctica. There, ocean currents flow along the coast. Deep, cold currents flow back from the South Atlantic, south of Africa and on to Australia. Cold, salty water off the Antarctic coast sinks into the depths, thereby boosting the push to the interconnected system of ocean currents. According to Wallace Broecker of Columbia University, Antarctic waters are sinking only at one-third of the rate of North Atlantic waters. All the data suggest, according to Broecker, that the rate of Antarctic deep-water formation must have changed dramatically over the last eight hundred years, from fast to slow. He adds, "about 12,500 years ago deep-water formation in the north virtually ceased during a pronounced cold event, while Antarctic deep-water formation accelerated in conjunction with a relative warming there."[3]

HAPGOOD'S WANDERING POLES THEORY

Charles Hapgood's wandering poles theory is perhaps the most fascinating of all ice age theories, and it caught the attention of Albert Einstein, who was "electrified" by the idea in its "great simplicity," and he believed that if it continued to prove itself, it would be "of great importance to everything that is related to the history of the earth's surface."[4]

Hapgood's theory began with an interest in geography and ancient maps, which led to his rediscovery of the Piri Reis map, a hand-drawn Turkish naval map that had been gathering dust since the sixteenth century. According to Hapgood's sources, the map was drawn a few years after Columbus launched his first voyage to the Americas. Admiral Piri Reis, cartographer of the map, noted that his world map was derived from very old reference maps. On close inspection, Hapgood recognized that spherical trigonometry was used in the map's layout, which required a detailed knowledge of global geography. The map also displayed the coastline of Antarctica at some remote time when it was free of ice. According to Hapgood, the map was accurate at a time when no one should have known the coastal areas of Antarctica. This prompted a search for an explanation and eventually led to his controversial theory.

According to Hapgood's theory of wandering poles, every twenty thousand to thirty thousand years, Earth's continental plates move as a single unit, rapidly and over great distances. This phenomenon, known as continental drift, occurs today, but at a much slower rate. If conditions arise that create an imbalance in Earth's gyroscopic rotation, Hapgood's theory stipulates that Earth's plates would move in such a manner as to return Earth to a balanced spin. Geologic evidence suggesting that the poles may have been in different positions during the Pleistocene epoch (1,808,000 to 11,550 years ago) is impressive, although the physics of such a pole shift remain problematic.

Based on geomagnetic and carbon dating, Hapgood identified the locations of the four previous poles and mapped out their transitional paths. Seventeen thousand years ago, the North Pole was located in the Hudson Bay and moved to its current position over the course of five thousand years. Before that, the North Pole was located in the Greenland Sea (seventy-five thousand years ago) and moved southwest to the Hudson Bay. Prior to the Greenland Sea site, the pole was located in the Yukon Territory of Canada.[5]

How this movement could occur is explained by the dynamics of Earth's composition. We live on the crust, the outer surface, which comprises six main continental plates and a few smaller ones. Earth's inner core consists of solid iron surrounded by an outer core of liquid iron. Surrounding the core is the mantle, which is composed of molten rock (lower mantle) and solid rock (upper mantle). The upper mantle and crust are loosely connected and are able to slide against each other, the least effect of which is continental drift. Theoretically, each layer is capable of movement independent of the other layers. According to Hapgood, the top two layers can slide, if certain forces are applied, while the core and the axis and orbit of the planet remain unchanged. But what force causes the slippage?

In Hapgood's opinion, the centrifugal momentum of ice caps, which is not in synch with the poles, provides this force. The weight of the ice on the poles creates an imbalance in the Earth's rotation. Eventually, this builds to a point where a change is required to correct the imbalance. Hapgood realized that the entire planet does not need to be repositioned around its axis to maintain its balance. Only the outer crust needs to move, just as the loose skin of a peeled orange can slide around the inner fruit. He envisioned a catastrophic and dramatic move of the entire crust that would allow the polar ice caps to melt in a new, warmer climate. Ice would then begin to build at the new poles, awaiting the next shift. The crust's rapid movement, of course, would create environmental mayhem. If the current level of seismic and volcanic activity is the result of plates shifting between one and four centimeters per year, a much faster rate of change would likely be apocalyptic.

After the poles shift, regional climates everywhere would change dramatically. The displaced polar ice would melt, causing incredible floods. The new polar areas would freeze in a relatively short amount of time, quickly killing life accustomed to a warmer climate. Areas of climatic convergence would shift; deserts would receive rain, and rain forests would become deserts. Plant and animal life would have to adapt to the new conditions or become extinct.

As this small survey of ice age theories demonstrates, discovering historical truths is a difficult venture, especially when those truths require the reconciliation of current fact with events in the remote past that we know little about. According to Professor Emeritus of Earth Sciences Doug MacDougall, "In spite of the great advances that have been made in working out the details of what actually happened during the ice age, there is still much uncertainty about how, and especially why, an ice age actually begins. To be sure, there are hypotheses, but none have yet attained the status of accepted scientific theory."[6] Thus, ancient history can be best described as a perception based on experiences, ideology, scientific inquisition, and cultural biases: a wobbling house resting on the shifting sands of evidence and interpretation. It's mostly ideas and part fact, sailing uneasily in uncharted waters somewhere between science and speculation. Ancient history is more supposition than hard data, and thus there are many opinions. However, one thing is certain concerning the end of the last ice age some twelve thousand years ago: *mass extinction*.

RECENT MASS EXTINCTION

Although scientists are uncertain what causes ice ages and what brought the last ice age to an end, they do know for certain that at the end of the last ice age, mass extinction occurred, and that extinction was violent. The destruction appears to have been the result of a terrible event. We don't know the nature of this event, but it appears to have been centered in the Northern Hemisphere, particularly North America, Europe, and Siberia. Two-thirds of North America's large mammals, birds, and reptiles suddenly became extinct. The European rhinoceros and cave bear, as well as the herds of bison and mammoth in Siberia, disappeared forever. Other than large mammals, birds experienced more loss than any other group; spectacular species such as the giant teratorns with their sixteen-foot wingspans, along with a variety of vultures, hawks, and eagles, are gone forever.[7]

In Australia, the extinction of large animals also occurred, coinciding with a period of great climatic change. Most large Australian mammalian species lived in woodlands, except for one small group of species that occupied the grasslands of southeastern Australia. Two other species occupied central Australia, and only those two species managed to survive.[8] Asia experienced modest extinction. Africa, however, appears to have suffered little damage and has been largely ignored by researchers because so few large mammals became extinct there, as opposes to elsewhere. In fact, Africa has been called "the living Pleistocene" because its current animals are as abundant and diverse as the now-extinct Ice Age animals of other continents, especially North America.[9]

Interestingly, current ecological and evolutionary theory predicts that most changes in the North American climate during the period of extinction *should* have resulted in an increase in large animals and perhaps an increase in diversity, because with warmer temperatures, glacial ice disappeared, and freshwater became available over most of the continent.[10] Nonetheless, an increase in large animals did not happen, and regardless of what created extinction at the end of the Ice Age, such animals seemed to be unfit to survive the new climate and ecosystem. The extinction began around 15,000 BCE, increased dramatically around 10,000 BCE, and reached a cumulative level around 6000 BCE.[11] Whatever the cause of extinction, it occurred suddenly, removing forever 45 percent of all mammalian species on Earth.[12]

Professor Frank Hibben, one of the pioneers of American archaeology, traveled from Arizona to Alaska in search of the first Americans. In his quest he discovered that "the Pleistocene period ended in death."[13] And this death wasn't ordinary. It was "catastrophic and all-inclusive."[14] Hibben found evidence for catastrophic death almost everywhere: Florida, New Jersey, Texas, California, and as far south as Mexico and South America. He compares the evidence of violence found in North America to scenes of liberated death camps in Nazi Germany: "Such piles of bodies of animals or men simply do not occur by any ordinary natural means."[15]

Across the breadth of the United States are hundreds of mammoth "death sites," concentrated mostly in the Midwest, along the Rocky Mountains, on the Great Plains, and on the West Coast. In Alaska, the evidence of cataclysmic death is clear. Frozen deposits of soil, rock, and plant and animal remains (known as muck), are common geological features. In many places, writes Hibben, this muck is "packed with animal bones and debris in trainload lot [including] bones of mammoths, mastodons, [and] several kinds of bison, horses, wolves, bears and lions."[16] They met their end in the icy waters of a monumental flash flood.

Hibben also found something unexpected. Within the frozen muck were parts of animals and trees mixed with chunks of ice interlaced with layers of peat moss. According to Hibben, "It looks as though in the midst of some cataclysmic catastrophe of ten thousand years ago the whole Alaskan world of living animals and plants was suddenly frozen in mid-motion like a grim charade. . . . Twisted and torn trees are piled in splintered masses. . . . At least four considerable layers of volcanic ash may be traced in these deposits, although they are extremely warped and distorted."[17]

Three thousand miles south of Alaska, a similar situation exists in southern California's La Brea tar pits. According to Canadian Professor of philosophy and geology George McCready Price (1870–1963), a large portion of the bones discovered were "broken, mashed, contorted and mixed in a most heterogeneous mass."[18] More than five hundred animal species were fossilized in the sticky black tar some eleven thousand years ago. In 1906, after the first season of excavations, more than seven hundred saber-toothed tiger skulls were found. The tiger skulls averaged an amazing twenty per cubic yard.[19] In the tar pits there were actually more bones than tar.

On the other side of the Arctic Circle, mammoths were dying in the same manner. In 1977, journalist and author John Massey Stewart estimated that more than half a million tons of mammoth tusks were still buried along Siberia's Arctic coastline.[20]

In recent times, several dozen frozen mammoth carcasses, such as the Jarkov mammoth, have been found with their flesh still intact.[21] Other mammoths have been found with undigested grass, bluebells, wild beans, and buttercups still in their stomachs.

Whatever catastrophe occurred also affected human cultures. The brilliant painters of the Magdalenian (Cro-Magnon) culture that populated Western Europe and were responsible for the beautiful works of cave art found at Pech Merle, Chauvet, and Cussac, among other places, seemingly disappeared around the same time as the mammoths and mastodons. Their successors, known as the Azilian culture, appear later as scattered communities peppering the land. Whatever happened at the end of the Ice Age, human cultures were certainly affected.

EVIDENCE OF A COSMIC CALAMITY

The cause of the catastrophe that resulted in the extinction of 45 percent of our planet's animals, roughly twelve thousand years ago, is a mystery. The Earth is a living environment that is always changing in a seasonal and cyclical circle of birth, death, and rebirth. Any evidence regarding the catastrophe's identity has been hidden, probably long ago, by nature itself. Furthermore, from the point of view of single lifetime, even many hundreds of generations, everything has generally been like it is, and is assumed to have been so, since the beginning of humankind. However, according to the archaeological evidence, everything has not generally been the same. The city of Jericho, in modern-day Israel, for instance, was established only some eleven thousand years ago. Before then, life was very different, and what happened to change that appears to be cosmic, literally.

While working in the northeast region of North America, archaeologist William Topping discovered that Pleistocene animal remains were producing carbon-14 dates far too young to be accurate, sometimes by amounts as great as ten thousand years when compared to like-kind remains from the western region. Such a mystery piqued the curiosity of another scientist, chemist Richard B. Firestone, prompting both of them to investigate. The result was an article titled "Terrestrial Evidence of a Nuclear Catastrophe in Paleoindian Times," published in the *Mammoth Trumpet* in March 2001. According to the article, radiocarbon dates for sites in North America were suspect, and the evidence pointed to Late Pleistocene cosmic ray bombardment that created vast amounts of radiocarbon in the atmosphere, the heaviest concentrations occurring in the region of the Great Lakes. This event reset the clock by which radiocarbon dating measures the passage of time. This catastrophe's radiation produced secondary thermal neutrons from cosmic ray interactions. So much energy was released that the atmosphere over the state of Michigan reached 1,832 degrees Fahrenheit (1,000 degrees Celsius) and melted vast amounts of glacier ice. For animal and plant life, the radiation would have been lethal.[22]

After further research, Firestone and Topping hypothesized that a 6.5-mile-wide comet, possibly resulting from a supernova, exploded over the Midwest thirteen thousand years ago. Furthermore, they added, "This event was preceded by an intense blast of iron-rich grains that impacted the planet roughly 34,000 years ago."[23] More recently, their theory has been published in the academically prestigious *Nature* magazine.[24] Two other archaeologists have reported similar dating results. In 1999, Robson Bonnichsen and Richard Will reported in *Ice Age Peoples of North America* that tests of thirteen prehistoric sites in the northeast United States all arrived at carbon-14 dates regarded as too young for the remains discovered. According to *Mammoth Trumpet* writer James Chandler, "Many anomalies reported in the upper United States and in Canada cannot be explained by ancient aberrations in the atmosphere or other radiocarbon reservoirs, or by contamination of data samples (a common source of error in radiocarbon dating)." The editors of *Mammoth Trumpet* were so intrigued by the story that they reprinted Firestone and Topping's article in its entirety. The investigators concluded that "the only phenomenon capable of creating such imbalances . . . is massive neutron bombardment, probably from a supernova."[25]

Firestone then teamed up with science consultant Allen West and geologist Simon Warwick-Smith in a book titled *The Cycle of Cosmic Catastrophes* in which they contended that the source of radiation was the Geminga supernova. Backed by years of study, the detailed geological and archaeological evidence describes a sequence of events beginning in 41,000 BCE and culminating in 13,000 BCE; according to the authors, these were responsible for Earth's last great extinctions.

Today, at five hundred light-years away, the Geminga pulsar is the closest pulsar to Earth. However, forty-one thousand years ago it was much closer, a mere 150 light years away. Also at that time the pulsar was an ordinary star. Unfortunately for us, it was at the end of its life. Geminga became a supernova and sent out a burst of radiation that set off a series of events that affected our planet for the next thirty thousand years.[26] This burst of radiation directly impacted the eastern portions of the southern hemisphere, eliciting widespread extinctions in Australia and Southeast Asia. For ten seconds, plant and animal life exposed at the surface was irradiated by dangerous levels of gamma rays. In those areas, the human race was decimated. For those alive at the time, the flash from the Geminga supernova was bright enough to be a second sun during the day or another moon at night. For six months Earth had two suns. Over a period of many years, the supernova's luminescence gradually faded until it was no longer visible.

Whoever survived the initial burst of radiation was subject to plummeting temperatures and unstable weather. The dead and dying vegetation served as kindling for devastating fires ignited by frequent lightning strikes. Along with the excess ozone created by the flood of radiation, nitrates in the atmosphere made a poisonous brew.[27]

The shock wave from Geminga's explosion finally reached Earth thirty-four thousand years ago, bringing with it more radiation and bombarding Earth with small ions and particles as well as comets and asteroids. It was so powerful it nearly reversed Earth's magnetic field. Then, a second shock wave struck Earth sixteen thousand years ago and brought with it another round of radiation, comets, and asteroids. The most devastating effects of the Geminga supernova, however, arrived thirteen thousand years ago.

From the Oort cloud, the outer shell of our solar system, the blast wave from Geminga pushed a vast amount of dust, debris, and ice into the core of the solar system. Some of the debris hit the sun, touching off a series of large solar flares. A large comet, traveling at thousands of miles per hour, entered Earth's atmosphere just above Lake Michigan and impacted the ice sheet.[28]

The impact of the comet ejected a vast amount of rock and ice across the northern hemisphere, creating a starburst of craters from the Carolinas to Texas and the West Coast. The impact of ejected rock triggered earthquakes and volcanic eruptions as well as intense fire-storms on a monstrous scale. In northern climes, heat from the impacts vaporized hundreds of thousands of cubic miles of ice and collapsed various regions of the glacial ice sheet. The rapidly melting ice quickly inundated coastlines, while trapped water surged below the ice, creating unique land formations called drumlins. The rain of exploding rock also triggered massive underwater slides, which produced enormous tsunamis that bombarded the Atlantic coast and released trapped methane gas from the ocean floor.[29]

The cascading effect of the comet impact devastated the climate, and for more than one thousand years, Earth returned to ice age-like conditions. Scientists refer to this period as the Younger Dryas. Rain and snow fell for weeks. Wildfires pumped untold amounts of carbon dioxide into the atmosphere. The cold water that was dumped into the North Atlantic stopped the climate-warming ocean currents. And the vaporized water and rock created thick clouds that covered Earth for many years.

It was the "nuclear winter" that the generation of the 1980s was so afraid of. The darkness and cold temperatures, along with fire, destroyed nearly all of the plant life in the northern hemisphere. With little to eat, the surviving animals faced starvation during the next few months. As a result, animals, including humans, were also destroyed. The most unfortunate species were those with large bodies; they became extinct. The biological void allowed disaster species to flourish. In the standing water left behind, algae grew exponentially and left a black mat of decay over the ground.[30]

Europe and North Africa were similarly affected. Drawing on the meteorite database in London's National History Museum, Firestone, West, and Warwick-Smith mapped the locations of 3,411 European, African, and Middle Eastern meteorite impacts.[31]

One other scientist has performed parallel research. Four years before Firestone and Topping published their article in *Mammoth Trumpet,* physicist Dr. Paul LaViolette published *Earth Under Fire,* putting forth the theory that our galactic core could become active for a time, raining high energy particles into our region of space. The immediate effect on Earth would be the arrival of an electromagnetic pulse (EMP), followed by a large gravity wave that would pull the planet at its seams (tectonic plates), resulting in a series of earthquakes. Darkness would follow as cosmic dust and debris from the outer shell of the solar system reached the inner planets. Enveloped with dust, the sun would react violently and behave like a T Tauri star, emitting excess X-rays as well as ultraviolet and infrared radiation. Solar flares would also result, increasing the sun's brightness.[32]

Over time, the cumulative effects on Earth's climate would be devastating. Dust filling the solar system would reflect radiation back to Earth and in effect create a "hothouse." The gaseous clouds surrounding the galactic core would become luminous from the cosmic radiation and form an oval shroud around the blue star. For those on Earth, this would appear to be a blue eye in the sky—the eye of Ra, a sign of cosmic punishment that nearly eliminated humankind, as told in the Egyptian myth of Hathor and the Eye of Ra. Those who survived the radiation burst would suffer through devastating environmental changes. People living in coastal areas would suffer from destructive floods. But more important, with the intense heat, weather patterns would become unpredictable, and the air would become toxic as nitrogen and oxygen broke down into brown smog. Famine would be the number-one killer. Only people who were fortunate enough to live near clean water and a ready supply of food would survive.[33]

More than sixty years ago, Immanuel Velikovsky published *Worlds in Collision* and proposed the same general catastrophic idea as Firestone, Topping, West, Warwick-Smith, and LaViolette. Velikovsky suggested that long ago the planets of the solar system orbited the sun in a very different path and that Earth was once a satellite of Saturn. Venus was ejected from Jupiter as a cometlike object and on its trajectory passed close to Earth, resulting in global cataclysmic events. Velikovsky believed that electromagnetic forces played an important role in the celestial mechanics of the planets. He also thought that some aspects of this cataclysm were remembered in mythologies by all ancient cultures. For Velikovsky, the human species was experiencing a cultural amnesia.

However, during the 1950s the scientific dogma of uniformitarianism reigned supreme, and Velikovsky's book was met with high criticism from the scientific community. Although Velikovsky was ridiculed by the scientific establishment for his theory, somehow his work touched a nerve in society, and *Worlds in Collision* spent two years on the *New York Times* Best-Seller list. Whether Velikovsky's theory has any substance to it is immaterial, although in the next chapter you will read about how accurate his theory might be. What is important is that Velikovsky seems to have touched a deep-seated nerve in society, perhaps a dim memory of an ancient catastrophic past that somehow has managed to survive within humanity's collective memory.

THE VELA SUPERNOVA "BULLET"

Science historian D. S. Allan and geologist J. B. Delair believe in this collective memory of the cataclysm and have put forth the most compelling and comprehensive theory that a solar system–wide catastrophe occurred 11,500 years ago. Like Firestone, West, and Warwick-Smith, Allan and Delair research believe that the source of the global catastrophe and mass extinction was a nearby supernova. In their model, a massive star in the Vela constellation exploded a mere eight hundred light-years away from our solar system, very close by stellar measures.[34]

The evidence for a nearby supernova 11,500 years ago is very compelling. According to the data collected from the HEAO 3 satellite, our solar system is enveloped in a high concentration of aluminum-26, virtually a cloud. Aluminum-26, an isotope with a half-life of one million years, is readily produced in supernova explosions and gradually decays into magnesium-26. According to the data, the cloud around our solar system is still very much composed of aluminum-26, suggesting that the supernova occurred very recently, about 11,000 years ago.[35] The Vela supernova debris cloud measures 230 light-years in diameter, indicating this is not your average supernova.

According to the Molonglo Radio Observatory and the German ROSAT X-ray mapping satellite, the Vela supernova was a type II supernova, the most violent of supernovae. In order to be categorized as type II, the exploding star must be at least eight times larger than the sun and then collapse violently only to explode with the greatest of intensities.

Today, the Vela supernova remnant, called a nebula with a pulsar near its center, still displays signs of past violent eruption. Six X-ray features (protrusions) extend outside the leading edge of the blast wave. Astrophysicists Bernd Achenbach, Reinhold Egger, and Joachim Trümper of the Max Planck Institute for Extraterrestrial Physics propose that these protrusions were formed during the collapse and subsequent explosion of the star.[36] Most likely, the Vela protrusions are "blobs of matter formed in the collapse of the progenitor star, and expelled in the subsequent supernova explosion,"[37] traveling largely unaffected through the hot, tenuous, postshock plasma behind the blast wave. Currently, these unimaginably hot "blobs" (5 million degrees Fahrenheit) have passed in front of the now much slower moving blast wave. In such an event, a supernova explosion resembles a "splinter bomb," which creates confined and long-lived explosion fragments. This occurs when the star's mantle becomes unstable, collapsing upon itself and giving rise to highly heterogeneous clumps of matter; in layman's terms, according to Aschenbach, "shrapnel."[38]

Richard Strom of the Netherlands Foundation for Research Astronomy is certain that this is the case. The velocities of these clumps, which have overtaken the blast wave, are "a clear-cut case of a 'bullet' of ejecta moving supersonically through the surrounding medium."[39] According to Strom, this bullet (a small portion of the star) has now traveled 160 light-years away from its origin.

In the Allan-Delair model, when the Vela star exploded, a small but dangerous mass of plasma—a solar bullet—shot through interstellar space with tremendous speed into our solar system. Such was the speed and energy of the star fragment that its composition can be thought of as a miniature sun. An object racing through space from the result of massive explosion would have been a disassociated mass of ions and electrons—plasma. Traveling at such high speeds, it would contain a high electromagnetic potential.[40]

As the Vela plasma bullet reached the combined electromagnetic and gravitational fields of the outer planets, it exploded again, creating the aluminum-26 cloud that now surrounds the solar system.[41] When this solar bullet passed Neptune, it pulled one of Neptune's moons into an all-new orbit separate from its former host, which became the former planet we refer to today as Pluto. As the Vela fragment headed toward the sun, it passed by Uranus, dislodging one of its moons; next, it swung by Saturn and then the inner planets, wreaking havoc on its fateful journey into the sun.[42]

According to traditional astronomical thinking, the orbits of the planets in the solar system have been stable since the spinning whirlwind of stellar gas condensed into the solar system we know today. Any hypotheses of an unstable solar system, such as that put forth by Velikovsky, is met with great suspicion and often jeered. However, a number of anomalies that exist in our solar system wouldn't be expected in an ever-stable solar system.

For instance, Earth's moon previously orbited closer to the Earth than it does today. Venus rotates extremely slowly for its size, and it does so in the opposite direction of the majority of planets, as does Pluto. Venus also demonstrates a very peculiar rotation. Although it orbits the sun in 225 days, a single rotation on its axis takes 243 days, which makes a day longer than a year. Mars rotates too slowly for its size and has an extremely eccentric orbit. Earth too has a noncircular orbit. Of the seven other planets in the solar system, only Mercury shows greater eccentricity. Mars has two irregularly shaped moons (Deimos and Phobos) that orbit Mars at extremely high speeds. For its mass and size, Jupiter rotates too fast, and unlike the other planets, its two outermost moons orbit from pole to pole, each in opposite directions. Saturn rotates at an unusually rapid speed and also follows a noncircular orbit. Several of its moons consist mostly of ice, and Saturn is orbited by numerous rings of debris that appear from a distance as a single ring, most likely the remnants of a destroyed moon. One of its moons, Phoebe, orbits in the opposite direction of all the other Saturn moons. Uranus follows a noncircular orbit and also rotates rapidly, with its equator inclined at an extreme angle. Several of Uranus's moons also possess tilts of extreme angles—90 degrees—and their surfaces display features indicative of a catastrophic collision. Neptune follows an eccentric orbit, with both of its moons orbiting in a backward fashion. The smaller moon is so elongated that it takes 359 days to complete a single orbit. Pluto, which is really a twin dwarf planet with Charon, orbits the sun at an inclination of 17 degrees, and at times its strange orbit intersects with Neptune's orbit. Even more suspicious is the asteroid belt that orbits between Mars and Jupiter. Whatever its origin, it represents the debris of some celestial affair.[43]

According to Allan and Delair, the circumstances behind the solar system's arrangement, the orbits of the planets and moons, indicate that certain changes have resulted in aberrant and anomalous motion. Although these "derangements" are of little importance to the overall mechanics of the solar system, they were apparently the result of one or more perturbations during the past. Perhaps the more important question is whether these strange features of the planets occurred as the result of many isolated disturbances or are the result of a single event.[44]

The solar system's unusual features, Allan and Delair theorize, are from a single event: ejecta from the Vela supernova blazing its way through the orbits of the planets. If all planets and moons were created together, then they would all rotate in the same direction and orbit near the sun. Yet, today, the planets are spread out, and we find the acute tilting of Uranus and the highly eccentric orbit of Pluto. This would require a very powerful force, and a force powerful enough to accomplish this would also have affected the rest of the planets. Such a system-wide event would have likely resulted in mass extinction on Earth, annihilation from cosmic rays and debris the star fragment brought with it from the outer region of the solar system. Allan and Delair believe such an event also explains the current geographic features and environment of Earth.

They also believe that the experience was remembered in myth as the story of Phaeton and the Chariot of the Sun, in which the young prince Phaeton, the son of an Ethiopian princess and the sun god, took his father's chariot for a ride across the sky. But Phaeton could not control the wild horses. The sun chariot raced away, into the outer reaches of the solar system, where the great chariot's heat awoke the sleeping serpent of the Pole Star. It hissed and exhaled a poisonous breath. Then the chariot blazed toward the giant scorpion. Its tail raised, ready to sting. In great fear the young boy dropped the reins, and the chariot headed back toward Earth. But the closer they got to Earth, the hotter Earth became. Rivers began to dry up, and cities and forests caught fire. Neptune raised his head from the sea and shook his trident angrily at the chariot of the sun. But the air was so hot that Neptune dove back into the sea. As the chariot crossed the continent of Africa, it set ablaze the great Sahara forest, turning the landscape into ash and burning sand. In fear for their lives, gods, humans, and every other creature cried out for help. Zeus then climbed on high, armed with a thunderbolt, and launched it toward the chariot of the sun. With a deafening crash, Zeus's thunderbolt shattered the chariot. Phaeton fell, engulfed in flames. The horses ran home, and what was left of the chariot fell into the sea.

This story represents a time of great catastrophe on Earth, preserved in myth and handed down through the ages. For Allan and Delair, the story captures the human experience on Earth as the Vela bullet shot through the solar system and right by Earth—echoing a real memory of the resultant upheaval.

George Michanowsky thought so too. In *The Once and Future Star,* Michanowsky revives a lost curiosity in Sumerian and Akkadian cuneiform texts. The experts who first looked at cuneiform tablet BM 86378 were quite convinced that the narrative referred to a certain group of stars in the southern sky. But they didn't know what to do with the information. Essentially, a phrase involving part of the southern sky translated to "giant star." At the time, in the early twentieth century, there was no knowledge of any giant star in the southern sky, so interest soon waned. Michanowsky reviewed the original work, and with the Vela supernova in mind, the Sumerian text made complete sense. Whoever made those tablets, or perhaps the ancestors who originally told the story, witnessed a star exploding in the southern sky that was so bright that at times it appeared as a second sun.

Beforehand, according to myth, Earth was a paradise planet where humanity lived in the abundance of a Golden Age.

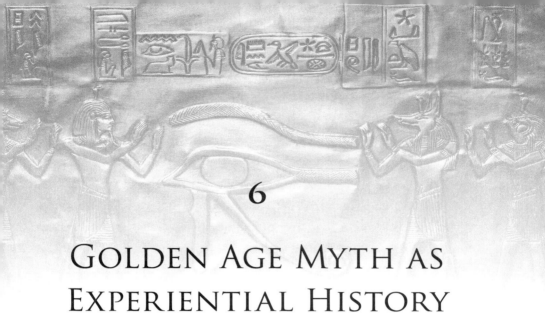

6

GOLDEN AGE MYTH AS EXPERIENTIAL HISTORY

The first time I heard of an ancient, mythical Golden Age was in grade school catechism. According to the biblical account, I learned, humankind began life on this Earth in a Golden Age of abundance and innocence. The second time I heard about an ancient mythical Golden Age was in high school, and that was in classical mythology, which was regarded as fiction. According to science, the evolution of life on the planet is linear, the first anatomically modern humans appeared between one hundred thousand and two hundred thousand years ago, and there is no evidence that an ancient Golden Age ever existed.

Understanding ancient history would be simpler if that were true. But evidence suggests the existence of a Golden Age around the world, most conspicuously in Egypt. In 1993, NBC broadcasted a documentary special hosted by Charleton Heston entitled "The Mystery of the Sphinx," based on the research of John Anthony West and Dr. Robert Schoch. West and Schoch visited Egypt in 1991 with the permission of Egypt's Supreme Council of Antiquities to perform a geological survey of the Great Sphinx. According to Schoch, the date the Sphinx was first carved is much older than Egyptologists recognize, based on their method of historical dating. Egyptologists believe that the Sphinx was carved in the middle of the third millennium BCE. According to Schoch, the Sphinx was first carved around 5000 BCE at least, and maybe even earlier.

A decade later, I met Christopher Dunn, the author of *The Giza Power Plant* and *Lost Technologies of Ancient Egypt,* who happened to live nearby. Over the course of the next four years, I learned from Dunn, an expert machinist and manufacturer of more than forty years, of the intricate and precise cutting of granite and basalt that was used in building ancient Egypt's temples, monuments, and pyramids. More important, I learned that Egypt's grandest pyramid—the Great Pyramid—was clearly built not as a tomb, but as a device. Exactly what that device was remains to be seen. Nonetheless, the precise cutting of chambers and hallways, not to mention the sheer size of the structure, requires a technology that did not exist during the third millennium BCE. They were clearly using a sophisticated technology; not only does the engineering testify to the fact, the economics does as well.

We could build an exact replica of the Great Pyramid today using the same materials as the ancient Egyptians. It wouldn't be simple or cheap. The limestone alone would cost $18 billion for 5.9 tons. For labor, fifty thousand workers for ten years would add another $255 billion. Add another 30 percent for general contracting costs, and the total cost of the Great Pyramid project comes to $380 billion. By using modern materials, we could lower the costs to around $35 billion, still a very large project by any standards.[1] Whatever the case, such high costs for any construction project, regardless of functionality, requires justification. In my opinion, why any society would devote such a huge amount of resources to a structure is a very important question, a question that has never been seriously considered. One would think that there needed to be some type of utility from which the entire civilization benefited. Furthermore, ten stone-block pyramids were built along the Nile River, not just one, with a number of temples and monuments. An additional nine pyramids would bring the cost of the project up to $350 billion. Add to that all the monuments, temples, palaces, and public works projects, such as canals and diversion dams. With such undertakings, the cost of this civilization's infrastructure would likely exceed a trillion dollars. Not to mention the fact that they built with limestone and sided with granite.

What kind of civilization builds with limestone and granite on a massive scale? The level of difficulty in quarrying, shipping, shaping, and setting limestone and granite, which is the hardest rock on Earth and must be cut by diamonds, is very high. We do it today, but it takes special equipment and is expensive.

As we touched on earlier, no equipment has ever been discovered that could possibly have been used in the construction of Egypt's magnificent granite temples and pyramids. However, the next best thing has been uncovered: a large granite stone that was obviously cut with a powered saw. Located just a few miles north of the Giza Plateau, this incredible stone lies on the east side of the Abu Rawash pyramid about a third of the way south of the structure's northeast corner. It is approximately four feet wide, six feet long, and ten inches thick. Workers from one of the past excavation teams must have pulled it from the rubble and placed it atop seven softball-sized stones. In pristine condition, a result most likely of being buried for thousands of years, it now rests about thirty feet from the base of the pyramid. Someday, this granite slab may be as important as the Rosetta Stone, and for good reason.

It has long been speculated by those intrigued with history's mysteries that an ancient technical civilization existed during remote times. Such speculation has never met the Sagan challenge that extraordinary claims require extraordinary evidence. This new "Rosetta Stone" meets that challenge, measuring approximately 56.75 inches long by 47 inches wide by 9 inches high. Its face or upright surface is smooth to the touch but not flat. Its surface is concave. At one end of the stone is an arc separating the smooth surface from the rough surface. Upon close inspection of the smooth portion of the stone, tiny lines—nearly microscopic—are visible across the width of the stone, in the same direction as the arc. You can't feel them with your hand, but you can see them if you look really closely. Whatever device did the cutting on this stone, it left grooves approximately 0.05 of an inch wide, which would normally be associated with the feed rate of the saw, but could also indicate a blade with multiple cutting teeth.[2]

There are five facts of great interest about this stone:

1. The tool that cut this slab of granite did so with relative ease, because the quartz crystals in the rock were cut as smooth and flat as the feldspar.
2. The tool that made the cut left an abrupt, exact terminating line in the shape of an arc between the smooth and rough portions of the stone.
3. The tool that made the cut also rendered the stone concave along its width.
4. Two slice marks (or steps) are exhibited on the stone's smooth surface. One is near the termination arc, and the other is on the opposite end.
5. There are machinist "feed lines" in the smooth part of the stone along its breadth the length of the stone.

Explaining these five features of the stone at Abu Rawash is impossible when claiming that simple hand tools were responsible. And when taking into account the feed lines, it is impossible. Because no tools that could possibly create these features have ever been found in Egypt, and there is no other evidence that such precise technology existed during Egypt's dynastic times, then there is only one alternative. A technical civilization must have existed prior to the beginning of Egypt's dynastic civilization. In other words, there is a distinct possibility that the Golden Age described by religion and ancient mythology isn't fiction. Rather, the Golden Age stories tell of history using metaphor. The problem is that as time passed, people's beliefs changed and the historical significance symbolized in myth was lost. So for us, many thousands of years later, trying to understand their meaning is like trying to solve a crime with a single piece of evidence and thirty witnesses, all with slightly different bizarre stories.

Egypt not only left us with a wealth of great structures to investigate, it also left us its history.

ANCIENT HISTORY ACCORDING TO THE ANCIENT EGYPTIANS

According to the Turin King List, an Egyptian papyrus, prior to Narmer, the first king of the first Egyptian dynasty, the "Followers of Horus" ruled for 13,420 years, and before them, "the gods" ruled for 23,200 years.[3] This provides the possibility that Egyptian civilization didn't begin in 3000 BCE; rather, it began in 39,620 BCE, a date that is consistent with other ancient writers. According to Diodoros of Sicily and several chroniclers, gods and heroes originally ruled Egypt for 18,000 years. Afterward, mortal kings governed for 15,000 years, bringing the length of Egyptian history to 33,000 years. Manetho, a third century BCE high priest of the temple at Heliopolis, attributes 15,150 years to prehistoric divine dynasties and 9,777 years to the kings reigning before Menes, for a total of 24,927 years. George the Syncellus claimed that the Egyptians possessed a tablet they referred to as an ancient chronicle, which mentioned thirty royal dynasties after the reign of "the gods," which comprised twenty-five Sothic cycles, or 36,525 years, one Sothic cycle being 1,461 years.[4]

Herodotus also mentions a long history for ancient Egypt in that, on four separate occasions, "the sun moved from his wonted course, twice rising where he now sets, and twice setting where he now rises."[5] Herodotus says that according to the Egyptians priests, from their current King Hephaistos to the first king of Egypt, there had been 341 generations of human beings. And because 300 generations are equal to 10,000 years (given that 100 years is three human generations), 11,340 years had passed from the first king to Hephaistos. During that time, the Egyptians said, "there had arisen no god in human form; nor even before that time or afterwards among the remaining kings who arise in Egypt."[6]

Herodotus was taken by the priests to a great temple and shown colossal wooden statues representing 345 men who served as chief priests during the 341 generations of kings. Each statue was a son succeeding his father. The priests, going from image to image, told Herodotus their names until he reached the one who had died last.[7] The Egyptian priests also claimed:

> In this time they said that the sun had moved four times from his accustomed place of rising, and where he now sets he had thence twice had his rising, and in the place from whence he now rises he had twice had his setting; and in the meantime nothing in Egypt had been changed from its usual state, neither that which comes from the earth nor that which comes to them from the river nor that which concerns diseases or deaths.[8]

In the ancient Egyptians' records, the spring equinox had twice been located in the constellation of Aries, and it also passed twice in the opposing constellation of Libra. In other words, one-and-a-half precessional cycles occurred during all of ancient Egypt's historic and prehistoric periods, approximately thirty-nine thousand years.[9] Manetho records the same story that the Palermo Stone and the Turin Papyrus record. According to Herodotus, "before the reign of kings that the priest spoke of the gods were the rulers in Egypt."[10] Although you will never come across such a statement in a current world history textbook, University of Southern California Professor Walter Wallbank, the 1951 winner of the Watumull Prize for *India in the New Era,* wrote in his world history textbook, *Civilization: Past and Present,* coauthored with Alastair Taylor:

Artifacts have been discovered in Egyptian tombs that go back as far as 15,000 BCE. These remains show that the early Egyptians passed through the main divisions of the Old and New Stone Ages and had even begun to use copper for tools before the time of the Old Kingdom. Progress was apparently rapid, and soon people lived in crude houses, had weapons of flint and copper, and engaged in agriculture. Examinations of grain and husks found in the stomachs of corpses in ancient tombs have shown that as early as 10,000 BCE the ancient Egyptians had developed superior strains of barley seed which could be easily cultivated and which produced heavy yields. The earliest Egyptians, whose race has not yet been conclusively ascertained, wore linen garments and were especially remarkable for their artistic skill, particularly in pottery. Their polished red-and black ware was never surpassed by their descendents, even in the periods of highest Egyptian accomplishments.[11]

How can this evidence of a sophisticated, technical—even anachronistic—civilization of the Nile Valley be explained?

There are only two choices. The first choice, which was adopted by nineteenth and early twentieth century Egyptologists, historians, and archaeologists, assumes that prior to 10,000 BCE, human beings were hunter-gatherers lacking advanced technology and a written language. And from 10,000 to 3000 BCE, human cultures were making their first attempts at agriculture, animal domestication, and construction, building villages of small dwellings from mud brick. So, for the ancient Egyptians of the Old Kingdom, living between 3000 and 2000 BCE, the urbanization of an agrarian culture was a natural progression. Therefore, they must have been able to erect, somehow, all the magnificent structures that still exist today regardless of the technology required to accomplish such a feat. Thus, in order to conform to the dogma of the day, the ancient Egyptians were able to build anything, whatever the scale or level of difficulty, through sheer manpower, an assumption that works as long as the precise cutting of granite and other hard stone and the lifting of multiton blocks of stone are not required. For example, the uppermost chamber of the Great Pyramid is made from seventy-ton rectangular slabs of granite, covering the floor, ceiling, and walls, and is situated approximately three hundred feet up the pyramid.

Copper hand chisels and stone hammers, however, could never be solely responsible for the precise cutting of granite used in building the massive megalithic pyramids, monuments, and temples of ancient Egypt. Not then and not now, as even today we cannot and do not build massive granite structures with hand tools. Attempting as much would be futile. Furthermore, the ancient Egyptians were well known for their record keeping. Some of the earliest texts, such as the Pyramid Texts, date back to the first dynasties of the Old Kingdom. Yet, there are no records left by Old Kingdom pharaohs chronicling their construction of pyramids or other monuments assigned by Egyptologists to the third millennium BCE.

Given the evidence, one is compelled to accept the notion that what we see as the history of dynastic Egypt actually is a re-creation, a reestablishing of a preexisting civilization I call "Civilization X." Because the technology to build precise megalithic structures did not exist during the third millennium BCE and did not exist up to modern times, civilization must have existed prior to the catastrophe we refer to as the end of the Ice Age.

So, when were these magnificent ancient structures of Egypt built, and by whom?

There is but a single reference to these concerns in ancient Egyptian texts, the Edfu Building Texts, inscribed on the wall of the temple at Edfu, located sixty miles south of Luxor. These texts contain a wealth of information concerning ancient Egypt's religion, politics, and history from the oldest epochs of pharaonic history.[12] According to the texts, the words of the "Seven Sages" were recorded by the god Thoth—the Egyptian principle of writing and wisdom—in a book entitled *Specifications of the Mounds of the Early Primordial Age*. This book listed the locations of sacred mounds along the Nile River as well as all the lesser mounds, or temples, along with the place where time began, the Great Primeval Mound. Furthermore, these sages were the only divine beings who understood how the temples were to be created. They were also the ones who began work on the Great Primeval Mound, planning out and erecting the mythical temple of the "First Time."[13]

In the ancient Egyptian language, the First Time was *Zep Tepi,* and in their mythology Zep Tepi was a remote age when the gods established their kingdom on Earth, in Egypt. According to Robert Thomas Rundle Clark (1909–1970) in *Myth and Symbol in Ancient Egypt,* certain principles were used in the creation of myth. First, the gods set forth the fundamental principles of life, nature, and society long before the institution of kingship was established, during Zep Tepi, a time when God first stirred in the Primeval Water to bring about the kingship of Horus and the redemption of Osiris. All proper myths must relate to events or manifestations of this age. Second, any authority or justice in society or natural phenomenon had to refer to the First Time. All rituals, royal insignias, temple plans, magical or medicinal formulas, hieroglyphic writing, the calendar—essentially civilization itself—had to refer to the First Time.[14]

According to Manchester University Egyptologist Dr. Eve Reymond, the Seven Sages described by the Edfu Building Texts were enlightened survivors of a cataclysm that nearly destroyed Earth, who then proceeded to help facilitate the beginning of a new age, referred to as the First Time. According to Reymond's translation of the texts, the First Time was an era that was based on what existed before. The general tone of the texts is that an ancient world or civilization had been destroyed, and from that death came a new period of creation, a re-creation or resurrection of what existed in the past. The Seven Sages originally came from an island, known as the "Homeland of the Primeval Ones," that was destroyed in a sudden flood. Although most of its inhabitants drowned, the few who managed to survive became the "Builder Gods, who fashioned in the primeval time, the Lords of Light . . . the Ghosts, the Ancestors . . . who raised the seed for gods and men

. . . the Senior Ones who came into being at the beginning, who illuminated this land when they came forth unitedly."[15]

In *The Message of the Sphinx,* Graham Hancock and Robert Bauval describe these builder gods as mortal men, and after completing the task of rebuilding, they handed down their duties and functions to their children. "In this way, just like the Followers of Horus, the generations of the 'Builder Gods,' or 'Sages', or 'Ghosts' or 'Lords of Light' described in the Edfu Texts could constantly renew themselves—thus passing down to the future traditions and wisdoms stemming from a previous epoch of the earth."[16] For Hancock and Bauval, these builder gods of the Edfu Building Texts are so similar to the Heliopolitan tradition of the Followers of Horus that it is "hard to escape the conclusion that both epithets, and the numerous others that exist, are all descriptions of the same shadowy brotherhood."[17]

ANCIENT MYTHS OF A GOLDEN AGE

The principles and character of the kingdom set forth by the builder gods—the Seven Sages/the Followers of Horus—were patterned upon the previous age, "before rage or clamor or strife or uproar had come about." There was no death or disease in this blissful epoch known by various titles in ancient Egypt: "the time of Re," "the time of Osiris," or "the time of Horus." According to Clark, the time of Osiris was "the model for subsequent generations" and "the driving force behind Egyptian culture for thousands of years." It was a Golden Age.[18]

The ancient Sumerians of Mesopotamia also recorded in the annals of their history a Golden Age. In an epic poem of the hero Enmerkar (cuneiform tablet 29.16.422 in the Nippur collection), the poet describes a "blissful and unrivaled state of man in an era of universal peace before he had learned to know fear and before the 'confusion of tongues.'"[19]

> In those days there was no snake, there was no scorpion, there was
> no hyena,

There was no lion, there was no wild dog, no wolf,
There was no fear, no terror,
Man had no rival.

In those days the land Shubur (East), the place of plenty, of righ-
     teous decrees,
Harmony-tongued Sumer (South), the great land of the "decree of
     princeship,"
Uri (North), the land having all that is *needful,*
The land Martu (West), resting in security,
The whole universe, the people *in unison,*
To Enlil in one tongue *gave praise.*[20]

We have a clue to an event that brought the Sumerian Golden Age
to an end. The epic poem of Enmerkar is retold in the biblical Tower
of Babel story. In Genesis, chapter eleven, the storyteller describes the
people of the world having a common language, literally "one pronun-
ciation and of the same words."[21] With such unification in society there
was nothing they couldn't achieve. So, they set out to build a city along
with a tower that reached to the heavens. Although we are not told why
God didn't approve of this venture to build a city and a tower, except to
state that "nothing they plan to do [literally dream of] will be impossible for them,"[22] God didn't approve, and to prevent them from finish-
ing their city and tower, God "confused their languages" and "scattered
them over all the face of the earth."[23]

There is only one reasonable explanation for the mythical tale of
the Babel story. The construction of the city and tower was halted as
a result of some devastating catastrophe. The story begins with "the
people in unison" and all speaking the same language. It ends with
people scattered across the face of the Earth, speaking many different languages. English is a new language, only one thousand years old.
However, speakers of English today would not understand Old English
and would have a difficult time with Middle English. Language, in

fact, is always changing, so a reasonable, historical understanding of the Tower of Babel myth is that the survivors of the catastrophe were drawn together in small pockets around the world and over many thousands of years and developed their own unique languages.

Other cultures, such as the ancient Hindus, also tell of a Golden Age. They viewed the human experience in a wider sense, as a universal or cosmic experience. According to ancient Hindu beliefs, the universe does not exist with a beginning and an end, but rather, being part of nature, is cyclical and is created and destroyed many times. This cycle is based upon the idea that the sun orbits around a twin star, as well as an area in space that is a seat of power, called "Brahma."[24] A single orbit, according to Hindu tradition, takes 24,000 years. When the orbit of the sun comes closest to this grand seat of power the mental virtues of people become highly developed, enabling them to easily comprehend things, even mysteries of the spiritual world.[25]

This grand 24,000-year cycle is divided into two 12,000-year cycles called Daiva Yugas, meaning "electric couple." One of the 12,000-year cycles is ascending, and the other is descending. For 9,600 years, when the sun is nearest the grand seat of power, Earth civilizations enjoy a Golden Age called Satya Yuga, where life is enjoyable and carefree. No one has to work because the climate is perfect and food exists in abundance. However, as the sun moves away from the grand seat of power this human intellect gradually loses its ability to grasp the knowledge of divine magnetism, and humanity enters an age called Treta Yuga. As the sun moves even further away from the grand seat of power, a lesser age begins called Dwapara Yuga in which humanity loses its ability to comprehend the power of energy and the creative principles of the external world. Finally, when the sun is at its furthest point from the grand seat of power, humanity enters a period of intellectual and spiritual darkness called Kali Yuga. During this period, the intellectual power of humanity diminishes to the point where no one can comprehend anything beyond the gross material world, resulting in widespread ignorance and suffering for all nations. Politically, there is no peace for any nation or kingdom. People then live in spiritual darkness and cannot separate what is true from what is false and don't care about the difference. Filled with jealousy and hate, they murder those who attempt to lead them out of the darkness and into truth. As a result, the world is filled with war over the most trivial of reasons. Resources become difficult to find, and in the end people resort to scavenging for food, eating whatever roots, fruit, and meat they can find or steal. As this dark age continues, people have few, if any, possessions.[26]

As the Kali Yuga age comes to a close, those living at the time have the opportunity to penetrate the illusions of physical life, embark on a spiritual, insightful path, and achieve peace of mind. At the 12,000-year midpoint of this 24,000-year cycle the intellectual and spiritual darkness ends, and humanity slowly begins to regain its intellectual and spiritual powers it once had during the ascending ages of Dwapara and Treta, reaching toward a new Golden Age.

The ancient Greeks also viewed the human experience as a cycle through successive ages. First there was a Golden Age of humankind, in which sadness didn't exist and people spoke directly with the gods and ate with them, and mortal women bore children by them. Work was unnecessary because food was abundant. When humans became too familiar with the gods, some say, they became arrogant and filled with contempt, believing they were as wise and strong as the gods. So the gods withdrew, thereby ending the Golden Age. Then came an age in which humans had to till the soil and earn a living, when they ate bread for the first time. This was a silver age. Even though men lived to be old, they were effeminate and dependent upon their mothers in a matriarchal society. Quarrelsome they were, and constantly complained about everything, so the great god Zeus destroyed them. Then there was a bronze age in which people were more industrious, but delighted in waging war—so much so that they killed each other off. Then, the gods fathered sons and daughters by human mothers, and the bronze age became an age of heroes. Men fought gloriously and lived virtuous lives; this was the age of Hercules and the heroes of the siege of Troy.

Now we're living in an iron age in which people no longer converse with the gods, but ignore them altogether. Life is materialistic, treacherous, and violent.[27]

The same general tale is told in the biblical story of Eden. Humankind first dwelled in a land of abundance, the Garden of Eden, where they lived solely off the abundant fruit and plants. Then some event, symbolized by eating the fruit from the Tree of Knowledge, brought them into an age in which they were forced to till the Earth, make bread, and eat animals to sustain life,[28] a world that became wicked and as a result was destroyed by a flood.[29]

The Vikings also tell in their myths of a time called the "Doom of the Gods," when the wolf swallowed the sun. This end of an age they called *Ragnarök*, and at the first Ragnarök, the stars fell down from their places, and it was said that time was forced upon the gods.

PLATO'S ATLANTIS

Plato's story of Atlantis didn't originate with Plato, according to his own words, but with his uncle, the statesman Solon (c. 638–539 BCE). Solon heard the story of Atlantis while visiting the priests of Sais in Egypt's Nile Delta. Although no researcher has ever discovered proof that Atlantis existed, such as a "Welcome to Atlantis" sign, the ruins of this mythical city are alleged to have been found in many parts of the world, including Spain, the Mediterranean, and even the Americas, which, incidentally, is the only place in the world where there exists a plain large enough to fit Plato's story. Atlantis is probably what Aristotle said it was in his treatise *On Meteorology,* a mythical place in a story.[30] Still, the fact that there are numerous ancient megalithic sites around the world, the most recent find dating to 10,000 BCE at Göbekli Tepe, Turkey,[31] needs to be explained. Perhaps Atlantis wasn't so much a city as a civilization that was spread across continents. The ancient Egyptians have another myth, called Denderah and the Eye of Ra, which also tells of a catastrophe that decimated humankind.

Mainstream scholars suggest that the devastating volcanic eruption on the island of Thera (modern-day Santorini, in the Mediterranean near Crete) is the source for Plato's tale. Although destructive enough to have destroyed a city, this volcanic event appears to have occurred too recently to serve as Plato's source. According to Plato, the event occurred nine thousand years before his time. Even if this number is only an estimate, it suggests that the cataclysmic event described in the story had to have transpired much earlier than the Thera eruption. Furthermore, other catastrophe stories predate the eruption on Thera.

The discoverer of an ancient Minoan port on the island of Thera, archaeologist Spyridon Nikolaou Marinatos has contributed perhaps more than any other researcher to the search for Atlantis. In 1939, he published the article "The Volcanic Destruction of Minoan Crete," which led to an association of Crete with Atlantis. According to Marinatos, "Plato's imagination could not possibly have conjured up an account so unique and so unusual to classical literature. . . . For this reason, the account is usually called a 'tradition' by Plato. I should also like to add that if in some parts the account chances to bear the stamp of the fable, this must be attributed to the Egyptians and not to Plato."[32] Marinatos further writes that the tale of this island that later vanished was clearly familiar to the Egyptians, claiming that the priests at Sais confused it with other traditional accounts concerning Atlantis.[33] What is noteworthy is that the tale of Atlantis is not a Greek story, rather an Egyptian one. And if the Egyptians confused the Thera cataclysm with another, older story, then it must be the case that the original version was significant enough to be remembered throughout many generations—in the same way that the biblical flood story was handed down orally for thousands of years in Mesopotamia. Furthermore, Crantor, a student of Xenocrates, who was a student of Plato, is said to have visited Egypt to verify the Egyptian story of Atlantis.

Although Crantor's commentaries on Plato are lost, Proclus (412–485 CE) declares in his commentaries on Plato that Crantor did visit Egypt and viewed the columns that contained the Egyptian story of

Atlantis. Plato never mentions any columns in his dialogues *Critias* and *Timaeus;* nonetheless, it might be the case that Solon heard the story from another Egyptian source. If the story was commonly known to the temple priests at that time, certainly there would be a number of ways to learn the story. Whatever the case may be, the tale of Atlantis was certainly an oral tradition in the ancient world that a previous civilization had been destroyed by cataclysmic events long before recorded history.

THE SATURN MYTH

With Göbekli Tepe, an archeological site in southern Turkey near the Syrian border, mainstream academics are starting to realize nineteenth and twentieth century interpretations of prehistory might be wrong. According to Dr. Schoch, Stanford University archaeologist Ian Hodder has commented that "[Göbekli Tepe] is unbelievably big and amazing, at a ridiculously early date . . . huge great stones and fantastic, highly refined art. . . . Many people think that it changes everything. . . . It overturns the whole apple cart. All our theories were wrong."[34] Schoch noticed similarities between petroglyphs he viewed at Easter Island and those of Göbekli Tepe, and observed that the glyphs were indicative of "powerful plasma events in the skies at the end of the last Ice Age."[35] Furthermore, Schoch thinks the evidence indicates that the ornate, megalithic Stonehenge-like structure at Göbekli Tepe was intentionally buried around 8000 BCE to preserve it from imminent disaster, because stone walls were built between the finely wrought upright pillars before its final burial.[36]

Plasma is a separate phase of matter different from solids, liquids, and gases. It is a collection of charged particles that respond strongly and collectively to electromagnetic fields, forming gaslike clouds or ion beams. According to physics, plasma is the fundamental state of matter, and physicists who specialize in the study of plasma have produced the same scarring effect in the laboratory as seen on the surface of Mars—

dendridic (tree-like) branching called Lichtenberg patterns, sinuous channels with scalloped walls, crater chains, domed craters, terraced craters, bull's-eye craters, hexagonal craters, dark spotting, and small pebblelike spheres known as *blueberries*. All these features, which were assumed to be a result of erosion and asteroids impacts, are actually the observed behavior of electric discharge on metal or stone surfaces. Smooth surfaces on Mars, when viewed up close, are actually fields of small, densely packed craters, indicative of electrical machining. Electric arcs can produce massive cratering of a planet in a short period of time, making it look a billion years old. Science is discovering that the universe is more electrically "alive" than has been previously thought.[37]

According to this electrical view of the universe, planets and other celestial bodies such as comets and asteroids are charged bodies seeking electrical equilibrium with the solar environment. The sun's corona emits charged particles scientists refer to as the solar wind, which envelopes the entire solar system. Planets and other celestial bodies trapped in orbit by the sun's gravity soak up these charged particles in much the same way a welding stick soaks up electrons when the wielding machine in turned on. Planets, like people, serve as capacitors for an electrical charge. So, when two celestial bodies of varying charge come into proximity with one another, the planet with the lesser charge will lose its charge to the other planet, and that transfer of electrical charge, if high enough in voltage, will be visible as a plasma streamer, often violently leaving craterlike pock marks and deep gouges on the surface of the planet receiving the discharge of plasma.

Mythologist and author David Talbott suggests that the surface of Mars was radically altered as a result of high voltage plasma discharge when another celestial body closely passed by. So was Earth.

Ancient mythology across the world tells the story of a solar system very different from the one we know today, and of a time of great upheaval in the sky. It has been a mystery why ancient cultures referred to the planets as "the gods." Today, the planets are difficult to see, and when they are in position where they can be seen, they appear to us as nothing more than bright stars. According to Talbott, the orbits of the planets were very different and much closer to the sun and Earth, so much so that they could be seen large and bold in the ancient sky, and because the planets were so close, the Earth received from them enormous streams of plasma energy.

During ancient times, Saturn was one of the inner planets, from an earthly perspective toward the north, where it served as the stationary "true" sun, Talbott suggests. As Venus and Mars came into proximity with Saturn, streamers of plasma flowed from planet to planet, creating an awe-inspiriting sight in the sky. For this reason, ancient cultures looked to the planets as "the gods." It's also why the ancient "cosmic wheel" is the greatest iconographic enigma recorded in myth by almost every ancient culture. Some images of a wheel in the sky, carved on stone, are older than civilization itself. Although mainstream archaeologists view this wheel to be symbolic of the sun rolling across the sky, in its most common form, the cosmic wheel is not depicted to be moving. It often rests atop a stationary pillar, stairway, or ladder, and it is sometimes being turned by a rope sitting on top of a table or altar. Furthermore, the spokes of the wheel are not functional but are fluidlike and etheric. A similar representation of a wheel with four filamentary spokes is found in Arizona, California, Ireland, Mesopotamia, Mycenae, Troy, Greece, and Israel.

Although the wheel might be drawn slightly different depending on the region, they all have the same three parts: a large circle or sphere, a central star, and a smaller, darker circle or sphere inside the starlike form. The inspiration for this, Talbott says, did not come from our sun. The images do not depict a single object, but three objects. These forms in the sky were the planets Venus, Mars, and Saturn in close congregation, which for people of Earth would be a spectacular view, leaving little confusion regarding why they would consider the planets to be gods. This cosmic wheel was also viewed to be the throne of gods and cultural heroes, and was replicated symbolically in the wheel-thrones of earthly kings. Archaic gods and heroes portrayed in art are sometimes depicted with a wheel in their hands, such as in the Hebrew Yahweh, or God; the Roman Fortuna, goddess of fortune and luck; and the Greek Triptolemos, a deity of agriculture. This alignment of planets in close proximity is even inspiration for the wheel-throne of Buddha. For Talbott, this wheel-throne underscores his point. It's also seen in the popular "footprint of Buddha."

In his book *The Saturn Myth,* Talbott writes that in ancient mythology Saturn was the dominant planetary body in the sky and that ancient races all over the world recorded that there was once a Golden Age, a time of cosmic harmony when a central light god ruled. That light god was Saturn, and it was close to the Earth, thereby appearing as the "primeval sun" of "terrifying splendor." Today, Saturn appears as a small speck of light. However, many thousands of years ago, Saturn stood at the celestial North Pole as a fiery globe fixed in place. Saturn ruled a celestial kingdom, serving as the "Universal Monarch" and the "Primordial Man." Ancient peoples drew pictures of Saturn incessantly and consistently depicted a central orb surrounded by a circle, the "enclosed sun"—the original hieroglyph for the planet Saturn. The band was Saturn's spouse, the Mother Goddess, and is his revolving temple, city, or island in heaven; together they form the stationary but ever-turning "world wheel." Saturn also dwells in its band as the pupil of the all-seeing eye. The same band was also symbolic of Saturn's throne, the receptacle of cosmic waters, and an encircling serpent. Four streams of light radiated from Saturn, dividing its band into quarters, which were symbols of the sun cross and enclosed sun cross, the universal image of the "unified state" on Earth. Mythically, they were described in stories as the four rivers of paradise, the four winds, and the four pillars of the cosmos. Ancient peoples also described a pillarlike stream ascending the world axis toward Saturn. From the human visual point of view, the pillar, a cosmic mountain—the mythical Mountain of God throughout the Old Testament—seemed to be sustaining Saturn's dwelling, the mountain being depicted as a circle atop a triangle—also referred to as the great god's single leg, the North wind, and the erect serpent or dragon.

When sunshine reflected on Saturn's band, a brilliant illuminated crescent could be seen. The light and dark portions of the band symbolically became the black and white cosmic twins, while the alternating positions of the crescent were the twins of the "right and left" or "above and below." When Saturn was in the polar configuration (symbolized by an orb with a crescent atop a triangle), the ancients saw "the cleft summit of the cosmic mountain, with the central sun standing between the peaks of the right and the left; the cosmic bull supporting Saturn between its horns; Saturn's crescent ship on the mountaintop; the heaven-sustaining giant with outstretched arms; the winged god or goddess; the plant of life; Saturn's turning sword; and the altar of the world. It was the relationship of the Saturnian crescent to Saturn's period of brilliance which produced the original symbolism of the four directions and of 'day and night.'"[38]

The Egyptian Legend of a New Sky and a New Sun

In the ancient city of Thebes, inscribed on the walls of a small chamber in the tomb of Seti I, is a legend that speaks of a time when the gods walked with humankind, the time of Re. For a long time Re ruled over humans. Then humans began to complain that Re was old. When Re heard their murmurings he ordered his bodyguard to summon all the gods living with him in the primeval world-ocean to privately assemble in the Great House, the temple of Heliopolis. Re was unwilling to slay the rebel humans and wanted advice from the other gods. They advised Re to send forth his eye in the form of the goddess Hathor, and she would accomplish the task. Hathor rejoiced in her destruction of humankind, and on her return she was praised by Re for what she had done.[39]

Re, however, suddenly had a change of heart and ordered messengers to bring him large quantities of the fruit *tataat,* which he ground up, then mixed with human blood and beer. Seven thousand vessels of this potion were carried up to where Hathor was destroying humankind. During the night the potion of beer, blood, and this mysterious fruit was poured out into the meadows of the Four Heavens. There, Hathor drank the drink, became intoxicated, and paid no further attention to her task. The men and women who lived carried forward the memory in a festival honoring Hathor and Re. Those who took part in these festivals consumed large quantities of beer, and under the influence of beautiful women engaged in "licentious orgies."[40] Re soon complained, and now grown weak, perceived humans as a worthless remnant and regretted that he hadn't killed more. To help Re, Nut changed herself into the Cow of Heaven, took him on her back with the help of Shu, and then fled. When the humans saw Re climbing onto the back of the Cow of Heaven, they repented and cried out for Re to stay with them. He refused, however, and Nut continued on, taking Re to "Het-Ahet, a town of the nome of Mareotis, where in later days the right leg of Osiris was said to be preserved."[41]

Meanwhile, the legend states, darkness covered the land. At daybreak, the repented men slew the enemies of Re, to his pleasure. From this time on, "human sacrifices were offered up at the festivals of Ra celebrated in this place."[42] Still, Re was intent on leaving and ascended into the heavens. Then, Re said, "Let a great field be produced and the Field of peace. Let there be reeds," and field of reeds came into being, which were the Elysian Fields of the Egyptians.

Then Re commanded the creation of the stars and to support them, the Four Pillars; he told Shu to protect them and hold up the sky in his hands. In this way, Shu (the air that holds up the sky we see today) became the new sun god in place of Re (Saturn). "Mankind would live and rejoice in the light of the new sun."[43]

In this case, Re's departure in the legend coincides with Saturn's change of position in the solar system, and the destruction of humankind in the legend have to do with a disaster associated with Saturn's movement.

Ragnarök: Legend of a New Sky and a New Sun

In Norse mythology, Ragnarök is the time when the gods are destroyed, a terrifying period ushered in by great wars around the world, and strife and hatred between men. Many believe Ragnarök to represent a future disaster in Norse mythology, but others think the legend depicts events that actually occurred in the ancient past, brought about by Saturn's shift to a new location in the solar system. During this time, family becomes meaningless, and appalling deeds are committed. The world sees a period of bitter cold in which the sun and the moon are swallowed up, and the stars fall from the sky. Mountains are crushed. The whole world trembles and shakes, and the World Tree quivers in the mayhem. The wolf Fenrir's great gaping jaws fill the gap between Earth and sky as the serpent rises from the sea, blowing out poison. The sea engulfs the land, and the ship Naglfar is launched, driven by Loki along with a crew of giants. Surt and his followers ride out from the fiery storm and join forces with the frost giants for their final battle with the gods.[44]

Heimdall blows his horn and alerts Aesir of the danger. Then Odin rides to the spring beneath the World Tree and chooses his champions to encounter his ancient enemy, the wolf. Thor battles the World Serpent, Freyr fights Surt, Tyr fights the hound Garm from the underworld, while Heimdall fights alongside Loki. The gods are destroyed except Surt, who throws fire over the world so that humans perish with the gods. The sun darkens, the Earth sinks into the sea, the stars slip out of the sky, and vapor and fire rage as the leaping flame licks heaven itself. The Earth, however, rises from the waves and returns to a fertile, green world. The sons of the great gods survive, and Balder returns to life to reign with them to rule a new universe. Two living creatures that sheltered in the World Tree come out and repopulate the world with men and women. A new sun outshining her mother in beauty journeys across the heavens.[45]

Recorded by the ancient ancestors in numerous stories, Saturn's change of location in the sky was catastrophic. According to Talbott, "the world-destroying deluge; the battle with the serpent-dragon of the deep; the birth of Jupiter, the Child-Hero; the resurrection and transformation of Saturn; and Saturn's eventual departure to the distant realm—these are the key elements in a story of incalculable impact on ancient imagination."[46]

Herein lies the reason that ancient cultures were so obsessed with the sky, particularly the Egyptians, who were terrified by the precessional movement of the constellations and converted observation of the sky into a science. Their world, their cosmic order of all things, was destroyed before their very eyes as was the civilization they had achieved. In Greek mythology, the Titans (elder gods) were supreme in the universe for untold ages. They were of enormous size and incredible strength. The most important was Cronus, in Latin, Saturn, who ruled over the other Titans until his son Zeus dethroned him and seized the power for himself. The Romans said that when Jupiter, their name for Zeus, ascended the throne, Saturn fled.[47]

Like other gas giant planets, Saturn is composed mostly of hydrogen and helium, and within its upper atmosphere fast winds combined with rising heat from its surface create its luminous yellow and gold banding. Interestingly, according to astrophysics, Saturn is sunlike, radiating more energy into space than it receives from the sun.

Saturnalia and the Roman Calendar

Among the Romans, Saturn was originally one of the *numina,* a divine power guiding the course of events, the Protector of the Sowers of the Seed. Every year during December, the people of Rome held the festival of Saturnalia in memory of the Golden Age, when Saturn reigned. The idea behind the celebration was that the Golden Age returned to Earth while the festival lasted. "No war could be then declared; slaves and masters ate at the same table; executions were postponed; it was a season for giving presents; it kept alive in men's minds the idea of equality, of a time when all were on the same level."[48]

According to Roman legend, long ago, Saturn was the righteous, beneficent king of Italy when the Earth brought forth food in abundance. War did not exist. No love of money and profits worked like a poison in the blood of the industrious and contented peasantry. Slavery and private property were unknown. All humans had all things in common. Saturn was responsible for agriculture and bringing the scattered people of the mountains together in order to teach them to till the ground, create laws, and live in peace. Then the good god, the kindly king Saturn, suddenly vanished. Saturn's memory from a distant age was cherished. Shrines were erected in his honor, and many of the hills in Italy bore his name. There was also a dark side to Saturn's memory. His altars were said to be stained with the blood of human victims, but in this age effigies were substituted.[49]

The festival of Saturnalia went on for seven days in the streets and public squares, from the seventeenth to the twenty-third of December, and during this time the distinction between citizens and slaves was temporarily abolished. Some masters even changed places with their servants and waited on them as if they were the masters. The purpose of this switching of positions was to imitate the state of society in Saturn's time; it was a temporary restoration of the equality of the monarch's reign.[50]

A fascinating story is connected to this Roman festival. In our understanding, by convention, it is the year 2013. The reason it is the year 2013, as opposed to any other number, is due to a Roman Abbott named Dionysius Exiguus, who, in the year 527, commemorated Christ by instituting a new calendar in which year 0 was assigned to the year Christ was born—in Latin, *Anno Domini Nostri Jesu Christi*.

Prior to 527, Western civilization followed a different calendar, instituted by the Roman emperor Julius Caesar in the year 46 BCE. In that year, Egyptian astronomer Sosigenes of Alexandria consulted with the emperor to reform the Roman calendar and achieve a more manageable and accurate structure. To compensate for past error, he added ninety days to the year 46 BCE. He also changed the number of days in the months to attain an accurate 365-day year. For year 0 in this new order of time, he chose 4713 BCE and started the clock on January first. This was not a random selection.

Why was 4713 BCE chosen? Assume that the Egyptian astronomer who Julius Caesar hired as a consultant studied in the Pythagorean School of Sacred Geometry. Pythagoras espoused an ideal reality based on "perfect solids," which could also explain the movement of the stars and planets. With this in mind, it is well within reason that Caesar was displaying his Pythagorean knowledge and honoring Egyptian astrology if, from the Egyptian's perspective, that year was cosmologically significant. To be sure, it was a very special year indeed. Here's why.

The rising and setting stars Aldebaran (in the constellation Taurus) and Antares (in the constellation Scorpio) were situated on the horizon at midnight on January 1, 4713 BCE. At this time, Antares was rising in the east and Aldebaran was setting in the west. Antares was fourteen minutes from the horizon. Also at that time, the sun was at a celestial longitude of 14 degrees (13 degrees, 43 minutes) in the constellation Aquarius. The moon's velocity, which is not constant and varies between 11 and 15 degrees, was 14 degrees (13 degrees, 59 minutes) per day. On day 0, year 0, these important celestial bodies were converging on the number fourteen. Fourteen is the sacred number of Osiris—an important god in Egyptian cosmology.

In addition to Aldebaran and Antares, Saturn played a crucial role in the selection of this date. The date—4713 BCE—was in conjunction with the most sacred star in Egypt, Sirius, 19 minutes away and 19 degrees in its own sign. The sun, whose birth was being celebrated on that day, was in Saturn's sign of Aquarius. Julius Caesar chose January 1, 4713 BCE, as the start of his calendar to honor the birth of the sun at the Giza Plateau. But at the same time, he honored the Roman festival of Saturnalia. For Caesar, that year, so long ago (even by Romans standards), seems to have been an obvious and logical choice.

Earth as Saturn's Moon

Ancient mythologies link Saturn to an astronomical event and to a previous Golden Age of peace and abundance. Before civilization as we know it existed, another civilization reached sophistication more than twelve thousand years ago, different but equal to our own. During that

Golden Age—what the ancient Egyptians referred to as "the reign of the gods" and "the time of Re"—Earth was literally a botanical paradise plush enough throughout its land masses to support large animals, most of which are now extinct.

The gods, however, of this era were not viewed in the same way as we view the Judeo-Christian God today. Their gods were never meant to be understood as omniscient, omnipotent beings, although they did believe in a creator god who fit that description. For the ancient Egyptians, the creator god was Atum. That is how we understand it. Their other gods were principles of nature and some of those gods were the planets, literally. Philosophically, those same planets represented the Archetypal Man from which all life arose. Viewing the universe as an interconnected system, a single entity, they believed the planets were a broader expression of the same life we live. In ancient Egyptian philosophy, the planets represented immortal man—what we today refer to as the human species as a totality.

There's only one way our ancient ancestors could have come up with the idea of planets as gods. The inner planets of the solar system followed very different orbits than they do today. Prior to twelve thousand years ago, Earth, Venus, Mars, and Saturn orbited the sun in close proximity to each other, as if in formation. Saturn, always visible to the north, possibly held Earth in its orbit, in effect making the Earth a moon of Saturn. Saturn was so brilliant it was the true, ever-present sun.

Immanuel Velikovsky theorizes a very different orbit of the planets in his unpublished manuscript entitled In the Beginning, describing the cosmic events narrated in the first chapters of Genesis, events that preceded those described in his bestselling book *Worlds in Collision*. Myths, Velikovsky realizes, are a description of real events, and at the center of mythology, in the beginning, is the fabled age of Saturn, remembered with nostalgia as an age of bliss. Hesiod tells of a golden race of mortal humans when Saturn reigned in heaven, living like gods without sorrow and free from toil. Earth bore much fruit, and everyone dwelt in ease. In *Metamorphoses*, book six, Ovid tells a similar tale of a Golden Age, when humans of their own accord lived out of good faith and did what was right, without the threat of punishment, and without laws. The Earth produced all things spontaneously as if spring was everlasting. Agriculture was unnecessary. Likewise, rabbinical sources, such as Louis Ginzberg's *The Legends of the Jews,* claim a similar state of the world before the Deluge. Humankind neither toiled nor had cares. However, as a consequence of their prosperity they grew insolent.

Velikovsky writes, "The dominance of Saturn at some remote period in the history of the life of the peoples on Earth was of such pronounced and all-pervading character that the question arises whether the adventures of the planet going through many exploits could by itself be the full cause of the worship of the planet and the naming of the Golden Age 'the Age of Kronos' (Saturn)."[51] According to Velikovsky, Saturn exploded, causing the planet Earth to suffer one of its greatest catastrophes. Saturn was "dismembered" like the mythical Osiris, and when it reconstituted itself, the planet was fettered by rings of debris.

The mystery in mythology is how could the myth makers concoct such a story without having being able to observe the events in the sky?

In Velikovsky's hypothesis, for ancient people, Saturn removed Uranus from its role as chief deity. However, Uranus is only faintly visible over Mesopotamia on a clear night. So, the distances between the Earth and Saturn and Uranus must have been very different than what they are now, or else Saturn would have never been considered to be such a spectacle in the sky as described in myth. Furthermore, according to Velikovsky, Saturn was more voluminous, and luminous, before the Deluge, but if in the ancient past it moved on today's thirty-year orbit of the sun, with Earth too orbiting along its present path, there would be no reason for our ancient ancestors to regard Saturn as the supreme celestial body of the sky.

Theoretically, Saturn could have satellites as large as the Earth because the moon is only one-fortieth the volume of the Earth, and Saturn is 760 times larger than Earth. Velikovsky speculates that if "the

Earth was once a satellite of Saturn, the latter must have revolved closer to the sun in order that the Earth should receive heat from it—Saturn exudes little heat—and if the age of Kronos was a Golden Age, then it is also proper to assume that the conditions on the satellite Earth were not unfavorable for life."[52]

Ancient Egyptian texts explain how Saturn went away violently, and with that violence inflicted on Earth, humankind was decimated. The stars were then "created" because our ancient ancestors had never seen the stars. Dismayed and traumatized, they instantly became astronomers, tracking the movements of the stars, because prior to the cataclysm everything was always the same. Now they anticipated more terror from the sky, but the stars moved slowly and life continued. After what must have been thousands of years, they switched their attentions to the new sun in the sky, and it became the life-emanating force that was previously Saturn's. The event that changed *life as they knew it* into *life as we know it* is called the Great Flood.

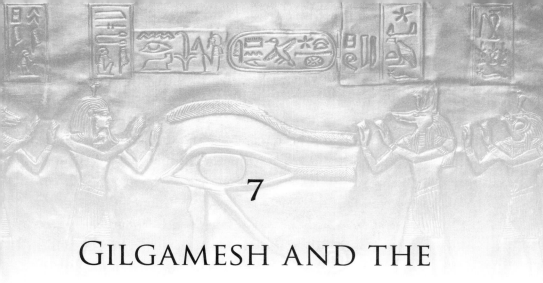

7

GILGAMESH AND THE GREAT CELESTIAL FLOOD

Flood stories exist in many ancient cultures. Ancient India, Babylonia, Greece, and Egypt tell of a great flood in their myths, as do the Native American peoples of the northern hemisphere—the Mandan, Knisteneaux, Choctaw, Creek, Natchez, Mojave, Apache, Cree, Algonquin, and Aztec.[1] The Incas of South America also tell of a devastating flood in which "it rained for months without end," and for those who sought refuge in the mountains, they looked on as "the entire world was being destroyed."[2] The most well known of flood myths, however, is the biblical story of Noah's flood, which some believe to be the oldest of all Near East flood stories. However, the oldest flood story is found in the Epic of Gilgamesh, who, according to the Sumerian texts was an antediluvian king.

In 1839, Austen Henry Layard began excavating the ancient Sumerian city of Nineveh. In time, he discovered buried beneath the sand a library of more than twenty-five thousand cuneiform tablets.[3] On some of those tablets was written the epic story of Gilgamesh. The flood story, however, was incomplete, so the search continued in

Nineveh for the remaining tablets. In 1888, an excavation team from the University of Pennsylvania led by John Punnett Peters began work on a mound in ancient Nippur, in southern Iraq. By the end of the following year, they had uncovered more than thirty thousand cuneiform tablets. Of these tablets, a small group contained the oldest versions of the Gilgamesh Cycle in the Sumerian language, dating to the end of the third millennium BCE.[4]

The Epic of Gilgamesh must have been widely known in ancient times. Other versions of the story have since been found in the archives of the Hittite capital at Boghazköy in Anatolia, written in the Semitic Akkadian language and translated into the Indo-European Hittite language, as well as the Hurrian languages. Parts of the story have been found at Sultantepe in southern Turkey and in the ancient city of Megiddo in Palestine, suggesting that the Canaanites also had their version of the epic. Recently, a case is being made for the existence of a Mycenaean tradition of the epic that somehow survived the Greek dark age and reappeared in Homeric and Greek poetry.[5]

In Sumerian literature, the story of the Deluge was not a part of the Gilgamesh saga, but was an independent poem, the role of Noah being played by the hero Ziusudra. In the tradition of Old Babylonia, the hero is Atrahasis, and the flood is the last disaster sent to destroy humankind in a series of disasters. Whether the Genesis flood is a later refinement of Sumerian, Assyrian, and Babylonian tradition is not entirely clear.[6] These myths do indicate, however, as in the Egyptian legend of the destruction of humankind, that at a remote time in our past, the world was nearly destroyed and with it, human life.

The Epic of Gilgamesh contains five stories: The Coming of Enkidu; The Forest Journey; Ishtar and Gilgamesh, and the Death of Enkidu; The Story of the Flood; and The Search for Everlasting Life. All are important in painting a contextual picture for the catastrophic event known as the Flood.

The saga is prefaced by the narrator explaining the mythic and heroic character of Gilgamesh. He was created by the gods, perfect in body. Shamash, the glorious sun, endowed him with beauty. Adad, the storm, endowed him with courage. The great goddess Aruru designed the model for his body and prepared his form, but Rimat-Ninsun, a notably wise goddess, known as the "August cow," bore Gilgamesh as her son. Gilgamesh was two-thirds god and one-third man. He was wise and knew all things, and as a king, he knew all countries. In Uruk, he built walls, a great rampart, and the temple of the blessed Eanna for the god of the firmament, Anu, and for Ishtar, the goddess of love. The temple still exists today, the narrator states, with an outer wall that shines with the brilliance of copper and an inner wall the likes of which no one can equal. "Take hold of the threshold stone—it dates from ancient times! Go close to the Eanna Temple, the residence of Ishtar, such as no later king or man ever equaled! Go up on the wall of Uruk and walk around, examine its foundation, inspect its brickwork thoroughly. Is not (even the core of) the brick structure made of kiln-fired brick, and did not the Seven Sages themselves lay out its plans?"[7]

Gilgamesh was a hero, the narrator exclaims:

It was he who opened the mountain passes,
who dug wells on the flank of the mountain.
It was he who crossed the ocean, the vast seas, to the rising sun,
who explored the world regions, seeking life.
It was he who reached by his own sheer strength Utnapishtim, the
    Faraway,
who restored the sanctuaries (or cities) that the Flood had destroyed![8]

THE COMING OF ENKIDU

The story begins with Gilgamesh behaving not like a hero, but rather as a tyrant, having no compassion for the people of Uruk, taking whatever he wanted, killing sons, and seizing daughters for his pleasure. The people complained, and Anu, the father of the gods—the Great God—listened. Then, the gods called to Aruru, the goddess of creation, who created humankind, and requested for her to create a *zikru* (an idea) that would be of equal balance to Gilgamesh's stormy heart so that Uruk might find peace. Within herself, Aruru created the zikru of Anu, washed her hands, pinched off some clay, and threw it into the wilderness, thereby creating the valiant Enkidu.

Enkidu was wild. Hair covered his body, and he ate grass along with the gazelles. One day, a notorious trapper saw him at a watering hole, and like all the other animals, Enkidu ran away in fear. The trapper told his father about Enkidu, and his father advised him to go to Uruk and tell Gilgamesh about this wild man of the mountains. He will tell you to take the harlot Shamhat with you to where Enkidu lives and have her take off her clothes so Enkidu might have his way with her. The trapper did so, and after Enkidu made love with Shamhat for six days and seven nights, the animals feared Enkidu.

Now having become like a god, Enkidu followed Shamhat back to Uruk. While on the way to Uruk, Shamhat told Enkidu that it was Gilgamesh whom she loved, and Anu, and Enlil (the god of Earth, wind, and air). She also told Enkidu that Gilgamesh had dreamt of him, that he saw the stars of the sky, and that some kind of meteorite of Anu fell next to him. In his dream, Gilgamesh saw the people of the land of Uruk standing around it; they thronged around it and kissed its feet as if it were a little baby. Gilgamesh's wise mother explained to him that the man Enkidu, whose essence fell from the sky, would repeatedly save him.

In Uruk, Enkidu ate bread and drank beer for the first time. He washed his body, rubbed oil onto himself, and became human. Then he put on clothing, became a warrior, and chased away all the predators so the shepherds could get some rest. Then one day, a young man came to Enkidu and explained that a wedding was about to take place. Further elaborating on the wedding details, the young man explained that Gilgamesh would first have the man's wife in bed before the husband could consummate the marriage. This angered Enkidu, so he went to the marital chamber and barred Gilgamesh from entering. They fought fiercely at the doorway, shattering the doorposts and shaking the walls. Gilgamesh threw Enkidu and suddenly lost all anger. They kissed each other and became good friends.

Gilgamesh dreamt and Enkidu interpreted the dream. The gods decided that Gilgamesh would inherit the kingship, but he would not be immortal. Do not be sad, though, Enkidu told him, because he had also been given the power to choose darkness or to enlighten human-kind. He would be given great power, but would also have to deal justly with that power—deal justly before Shamash (the sun).

Gilgamesh saw that Enkidu was physically weak and turned his thoughts to the Country of the Living, to the Land of Cedars. "This is my destiny," Gilgamesh thought and decided they would go to the country where the cedars were cut. There he would become famous. However, they would encounter the terrible Humbaba, a monstrous giant, whose "roar is a Flood, his mouth is Fire, and his breath is Death!" Humbaba was assigned the task of terrorizing human beings. Still, Gilgamesh understood that he must go anyway and kill the terrible Humbaba. Together, Gilgamesh and Enkidu would face death.

THE FOREST JOURNEY

On the journey to the Cedar Forest, Gilgamesh had five dreams, the fourth and fifth of which he found disturbing. When Gilgamesh and Enkidu confronted Humbaba before he could enter the Cedar Forest, Humbaba kept changing faces. Gilgamesh was terrified and cried out to Shamash, who sent Demon Wind, Ice Wind, and a sandstorm—a total of thirteen winds—against Humbaba. In fear for his life, Humbaba offered to be Gilgamesh's servant. However, Enkidu warned against taking the offer. So Gilgamesh took out his axe and his sword. Taking turns, they struck blows, and on the third blow Humbaba fell. They took down the cedars; the seven splendors of Humbaba were extinguished. Next, they moved into the forest and discovered the sacred dwellings of the Anunnaki. Gilgamesh felled the trees while Enkidu cleared the roots. From cedar wood they crafted a raft and carried Humbaba's head away to show to the gods.

ISHTAR AND GILGAMESH, AND THE DEATH OF ENKIDU

The saga continues with Ishtar (comparable to the Roman Venus) making advances to Gilgamesh and asking him to marry her. He declined and insulted Ishtar by accusing her of being wicked because she turned her last lover, Ishullanu (the gardener of Anu), into a dwarf and made him live in the garden of his labors. Ishtar was furious and asked Anu, her father, to give her the Bull of Heaven in order to kill Gilgamesh. Anu saw that it was Ishtar who provoked Gilgamesh and knew what Gilgamesh had said about Ishtar was true. Ishtar threatened to knock down the gates of the Netherworld by causing famine in the land of Uruk. Anu gave in to her threats and handed her the nose rope of the Bull of Heaven. The bull snorted and opened up a huge pit, into which fell a hundred men. With a second snort, another pit opened up, into which fell two hundred men, and with a third snort, a third pit opened up, which Enkidu fell into up to his waist. Gilgamesh and Enkidu were ready, however, and devised a plan to thwart the bull's attack. Enkidu jumped out of the pit and wrested the bull by the tail, and Gilgamesh, like an expert butcher, thrust his sword into the bull's nape. With the bull dead, they ripped out its heart and presented it to Shamash (the sun) with a humble bow.

In mourning, Ishtar cried out and cursed, "Woe unto Gilgamesh who slandered me and killed the Bull of Heaven!" In anger, Enkidu ripped off the bull's hindquarter and flung it in Ishtar's face. Ishtar assembled the cultic women of lovely-locks, joy-girls, and harlots, and set them to mourning over the hindquarter of the bull. Gilgamesh summoned all the artisans and craftsmen, and they celebrated into the night until they fell asleep.

While asleep, Enkidu dreamt that the Great Gods Anu, Enlil, and

Shamash held council over the deeds of Gilgamesh and Enkidu. Anu said that because one of them went up the Cedar of the Mountain and killed the Bull of Heaven, then one of them must die. Enlil exclaimed that it must be Enkidu who dies. However, the Sun God of Heaven decreed that it was by his command that they killed Humbaba and the Bull of Heaven. Enlil became angry and told Shamash that it was his fault because he traveled daily with them as their friend. In the Cedar Forest where the Great Gods dwell, Enkidu lamented that he must die and become a ghost, and declared that he did not kill the Cedar of the Mountain.

Gilgamesh told Enkidu that the dream was important even if it was frightening and said that he would pray and beseech the gods for an appeal. At dawn, Enkidu raised his head and cried out to Shamash for his precious life and cursed the harlot who had turned him into a human. Shamash consoled Enkidu and calmed his heart, reassuring him that it was good that the harlot Shamhat served him so. Enkidu then blessed Shamhat with many words and decreed that her fate held riches.

Enkidu then had another dream in which the heavens cried out and the Earth replied. He was standing between them. There appeared a man of dark visage whose face resembled Anzu (whose name means He Who Knows the Heavens), although his hands were the paws of a lion and his nails, the talons of an eagle. He seized Enkidu by the hair, overpowered him, and took him down to the House of Darkness, the dwelling of Irkalla, where those who enter never come out. When Gilgamesh woke up he discovered that Enkidu had died, and he ordered that the blacksmith, coppersmith, goldsmith, and jeweler fashion a statue of him.

THE SEARCH FOR EVERLASTING LIFE AND THE STORY OF THE FLOOD

Gilgamesh cried bitterly over his friend Enkidu and roamed the wilderness thinking that he too was going to die. Fearing death, he set out to the homeland of Utnapishtim (comparable to Noah in the Hebrew story of the flood and to Ziusudra in the Sumerian version), who they called the "Faraway." On the journey, he passed Mount Mashu, the guardian for the rising and setting of the sun, above which lies only the dome of the heavens. There Gilgamesh found two scorpion beings, a male and a female, watching over the gate, and told them he had come a long way in search of his ancestor Utnapishtim, who was given eternal life and now dwelled in the Assembly of the Gods. He wanted to ask him about life and death. Even though no mortal had crossed the mountains, the scorpions allowed him to pass, so along the Road of the Sun Gilgamesh journeyed. For ten leagues he traveled in darkness, but in the eleventh league he could see a glimmer of light. In the twelfth league the light grew brilliant. When he entered its brilliance, Gilgamesh discovered that it was a garden with trees bearing beautiful blue gemstones as foliage. There he met a tavern keeper named Siduri living by the seashore. Because of Gilgamesh's haggard appearance, she thought he was a murderer and locked the door.

Gilgamesh identified himself as the one who had killed Humbaba and the Bull of Heaven, then asked for the way to Utnapishtim. The tavern keeper replied that there had never been a passage and that no one since the days of old had crossed the sea. Only Shamash (the sun) could cross the sea because it was difficult and its ways were treacherous through the Waters of Death. Nonetheless, she pointed Gilgamesh in the direction of Urshanabi, the ferryman of Utnapishtim, and both of them cut three hundred punting poles for the boat they would use to cross the sea. They launched the boat and sailed away. By the third day they had traveled a stretch equal to a month and a half of a normal voyage and arrived at the Waters of Death. Gilgamesh took punting poles, one after another, and used them to move their boat past the treacherous waters.

Finally, Gilgamesh faced Utnapishtim, "Enkidu, my friend whom I love, has turned to clay! Am I not like him! Will I lie down never to get up again?"

Utnapishtim replied, "Why, Gilgamesh, are you sad? You were created from the flesh of gods and mankind. . . . Yes, you are a human being, a man." After Enlil had pronounced the blessing, the Anunnaki, the Great Gods, assembled, and Mammetum, the goddess of destiny, determined their fate. They established death and life, but they did not make known "the days of death." While Utnapishtim spoke, Gilgamesh had been looking at him and was surprised that he looked like a man. He asked him how it came about that he stood in the Assembly of the Gods.

"I will reveal to you, Gilgamesh, a thing that is hidden; a secret of the gods I will tell you! Shuruppak, a city that you surely know, situated on the banks of the Euphrates—that city was very old and there were gods inside it. The hearts of the Great Gods moved them to inflict the Flood."

Utnapishtim told Gilgamesh that the clever prince Enki told him to tear down his house, build a boat, and bring all living beings into the boat. So he did and loaded his silver, gold, all the living beings, his family, craftsmen, and all the beasts of the field into the boat. Then the Flood came as the Anunnaki lifted up their torches and set the land ablaze. Enlil's deeds overtook the heavens and turned the light into blackness. The land shattered like a pot. All day long the south wind blew and submerged the mountains in water. No one could see his fellow man or recognize each other in the torrent. The gods were frightened by the Flood and retreated into the heaven of Anu. They cowered like dogs, crouching by the outer wall of the temple. Ishtar shrieked like a woman in childbirth, wailing, "The olden days have alas turned to clay because I said evil things in the Assembly of the Gods! How could I say evil things in the Assembly of the Gods, ordering a catastrophe to destroy my people! No sooner have I given birth to my dear people than they fill the sea like so many fish!"

Sobbing with grief, the Anunnaki gods wept with her, their burning lips parched with thirst. The wind and the Flood lasted for six days and seven nights, and the land was flattened. Then, on Mount Nimush,

Utnapishtim's boat lodged. After the seventh day, Utnapishtim sent out a dove, but it came back to him because no perch was available. Then he sent out a swallow, and it flew back to the boat too. Later, the raven Utnapishtim sent out did not fly back to the boat, so he sent out the animals in all directions and sacrificed a sheep. He also made incense offerings of reeds, cedar, and myrtle, which the gods savored, except for Enlil, because it was he who brought about the Flood and ordered death for humankind. When Enlil saw the boat, he was furious and cried out in rage at the Igigi gods, "No man was to survive the annihilation!" Ninurta (the god of war) claimed that it was Enki who alerted Utnapishtim because he knew every machination.

"It was not I who revealed the secret of the Great Gods," Enki replied. "I only made a dream appear to Utnapishtim, and thus he heard the secret of the gods. Now then! The deliberation should be about him!" With that said, Enlil brought Utnapishtim and his wife into the boat, had them kneel, touched their foreheads, and pronounced that they were no longer human. They were now gods and would reside far away at the Mouth of the Rivers.

After hearing this story of how Utnapishtim survived the Flood, Urshanabi and Gilgamesh sailed away. While on their way back to Uruk, Urshanabi noticed that Gilgamesh was exhausted and offered him another secret: that there is a plant with thorns, like boxthorn, called "The Old Man Becomes a Young Man," and it prevented humans from decaying. Gilgamesh planned to eat the plant, but before he could, a snake smelled the plant's fragrance and quietly snatched it away. As it retreated, it shed its skin. Gilgamesh sat down and wept.

When they arrived in Uruk, Gilgamesh said to Urshanabi, "Go up, onto the wall of Uruk and walk around. Examine its foundation; inspect its brickwork thoroughly"; that it is not a brick structure of kiln-fired brick, and "did not the Seven Sages themselves lay out its plan!"*

---

*Here, we see that the Seven Sages had built the city and the wall, because it was not made of simple kiln brick, rather they used stone. It is a hidden nugget because it implies that the structure survived the Flood catastrophe.

DRAMA IN THE SKY

Gilgamesh's exploits are reminiscent of the mythologies surrounding Ulysses and Hercules. He was the most popular hero of Mesopotamia as late as the Babylonian Kingdom, and the story was translated into numerous Assyrian and Babylonian editions as well as the Hittite and Hurrian languages. In that respect, *The Epic of Gilgamesh* served, like the biblical Genesis, as sacred cultural history. Typical of ancient myth, many of the characters in the Gilgamesh epic are not human. They are gods or demigods. The immortal hero Utnapishtim, who escaped the Great Flood, lives in a realm beyond the rising and setting of the sun, within the dome of the heavens in the "Assembly of the Gods." As such, like the Greek myths, *The Epic of Gilgamesh* is a drama in the sky. Such a story, obviously steeped in symbol and metaphor, can be difficult to interpret. Understood literally, *The Epic of Gilgamesh* is terrestrial. Yet, many of the main characters are planets or other celestial phenomenon. Ishtar, the goddess of love and fertility, corresponds to the Roman deity Venus and to the planet Venus. Shamash, although understood in ancient times to be the sun, according to the earliest translations cannot be the same sun we see in the sky today.

According to Reginald Campbell Thompson (1876–1941), a British archaeologist and expert in the translations of cuneiform texts, there is reason to believe that the sun (Shamash) being referred to in the Gilgamesh story is actually Saturn. While translating Sumerian omen texts, Thompson noted that halos of the sun and moon were sources from which omens were derived. However, in one tablet (K. 200), omens correspond to the four cardinal points and are derived from the presence of planets or constellations within the halo of the moon. The tablet also refers to an omen "when the Sun stands within the halo of the Moon," which would be impossible for the sun in our sky today. In reference to the word *sun*, Thompson writes, "we must understand the 'Star of the Sun,' i.e., Saturn, and we now know that the omen for the Sun in such a case would be given just as if the Sun were occupying the place of Saturn. From Eratosthenes, too, we learn that Saturn was called Sol."[9] Thus, Shamash, in the proper context of the story, is a reference to Saturn. Therefore, Saturn traveled with Gilgamesh and Enkidu daily on their journey to the Cedar Forest to confront Humbaba, a shape-shifting creature that existed to terrify human beings.[10]

In support of Thompson's research, University of Pennsylvania professor of Semitic languages Morris Jastrow (1861–1921) identifies a number of other "sun omen" passages in which Shamash must refer to Saturn. "The Reports Nos. 173-183B he [Thompson] has grouped under 'Omens from the Sun' whereas it is clear that in Nos. 174, 174 A, 175, 176, and 180(3), Shamash must refer to Saturn, just as in Nos. 89 rev. 6; 90 obv. 3; 99 obv. 6; 101A obv. 5; 102 obv. 5; 107 obv. 3 (to be restored); 114A obv. 3; 115C obv. 3; 144 rev. 1—many of which were correctly so regarded by Thompson; also in Nos.107 obv. 3 and 216B obv. 3."[11]

The proof, writes Jastrow, is furnished by the astrologers themselves in a number of passages. "Mul Lu-Bat Sag-Uš ina tarbas Sin izzaz" means "Saturn stands in the halo of the moon." In Nr. 176(6) rev. 3 there is an inference, "(Mul) Lu-Bat Sag-Us Mul (il) Samas su-u," meaning "the planet Saturn is Shamash." In a number of cases the explanation is added, such as "(Mul) Lu-Bat Sag-Us ina tarbas Sin izzaz," meaning "Saturn stands in the halo of the moon." In other references the text states that "The moon has a halo around it and Saturn (Lu-Bat-Sag-Us) stands in it." Another omen reads "if Shamash [(An) Ut] enters into the moon," and elsewhere is a note observing that "Saturn (Lu-Bat Sag-Us) entered the moon."[12]

The reason there has been such confusion with the translation of the word *Shamash* is that it was also used to describe the daytime sun. For example, in the omen "If Shamash has a halo around it, there will be rain." Here, the sun that we are familiar with is meant by the notation "Samse it-mi," in other words "Shamash of the day" or "the sun of the day," distinguishing it from Saturn, which is referred to as "the sun of the night." The same is true for the omen when Jupiter (Sag-Me-Gar) stands in the sun (An-Ut). It is evident, Mastrow writes, that Saturn and not the sun is meant, because the phenomenon in question belongs to the night.[13]

Who then is Humbaba?

According to Giorgio de Santillana and Hertha von Dechend's *Hamlet's Mill: An Essay on Myth and the Frame of Time,* Humbaba was called a god because *hum* means "creator." Hum is the father, the "guardian of the cedar of paradise" and corresponds to the Elamite god Humba or Humban, who shares the title of "prevalent" and "strong" with the planets Mercury and Jupiter and with the star Procyon (Alpha Canis Minoris). Humbaba also occurs in the Sumerian star list carrying the determinative *mul,* which appears in the names of stars such as mulHumba. In art, Humbaba is depicted as being made from intestines in a single winding line, and his head is depicted as intestines. Santillana and Dechend believe that Humbaba refers to the planet Mercury because Mercury's orbit is the most erratic of the major planets. It winds around and can be likened to intestines twisted around in the abdominal cavity.[14]

As for Gilgamesh, he cannot be a biological man because he is two-thirds god. Nor can he be pure god because he searches for the secret of everlasting life. Gilgamesh is described as a "man of extreme feelings," "beautiful, handsomest of men," and "perfect." He is the "man of might" and is "wise in perfection." His mother is Rimat-Ninsun, the goddess of wisdom—the Wild Cow of the Enclosure—who is all-knowing and bore Gilgamesh "unique." His father, Lugulbanda, is Gilgamesh's guardian god.

Enkidu, however, is clearly mortal. He dies in the story and yet has no father or mother. Like the biblical first man, Enkidu is made from clay. Unlike the biblical Adam, Enkidu must be transformed from a wild beast that eats grass into a human able to eat bread and drink beer. Eerily, like Harner's ayahuasca vision of DNA falling from the sky, the "meteor of Anu" also fell from the sky to Earth in Gilgamesh's dream, a symbolic and esoteric expression of how the wildman Enkidu was created and somehow became human.

Mostly a god (a celestial body) and partially human (a terrestrial body), Gilgamesh is the personification of Earth, and Enkidu, the man Gilgamesh loves "like a wife," is the personification of terrestrial life, particularly human life. Such a consideration is evident in that Gilgamesh has been given the power to be in the darkness or light of humankind, where light represents the use of knowledge in harmony with nature; to create as opposed to destroy. The terror of global upheaval and a changing sky during the Great Flood is a primary focus of the saga, and Gilgamesh represents the planet trapped during this time of great celestial turbulence.

From the perspective of the gods (the planets), humanity must be dealt with, removed from the face of the Earth by a Great Flood. Of course, this is purely the human author's point of view based on the culture existing at the time. For a catastrophe of such magnitude, the surviving people had to ask themselves "why?" and "what did we do?"

This confusion provided the emotional tone for the myth, and the story itself explains the literal, celestial events that occurred in the heavens. People were left to conclude that they are disobedient, evil, and had to be punished, a notion associated with the biblical Fall of Man. In *Hamlet's Mill,* Santillana and Dechend view Utnapishtim's construction of an ark not as a way to escape a literal flood. Rather, it was symbolic of Earth's survival of a great celestial flood. The ark corresponds to the constellation of Argo, and in ancient times "floods refer to an old astronomical image, based on an abstract geometry."[15] This celestial flood is not an easy picture to see, considering the objective difficulty of the science of astronomy. However, simply put, the plane of the celestial equator divides the constellations into two halves. The northern half of the constellations, those between the spring and autumn equinoxes, represents dry land. The southern half, those between the autumn and spring equinoxes, including the winter solstice, represents the waters below. The four points on the zodiac (the two equinoxes and the two solstices) define the conceptual plane of the flat Earth. Therefore, a constellation that ceases to mark the autumn equinox, thereby falling below the equator, sinks into the depths of the water. It is in this abstract way that the flood was celestial.

THE BEGINNING OF TIME

Precisely what happened within the heavens—in the solar system and perhaps the galaxy—to cause this great celestial flood is not entirely clear, although the terrestrial evidence of global cataclysm and mass extinction is unmistakable. Whether it was due to the Geminga supernova or a galactic core burst or some other celestial event yet to be discovered, Earth was devastated, and according to myth, that horrific destruction emanated from the sky. In the annals of ancient Egyptian history, describing a civilization that spanned three thousand years, a story is told, an astronomical story recounted by Jane B. Sellers in *The Death of Gods in Ancient Egypt.*

After sixty years of studying myth and astronomy, Sellers concluded that the myths of ancient Egypt were "the carriers of information of celestial movements and events, and that they existed for a long time before being put down in written form."[16] For the ancient Egyptians, according to Sellers, the discovery of precession—that the stars gradually shift position over a very long period of time—was terrifying. The Age of Terror had begun.

The Earth's axis of rotation varies between an angle of 20.4 degrees and 26.2 degrees. In other words, the Earth wobbles very slowly as it orbits the sun. One wobble takes approximately 25,900 years. This slow change in the angle of the Earth's axis causes the position of the stars to change over time, as the stars are viewed from Earth's surface. Today, Polaris is referred to as the North Star because it remains stationary above the North Pole, and all other stars appear to move around the Earth. In 3000 BCE, the North Star was Thuban, and two thousand years from now it will be Alrai.

This slow change in the angle of the Earth's axis also causes the constellations of the zodiac to change their position in the night sky relative to the vernal (spring) equinox. Known as precession, this phenomenon causes the zodiac constellations to appear to be moving backward as the arrow of time proceeds forward, moving to the next constellation approximately every 2,150 years. In our time, each April 21 the sun rises into the constellation of Pisces. Within a few hundred years it will rise on that date into the constellation of Aquarius. Before the Common Era, between 2000 BCE and 1 CE, the sun rose on April 21 into the constellation of Aries. After 25,900 years, each zodiac constellation will have had its turn positioned in the eastern sky as the sun rises on the equinox.

For the ancient Egyptian skywatchers, the precessional, backward movement of the stars was an extraordinary discovery, and until they were able to rationalize this movement, "the stability of their world was severely threatened. The skies were out of kilter: the axle of the heavens had shifted, and most certainly the stars were finally understood to be irrevocably on the move."[17] In great detail, Sellers puts forth the theory that in order to deal with the distressing changes in the sky, the ancient Egyptians not only created specific myths, but captured within those myths the scientific knowledge of precession. Those myths imposed an artificial duality, or symmetry, on the deities as well as their centers of worship, which remained constant throughout ancient Egypt's history. They were created as a tribute to a lost Golden Age, when the skies were balanced and their religion was new and unchanging.[18] Over time, however, the ancient Egyptians grew accustomed to the precession of the stars and established the sun as the new core of their worldview. According to Sellers, "From the New Kingdom on, Osiris is firmly established as a legitimate occupant of the throne of Re. No longer must the throne be subject to the precessional movement. It is though the priests had decided that enough was enough."[19]

Sellers painstakingly surveyed the changes in Egyptian mythology and matched those changes to the changes in the nighttime sky.

According to Sellers, Osiris as the constellation of Orion ruled alone in the sky between 7500 and 6900 BCE, when Orion's brightest shield star reappears in the east just before dawn on the spring equinox. When Horus and Seth ruled equally, the V-shaped head of Taurus (the star cluster Hyades) reappears just before dawn on the spring equinox and Scorpius reappears just before dawn on the autumn equinox. Then, around 4867 BCE, associated with the Pleiades reappearing before dawn and the head of Taurus rising invisibly with the sun on the spring equinox, Horus in the solar boat became the ruler of all.

The ancient gods—the planets and stars—were not like the Judeo-Christian God of today, which we understand to be an omniscient, omnipotent being. Rather, the Egyptians understood gods as principles of cosmic nature. They were a metaphor for order, and when that order was altered, myths were created to quiet the fear and still the terror.[20] In explaining the order of the world that now exists, in the mythical tradition, it was Saturn who gave the measures of the world to Zeus. "Saturn has always been credited with giving the measures," Sellers writes. "Why should this be so?"[21]

One tidbit of information found in Plutarch's story of Isis and Osiris may be there, Sellers believes, solely to transmit a secret regarding the mythical connection between Osiris and the constellation Orion. In Plutarch's long account of Osiris's family tree, he uses Greek names instead of Egyptian names. Osiris's mother is Rhea instead of Nut, and his father is Cronus in place of Geb. The Greek Cronus, of course, is the Roman god Saturn, and is credited with the invention of time, because it is Cronus who determined the important measures of the year. In mythology, Cronus was the son of Uranus (Father Sky) and as we have previously discussed, ruler of the Golden Age. Cronus (Saturn) usurped his father's throne (the sky) but was destined to lose his throne to one of his children. To prevent such a fate, Cronus swallowed one of his own children, only to later disgorge the child.[22]

Sellers believes that the story of Cronus reflects the idea that even though the cosmos goes on forever and there is a creator god, there were other gods in the heavens who ruled for specified periods of time. Sellers writes, "As there was boundless time, there was also finite time: a time whose length of reign could be measured. This latter type, reflected in the movements of the heavens, is measurable time, and I believe this discovery struck awe in the hearts of ancient man."[23] She also hints at the cause for Cronus being remembered as the Father of Time. Because positive proof is lacking for the early division of the sky into 360 degrees by our ancient ancestor, it proves that the sky was not early divided, and this leaves space for speculation. "This argument has always seemed similar to that of those who would insist that, since positive proof is lacking that the orbits of the solar system have always been as they are, it proves that our solar system is *not* stable."[24]

The idea that mythologies involving Cronus (Saturn) and Osiris, as interpreted by Jane Sellers and David Talbott, reflect ancient scientific observations of the sky is profound. Time, as we know, is measured using the movement of the stars, and without precession there would be no way to measure time because the night skies would eternally be the same. Furthermore, if Saturn's loss of gravitational grip on Earth was responsible for the creation of time, in the view of the ancient Egyptians, then Saturn was also responsible for the creation of precession—the backward movement of the zodiac constellations measured by the spring equinox—because it is through precession that time is measured. For this reason, Cronus (Saturn) is considered the Father of Time, or as he is known in modern times, Father Time.

We are discovering that our ancient ancestors were highly sophisticated and left for us a record, intentionally or not, of Earth's previous planetary state not so long ago: a Golden Age of abundance and peace. It's why the ancient Egyptians, Sellers writes, "were a people who needed and depended on a vision of an unchanging universe."[25] They had experienced—lived through—humankind's fall from paradise, and they searched the skies seeking a new order from the gods.

HUMAN EXPERIENCE AND HISTORY

Members of Western civilization should never be so arrogant to assume that their linear understanding of Earth and human history is correct. The physical evidence of sophisticated cutting equipment used by builders of ancient Egypt's pyramids and temples, as described in my last book, *Ancient Egypt 39,000 BCE: The History, Technology, and Philosophy of Civilization X,* and other sources, such as Christopher Dunn's *Lost Technologies of Ancient Egypt: Advanced Engineering in the Temples of the Pharaohs,* indicates with high probability that a technically advanced civilization is part of our planet's ancient past.

Likewise, we should never be so naïve to believe that our planet and solar system are stable and have always been stable, following the orbit that they do today. We've known for many thousands of years that the stars in the sky seem to move according to the time of year and the millennium. What reaction would people have if the stars suddenly changed direction or perhaps disappeared altogether? Or, worse, if we encountered a devastating global catastrophe?

It would be terrifying.

Ancient myth has long been veiled by cultural prejudices, and such biases have kept us from learning about a past that helps explain why society exists as it does today. History, as a tool for explaining the human experience, is as powerful as any other academic discipline. Knowing how the universe exists in accordance with the laws of physics is important and provides a foundation for understanding how life came to be. However, there is a progression from these fundamental laws to more intricate laws of chemistry and biology, then to a complexity of the abstract with the emergence of sentient life, of which there forms humanity and ultimately, history.

The human experience began in paradise, a Golden Age of abundance and peace. There was no time as we know it because its perception didn't exist. Earth's orbit was close enough to those of Venus, Mars, and Saturn that these planetary bodies were visible to the naked human eye as much as the moon is to us today. Such a scene, as filmmakers have presented in animations, is as alien as it is awe-inspiring. Or, perhaps, Earth was a moon of Saturn, like Titan, which fascinates scientists. Titan is enveloped in a haze of smog and bears a striking resemblance to Earth, with mountain ranges, dunes, numerous lakes, and possible volcanoes. And with an active environment, as on Earth, the evidence of impact craters has been largely erased.[26] Furthermore, rich in hydrocarbons, Titan's atmosphere resembles Earth's early atmosphere. Of even more interest, laboratory experiments suggest that Titan's atmosphere may be rich in amino acids and other DNA-like material, the building-blocks of life.[27]

The Golden Age that once existed, both technical and philosophical, was overcome by a celestial flood, a great conflagration that knocked the planet into a wobble, destroying its fertile climate. That event dispersed the "the gods"—Saturn, Mars, and Venus—nearly destroying civilization in its entirety. Those who survived, however, were able to quickly rebuild a small fragment of what once was in order to reestablish civilization. For the survivors, the harsh new climate meant that labor would have to be set up as a force in acquiring and cultivating resources from the land. And with the continuing struggle to survive, the "fear of lack" became a mindset and a motive.

Because we today live in a time many thousands of years removed from our ancient ancestors, it's difficult to conceive that an event that occurred so long ago has affected the way modern society thinks and behaves. Barbara Hand Clow's *Awakening the Planetary Mind* convinced me otherwise; it discusses history from an experiential point of view, tying our global, present-day conscious existence with all its political, academic, and religious dogmas to a great catastrophe of our remote past.

Clow describes our society as a collective, a point of view that is the product of a devastating catastrophe around 9500 BCE, the effects of which can still be seen today. Humanity, she writes, suffers from what she calls *catastrophobia,* an undercurrent of social paranoia that the world will soon come to an end. Such a notion of destruction does indeed span our history, beginning with mythology, and is apparent too in the religious texts of the Hebrews and the Christians. In modern times, the fear of cataclysm is evident in the Millerites of the nineteenth century, the mutually assured nuclear destruction of the twentieth century's Cold War, the new millennium collapse, and the modern concern regarding the Mayan calendar. Even today, many Christians believe the world will soon come to a violent end with the return of Christ. Science also contributes to this view, pointing out that an asteroid a mile wide impacting Earth would create sufficient energy to destroy the planet, inspiring such movies as *Armageddon, Deep Impact,* and *2012.* Total destruction of the world fascinates us.

In our past, there has always been a dividing line between historical and mythical times. In reality, there is no line, only human experience. How we now and in the past, individually and collectively, relate our lives to the life of this world is passed along from generation to generation. Such a traumatic experience as living through mass extinction and the decimation of civilization would certainly have been carved into our ancestors' mindset. With the survivors who once lived in a paradise, a world of scarcity would bring new pressures in thought and behavior. Hoarding would become a necessity and the collecting of wealth a way of life.

When catastrophe struck the rat race started and the dog-eat-dog world began. Time existed, and the Age of Terror commenced.

8

THE COMING GLOBAL
GOLDEN AGE

As members of Western society, we should never be so arrogant to assume that our contemporary socially hierarchal and linear approach to everything are beyond questioning. Neither should we assume that the redistribution of wealth through democratic socialism will render a better and more equitable society. Likewise, we must not assume that capitalism is humanity's salvation, the resource distribution mechanism through which humanity will realize a new Golden Age. Capitalism has a deep, inherent, social flaw.

Underneath the capitalistic worldview lies the assumption that individuals look out only for their own best interests, meaning that people are inherently selfish and that the most successful capitalists are not only selfish, but miserly and even greedy. While this is certainly not true of all business owners, when the measure of success is popularly *perceived* to be wealth accumulation, then everyone will seek to attain wealth, often doing so to their own detriment, turning what was meant to be a pleasurable, prosperous life into a game of profiteering whenever and however possible. Such a cultural philosophy of life leads to crime, poverty, hatred, and violence, because competition always demands placement, which creates a first place, a second place, and a multitude of last places. Everyone realizes crime, poverty, hatred, and violence are unwanted consequences of the society we've built, and we do our best to eliminate them. We also must realize our attempts fail despite all the laws and regulations passed to reduce such unwanted consequences. In a technologically advanced civilization, why do these burdensome things exist in the first place?

They exist because capitalism, the prevailing method of resource distribution, is as antihuman a philosophy as any conceived philosophy can be. Democracy values each person in that everyone is understood to be endowed with an innate worth that must be honored—that "these truths [are] self-evident, that all men are created equal, that they are endowed by their Creator with certain unalienable Rights, that among these are Life, Liberty and the pursuit of Happiness."[1] Capitalism, however, pits individual against individual in a competition for resource accumulation. Such a race polarizes society between owners and laborers at every level, whether local, regional, national, or international, rationalized by the quest in the Land of Opportunity for the American Dream. As we have found out, in a democratic society such animosity creates long lists of rules and regulations in a continuing legal battle between labor and ownership. In the United States such a battle has been going on within state governments since the nineteenth century, beginning in Massachusetts, and that battle became federal in 1924 when Congress amended the Constitution to provide the federal government with the authority to regulate child labor.

The potential existence of a contemporary "power elite" is much more real than fantasy. More than fifty years ago sociologist C. Wright Mills characterized the governing elite of the United States as the highest political leaders of the country, such as the president, his cabinet members and close advisers, the executives and owners of major corporations, and high-ranking military officers. Although these individuals revolve in their private circles, they are not truly conspiring because they are looking out for their own self-interests and working toward their common goals. In general, they operate openly and peacefully, allowing the mass media to form public opinion in conjunction with their goals, which is why federal laws and Presidential Directives have become so important in the last hundred years. Since 1956, when Mills's *The Power Elite* was published, federal laws and regulations have grown exponentially. Federal laws gain more power and become more prevalent, Mills writes, when the highest political positions and the top echelons of the business hierarchy share the same values and beliefs. That, however, is not just capitalism. Rather, it is a monopolistic style of capitalism because elected officials can pass legislation affecting the regulation of commercial industries. Throughout history this relationship between wealth and government has always existed, even though governments have taken on various forms over the millennia, as if this need to fight over land and control resources is a genetic memory of our ancient ancestors—the fear of lacking sufficient resources.

Perhaps our society, which is driven by experience from generation to generation, breeds crime, poverty, hatred, and violence because it is what we are being taught and teaching our children, not on a conscious level of awareness, but rather in a subtle way through the media, such as television and radio broadcasting. That's where we are taught to be consumers and competitors and is what some anthropologists, such as Neil Whitehead, call the "cannibal war machine."[2] It really is a dog-eat-dog world, and we are the dogs in an economic way. We are taught to be consumers while at the same time taught to believe that if we are smart enough and work hard enough, we too can be successful in the game we grew up with, Monopoly.

Today, with ever-increasing technology, commerce has been pushed to all-new limits. So have news, knowledge, and alternative points of view, otherwise unheard in the past. YouTube, for example, has become the people's television, available to anyone and everyone to broadcast ideas, concepts, opinions, and documentaries covering just about any topic of interest. YouTube is equivalent to 385 always-on television channels, but with 88 percent new and original content, according to Kansas State University anthropologist Michael Wesch. Wikipedia has become the people's encyclopedia, written, edited, and updated by volunteers and funded almost exclusively by public donations. Social networks such as Facebook have been powerful as the people's medium for organizing, as the now-overthrown Mubarak government of Egypt has discovered.

Governments of the world too have benefited from technology, most notably the United States and other Western countries. However, technology has changed so rapidly in the past thirty years that governments have yet to catch up with laws and regulations. The invasion of privacy has become an important issue, as both a crime and a government policy. Society is becoming increasingly more regulated, and its commercial ownership is so concentrated that some social critics and investigative journalists, such as Jim Marrs, are becoming concerned.

According to Marrs, who is also a bestselling author, America, "is a National Socialist's dream come true."[3] Individuals are computerized, databased, logged, and categorized. Video cameras, motion sensors, metal detectors, and spy satellites monitor our movements, while think tanks and foundations study our every habit. And like the dark world portrayed in George Orwell's *1984,* Marrs sees America as a society being bombarded constantly with official pronouncements and advertisements from Big Brother televisions everywhere. He sees big corporate business being governed by faceless directors who answer only to shadow owners, and they control everything from water to wing nuts. All the while the American taxpayer foots the bill.[4]

Fascism, Marrs claims, is on the rise in the United States, masquerading as something else and challenging everything the country stands for. We haven't learned from history, he writes, and he says that a careful study of past fascist regimes by Dr. Laurence W. Britt in an article for *Free Inquiry Magazine* shows that what happened in Germany during the 1930s sounds "ominously close to what's happening today in the United States."[5] Concerns include a controlled mass media, obsession with national security, the power of corporations protected, the power of labor suppressed or eliminated, cronyism, corruption, and the identification of enemies or scapegoats as a unifying cause.[6]

According to Marrs, in light of Britt's fourteen characteristics of a fascist regime, the argument can be made that "global fascists" are turning the United States into "a subsidiary of their global corporate structure— their empire of the super rich."[7] When various groups of people with different perspectives—secular humanists, conservative Christians, Jews, liberal Democrats, conservative Republicans, as well as moderates—all start saying the same thing about the government, we need to pay attention. He adds, "Even mainstream centrists like Bill Moyers and attorney Gerry Spence have warned of the abuses of a 'secret government.'"[8]

Global National Socialists—Marrs calls them *Nazis* (from the German term *Nationalsozialismus*)—plan well in advance, up to a hundred years into the future. They are the owners of multinational corporations and congregate in secret societies knowing that their goals cannot be reached overnight, although since the events of 9/11 they seem to have stepped up their efforts in establishing a social global order of politics and commerce. It's why political and corporate leaders continually swap roles and in effect are attempting to create a merger of state and industry, which is the definition of fascism. According to Marrs, "mergers and leverage takeovers have concentrated corporate power into fewer and fewer hands, many of those directly connected through banking and corporate ties to prewar support for the Nazis."[9] In truth, Marrs asserts, this is not a new world order but an old world order being reasserted with new advertising slogans, names, and logos. In recent history the ideals of National Socialism have been infused into the military-industrial complex, and with innovation being a necessary process of defense systems, those ideals then spread into science and are now infiltrating corporate life, the mass media, and even political parties. All of this is engineered by the global elite who have monopolistic "power over basic resources, energy, pharmaceuticals, transportation, and telecommunications, including the news media."[10]

Why they are doing this, Marrs concludes, is that it is "the only means of maintaining their power and control, the only way—in their view—to maintain the purity of their race and class. They laugh at the concepts of true individual freedom and multiculturalism, for they have no faith in the innate goodness of humankind or its ability for self government. They have no real faith in God and use religious ideals and concepts merely as another tool for social control."[11]

GROWING GLOBAL POLITICAL AND ECONOMIC AWARENESS

In Montreal, Canada, May 2010, Zbigniew Brzezinski spoke to members of the Council on Foreign Relations. One of the primary messages was that of a massive global political awakening. Brzezinski stated, "For the first time in all of human history mankind is politically awakened. That's a total new reality."[12] He added that "no matter where you go, politics is a matter of social engagement, and most people know what is generally going on, generally going on in the world; and are consciously aware of global inequities, inequalities, lack of respect, exploitation."[13] Such a state of "awakening" worries Brzezinski because the combination of "mankind," as a totality, being aware of how the political and economic systems functions, and how the people that manage those systems take advantage of people, coupled with a "diversified global leadership"[14] makes it more difficult for that leadership to promote its agenda. In fact, he calls it a "central global menace" that is "obstructing our ability to deal effectively with the global political turmoil that this awakening is generating."[15]

The "turmoil" to which Brzezinski alludes is the fact that technology, primarily the global Internet now available as a handheld "smart phone," has created a wealth of knowledge, an all-new type of free press. And, with its use, people are becoming aware of the political/economic system and how it works. More important, they are aware that our minds are shaped into the worker mold at a very young age—what a capitalist system along with its governing body must have in order to manufacture their products or offer their services: labor. As a result, the labor force, which is a large majority of the population, is also, largely, the consuming force.

In the last two hundred years, people en masse have moved out of an agrarian-based society into an industrial and then a technical society, all fueled by the demand for goods and services, which has always been pushed by innovation, often by war. Over the centuries the progression of innovation and its need for extending knowledge have carried the human species forward into a state where intelligence is generally homogenous throughout society. In general, but not always, any citizen has the mental capacity to perform in a social leadership role, the desire to do so being another matter.

According to the U.S. Census Bureau, 52 percent of the U.S. population has completed at least some college education. International student enrollment is at an all-time high, with some colleges having anywhere from 12 to 25 percent of their student body hailing from abroad. Such a condition for human societies around the world makes it difficult to manage people, particularly when a large portion of them are highly intelligent and well educated. In the drive for more and better technology, the human species has educated itself into a whole new understanding of life and the social principles that guide civilization. Such a situation makes governance an issue, as we have seen over the past one hundred years with the growth of government agencies and associated regulations everyone has to follow.

Controlling a large population of people is a difficult task. Governments try, but are always playing catch-up with the latest innovations, commerce, and social trends, domestic and international. From the perspective of the governing officials, a global political awakening can be viewed as a "menace" in that the way affairs are conducted might have to change to accommodate the wants of the masses.

From the point of view of the masses, people can consume only so much and then business has to expand its operations in order to continue profiting. It's why business gradually and eventually becomes big business and why labor suffers the consequences when jobs are spread across the world through the rationale of reducing labor costs. Such a movement in human business affairs has created a situation in which large corporations have transcended national boundaries and in effect have become as powerful, if not more so, than governments. Government officials know this and know jobs are vital to the success of their governments. So, when civil authorities pass laws favoring certain industries in exchange for wealth, thereby gaining power, there's no need to call it a conspiracy. Substantial and wealthy interests are converging on a common goal. It's just business. Unfortunately, throughout human history weapon and defense industries have been some of the highest growing and grossing businesses. Therefore, they tend to influence the rules and shape society.

On the other hand, such wealth has provided the opportunity to invest resources in knowledge that has radically improved our lives, which brings up an important fact. Neither business nor government is responsible for all of our modern conveniences. Science is, along with the application of science to meet human needs. World War I, World War II (in particular), and the Cold War shaped the society and economic system we live in today. The victors of the Second World War became competitors and enemies, and faced off regarding who could build the biggest empire and the best weapons. It became a war of economics and technology, and the western half of World War II's alliance won. All the world's leading countries now have decided that capitalism and commerce are the way to manage their domestic and international affairs, with science and innovation serving as the foundation.

The evidence is convincing that we are already living in a Golden Age of science. In the grand course of history, human consciousness— the human perspective—has moved from a very limited worldview, say that of a village, to one that sees the world and sees it instantly. Now, instant communication is affordable to almost anyone, and a wealth of information is available on the Internet to read, whether it's the latest political debate, the growing "emerging church" movement, or AC-DC—anything. Allowing one's mind to wander around the Internet has become as popular as channel surfing the television, if not more so. You can focus on any subject you want at any time you want. And in doing so, people with similar interests have created social networks and message boards to discuss just about anything. A website or forum can quickly be found. Society has become global in a communicative way, and the anonymous masses, particularly the young, are taking advantage of it and making it easier to form new and different opinions on their lives and the world they live in. Science and innovation have brought us to this point in life through its commercialization, and commercialization has made big business a powerful force needing to be regulated by government.

With three generations that have now grown up with personal computing and the Internet—those born during the 1980s, the 1990s, and the 2000s—and another generation that created the personal computing age, there are a lot of people browsing the web for news and information. This now mature "free press" is changing the way people think, as Marrs writes; there is "a sea of change in the public consciousness."[16] Brzezinski seems to agree, although from the opposite social perspective.

MASS MOVEMENTS

If you browse for news on the Occupy Wall Street Movement, you can find a deeper story from such groups as The Venus Project, Zeitgeist (meaning the spirit of the times), and Thrive, to name a few. All have the same basic message, that the socio-political-economic system we live in is destined for failure if it continues as it has been since the early part of the twentieth century, when the United States began playing a more progressive role in international affairs.

The Thrive Movement is led by Foster Gamble, the great-great grandson of Procter & Gamble Corporation founder James Gamble, with the intent of building "a self-creating movement that aims to empower a world where all can thrive." According to Gamble, what is keeping the human species from thriving is that "a small group of financial elite have gained control over key areas of our lives—energy, food, health care, education and more."[17] Gamble adds, "we've been duped into a system that is designed to consolidate wealth and power,"[18] and it works like this: Those at the top, the financial elite, use international and national banks to control corporations and manipulate national economies and their governments with their financial leverage. The result is that people, companies, and governments are all in debt to the banks and ultimately to the wealthiest men in the world. According to Gamble's research, "As of 2007, the richest 2% of adults owned more than 50% of the global assets and as of 2010, one out of every seven people didn't have enough to eat."[19] Even though the other 98 percent of the people do the work, the material wealth flows upward to the controllers and directors of the commercial system we call the free market, while the mass media operate like gears in a hypnotizing clock.

The Zeitgeist Movement's mission is to create awareness that "the majority of the social problems which plague the human species at this time are not the sole result of some institutional corruption, scarcity, a political policy . . . [and] that issues such as poverty, corruption, collapse, homelessness, war, starvation and the like appear to be 'Symptoms' born out of an outdated social structure."[20] The movement is led by independent filmmaker Peter Joseph. And according to Joseph, the movement has no allegiance to any country or political organization and views the world in a holistic manner. In his view, the nations of the world must de-arm and learn how to share their resources in order for the human species to survive.

Joseph has written and directed three documentary movies, the first of which is *Zeitgeist: The Movie,* released in 2007. In the film, Joseph puts forth the notion that the masses of people in the United States and the world are being manipulated to view history and their lives in a certain way. Christianity, he claims, is a fraud, and like Thomas Paine (1737–1809), he believes that the Christian religion is based on the worship of the sun, not an unseen, omnipotent, omniscient God. The Christian religion, in his view, serves only to detach people from their natural living environment and from each other. Such a condition, Joseph states, lulls people into blind submission to authority to "reduce human responsibility to the effect that 'God' controls everything, and in turn awful crimes can be justified in the name of a Divine Pursuit. And most critically, it empowers the political establishment, who has been using the myth to manipulate and control societies. The religious myth is the most powerful device ever created, and serves as the psychological soil upon which other myths can flourish."[21]

The film also builds, through numerous pieces of news footage and interviews, the case that the bombing of New York's twin towers was an inside job. More than one person in tower 1 heard and felt a blast coming from the basement before the first plane hit. Then, there is the collapse of the towers and building 7, which all crumbled in a manner indicative of a planned and controlled demolition. The buildings came straight down at the speed of freefall. Furthermore, more than one firefighter at the scene testified on camera that molten metal existed in rubble and basement areas of the World Trade Center for weeks after 9/11 and that it was a fire too hot to have been caused by jet fuel. In some instances, the "lava," as one firefighter called it, was over 2,000 degrees Fahrenheit and lasted for five weeks. A team of scientists from the University of Copenhagen and Brigham Young University analyzed some of the dust from the rubble and discovered an active thermitic material,[22] dangerous evidence that there is more to the World Trade Center bombing than two jet airliners running into the two towers. Demolition experts use thermite explosives to severe the steel support beams when bringing down a building. In 2005, the National Institute of Standards and Technology released its report on World Trade Center towers 1 and 2 and did not address the actual collapse of the buildings. Then there is the fact that NORAD was performing an exercise on 9/11 that involved the insertion of false radar blips and that another exercise on the same day involved airline hijacking. So the intercepting pilots were confused about which hijacking was real. In 2000, NORAD had sixty-seven intercepts with a 100 percent success rate. On 9/11, they failed four times in a single day.[23]

Why would the American government carry out such a crime?

The documentary states that the bombing of the World Trade Center on September 11 was a "false flag operation, intended to authorize the doctrines and funds needed for a new level of imperial mobilization."[24] The ruling elite of the United States of America view terrorism as the only way to provide social cohesion through an enemy, with the goal of "world hegemony, built around securing by force command over the oil supplies required to drive the whole project."[25] They do so for power. The people behind this are the "network of Centralized Banking, the Military Industrial Complex, and the Media Culture." The same people Foster Gamble claims have "designed [a system] to consolidate wealth and power," and both Joseph and Gamble seem to agree that money is the most important aspect of controlling people and resources, in essence controlling the world.

Money buys resources, and resources provide the means to live. More money means more resources and better living. An extraordinary amount of money means an extraordinary amount of resources, so much so that an extraordinary amount of resources means you can do almost anything. That's what Joseph cites as the primary means by which the networked elite maintain and increase their power: money and banking. It started with the Federal Reserve Act of 1913, an act of Congress that created the Federal Reserve System in use today. The American banking system is based on a concept called fractional reserve banking in which the government issues currency to the central bank and its member banks, which then loan out 90 percent of the currency and keep 10 percent as a reserve. The banks then loan 90 percent of their deposits to individuals and businesses for the purchase of assets. Sellers who receive monies from buyers turn around and deposit the money from the sale in their bank, which, in turn, is available to be loaned out again. A $100,000 deposit can be used to create $90,000 in loans, and the loan proceeds are deposited in another bank, which creates $81,000 in loans. The cycle repeats, creating loans for $72,900, then $65,610, and so on. In the end, the original $100,000 deposited in currency becomes $1,000,000 in loans.

An easily overlooked aspect of this type of banking system, from an outsider's point of view, is that the money created through loan operations *doesn't physically exist.* Furthermore, in the act of repaying loans, there is always an interest charge to be paid by the borrower in addition to the principal amount borrowed. This is why the Federal Reserve

Bank, the central bank for all banks in the United States, is so careful in conducting monetary policy, which is a term for controlling the money supply in the banking system through buying and selling Treasury bonds. When the Federal Reserve buys Treasury bonds, the currency used becomes available for member banks to lend. On the other hand, selling Treasury bonds removes currency from the banking system.

However, there are also a number of factors outside the Federal Reserve System that play a role in economics. The Fed cannot influence the production of goods and services by corporations nor can it control the level of unemployment. These factors depend on private enterprise and the population. Nor can the Federal Reserve control inflation, which, today, is primarily a function of the price of oil on the world market—oil being a critical part of any modern nation-state's economy. (In order to control inflationary pressures, a global central bank would be required.) There are also roles played by private investment and savings as well as the government fiscal policy, each of which also affects economic growth or recession. Despite the intricacies of economics, a fractional reserve banking system requires that as the money supply increases, so does the debt. This can be seen as a historical fact, which draws Joseph to the conclusion that *money is debt*. And as the economy grows and recedes, over time, more and more wealth is consolidated in the hands of a few, as businesses fail and individuals lose their property through foreclosure. It's a never-ending pattern. It is noteworthy to add that if all debts were paid off, there would be no currency in circulation. All existing currency would be in bank vaults. And, then, who would have ownership of the cash deposits in the banks? Only those who previously held more cash than liabilities.

Former Republican congressman Ron Paul of Texas wants to make it law that the Federal Reserve System regularly undergoes an audit, and on February 26, 2009, he introduced HR 1207, a bill to audit the Federal Reserve:

I rise to introduce the Federal Reserve Transparency Act. Throughout its nearly 100-year history, the Federal Reserve has presided over the near-complete destruction of the United States dollar. Since 1913 the dollar has lost over 95% of its purchasing power, aided and abetted by the Federal Reserve's loose monetary policy. How long will we as a Congress stand idly by while hard-working Americans see their savings eaten away by inflation? Only big-spending politicians and politically favored bankers benefit from inflation.[26]

According to Paul, the Federal Reserve System is not a private company in the same way other U.S. corporations are private companies. The Federal Reserve was created by an act of Congress, "but what is so sinister about it" according to Paul,

is that it was turned over to private individuals who can run everything secretly. That's why, of course, the audit is so important. So it's been federally created. It's special, it's secretive. It has privileges far beyond any private corporation. Private corporations would have to yield to anti-fraud laws. But the Federal Reserve commits fraud by counterfeiting money. The fact that they can create money out of thin air and place it in banks for their benefit, the fractional reserve banking system is also something that benefits the bankers. They can loan out money they don't really have. So it's all based on fraud.[27]

Paul also recognizes that the big banks make up a cartel because they dictate monetary norms; whereas, the market itself has no control over the money supply or the availability of money. There is nothing of intrinsic value underlying the U.S. currency, except the wealth and word of the country, and for Paul this is a problem. Because the U.S. dollar is the reserve currency of the world, the U.S. banking cartel "is probably the most powerful cartel in the whole world; might have been the most powerful cartel ever in the history of the world, as far as I can see."[28]

Paul explains that governments have been behaving in this manner toward money for a long time. Whatever the country, its government has a monopoly on the money supply, and those in office will always abuse their power for their own benefit. When gold and silver were used as coinage, "they would maybe just clip the edges off a gold coin in order to get more gold. Or they would dilute the metals like we did in the 1960s with the silver coins." Then, the government went to printing currency. Today, it's all done with computers.[29]

The power advantage it gives them is that they get to use the money first. "So, if you're in the government and the government is spending the money or the military-industrial complex that might get money or the banks that get to spend it early on; they all benefit because the dollar has more value than after 2 or 3 years. It circulates and then the average person might say, 'Oh, the cost of energy has gone up, the cost of education has gone up, the cost of medical care has gone up.' And they don't see the connection."[30]

Western civilization is all too preoccupied with our differences, our beliefs—the giant belief system that we live in—to focus on what's truly important, the economic and banking systems. People are more interested in being entertained by sports, movies, and television programs, which alleviate the monotony and stress of working for a living. Perhaps that is just what Mills's "power elite" want, a dumb-downed labor force without opinion.

For Peter Joseph, the single most important statement of the film's narrative is that "the social manipulation of society through the generation of fear and division has completely inhibited the culture. Religion, patriotism, race, wealth, class and every other form of arbitrary separatist identification and thus conceit has served to create a controlled population utterly malleable in the hands of the few. Divide and conquer is the motto. . . . And as long as people continue to see themselves as separate from everything else they lend themselves to being completely enslaved."[31]

This notion that human beings are separate from nature, including each other, is the binding force between the Christian religion and a capitalist free market system. In fact, it has been the determining force in building the modern industrial state and society. For the Christian, the belief that people are inherently evil (needing redemption through an authority) is nearly synonymous with the capitalist belief that all people are selfish and will always act according to their own best interests. And the separatist idea offers the theological and economic basis that resources, including people as labor, exist to be exploited for gain. Such is the reason why Christian fundamentalists often find common ground with conservative "free enterprise" politicians. So, from a world of beliefs comes this social order in which competition is necessary and good—the ultimate competition being war. As a result, the population competes against itself objectively and pays the price subjectively in hate and violence, which turns into crime. This is true for every country regardless of whether that country's government structure is democratic, communistic, socialistic, or fascist. The use of resources always requires capital and labor, and a medium of exchange between the two, which is what we call money.

Industrial designer and social engineer Jacque Fresco was born on March 13, 1916, and in his ninety-five years he has experienced many great events in history. He lived through the roaring '20s, the Great Depression, World War II, and everything after. During the Great Depression he had difficulty understanding why millions were unemployed, homeless, and starving, even though all the factories were just sitting there. The resources were still there too, unchanged. At that time he realized that the rules of economics were "inherently invalid."[32] After World War II he calculated that all the resources used in that war could provide for every human need. Since that time he has watched "social values of society be reduced into a base artificiality of materialism and mindless consumption . . . as precious finite resources were perpetually wasted and destroyed in the name of profit and free markets . . . as the monetary powers control the political structure of supposedly free society."[33] Humanity, he believes has set the stage for its own destruction.

According to Fresco, our current economic system is not capable of providing a high standard of living for the people. The money system that is used to allow access to needed resources inherently creates social stratification and elitism. Money is not what people really need. Resources are what they need. However, money being the chosen medium of exchange, whoever has an abundance of it has purchasing power. In other words, money buys resources. State governments take advantage of this need for money and help fund their programs through lottery systems, because everyone is in need of resources and in our system only money can buy resources. Thus, at a dollar a ticket, hitting the multimillion-dollar jackpot appears to be worth the risk of losing a dollar.

For people who don't have enough money, whether merely a perception or actual fact, the drive to "have more money" creates tremendous corruption, greed, embezzlement, and crime. Noncriminal corruption also exists. Whole industries and large corporations with enough money can exert influence on government officials through lobbying. Furthermore, corporations are dedicated to increasing the value of their stock for the shareholders, and they do so through profit. Thus, corporations are not inherently concerned about benefiting the people or the environment. Rather, they are concerned primarily with the acquisition of wealth, property, and power. For Jacque Fresco the meaning of the current socioeconomic system is simple: "The Earth is being plundered for profit."[34]

Even *National Geographic* has voiced an opinion on the matter of a sustainable economy. In 2010, the National Geographic Channel aired a special television documentary entitled "Collapse: Based on the Book by Jared Diamond." In the documentary, the year was 2210 and a group of scientists set out to discover why civilization, two hundred years earlier, had collapsed. They discovered that history had repeated itself. Like the Mayan and the Roman empires of antiquity, the global civilization of the twentieth and twenty-first centuries failed to properly manage their resources. Although there was not a single cause of civilization's collapse, the twenty-third century scientists of the documentary concluded that our demise was a psychological one. With ever-increasing consumption rates and far greater destructive power than ever before, we failed to see the short-term thinking that created the conditions for our collapse. With competition for limited resources and an economic system designed around the principle of capitalistic competition, society collapsed from within. Yet, unlike the civilizations of the Romans and the Maya, we have the technology and the knowledge of the past, and we can have the vision of the future to avoid such a fate, if we want to.

HUMANITY'S TWELVE-THOUSAND-YEAR-OLD QUEST TO RETURN TO A GOLDEN AGE

Geologists and paleontologists have labored over the past 150 years piecing together the mysterious history of our planet. During the late nineteenth century, with the abandonment of the Great Flood as a means of explaining geologic history, geologists adopted a theory of uniformitarianism to explain the past. However, because science is an ever-correcting discipline, recent theories put forth the notion that life on Earth has been nearly annihilated five times during the past, each catastrophe bringing with it new forms of life. The most recent destruction, which brought an end to the age of dinosaurs also gave birth to the age of mammals, of which humans are the most recent expression.

Today, through our fascination with "who we are" and "how we got here" as a species and through scientific diligence, we are discovering the truth of human history, a multidisciplinary task blending history with geology, archaeology, biology, and physics, involving many people over the last fifty years. Mythology, we have discovered, is not only history in its truest sense, but a record of the beginning of history and time as we understand it. Humanity suffered a global cataclysm twelve thousand years ago, spurring the many cataclysmic myths told around the world a very long time ago, and passed down the generations. Like the events it portrayed the story was cataclysmic. Humanity's first story was *the death of the gods* and the Fall of Man from paradise to a world of scarcity, labor, and war. This memory has been repressed and suppressed for many thousands of years. Now, "we are waking up from a collective amnesia as we hear the correct version of the past," writes Barbara Hand Clow in *Awakening the Planetary Mind*.[35]

The whole world is in a very nervous mood, which bears all the signs of people with terribly painful memories. Of course, the popular media stirs these murky fears with disaster scenarios and constant reports of violence and chaos. Why? Just so the elite can prolong selling both pharmaceuticals and guns to get more corporate profits. People feel cornered, as if there is no future.[36]

Since the beginning of the twentieth century, we have known that a very different Earth existed twelve thousand years ago and that mass extinction was the result of devastating climate change. We also have known that with climate change, humankind endeavored to farm and domesticate animals in order to establish a ready supply of food. The mystery has always been what happened to the climate. Now we know. The Earth was a literal paradise, lush with vegetation and fruit, able to support a kingdom of large animals on all its continents. Humanity didn't need to farm because farming wasn't necessary. Likewise, there was no desire to hoard food or accumulate wealth. Such actions were simply unnecessary. Living with such abundance provided the leisure and the freedom to create a sophisticated civilization of unimaginable technology, a Golden Age of humanity, the evidence of which still exists to this day among the ruins and the abandoned temples and pyramids of Egypt.

Then the gods (the planets) died in a celestial flood of cosmic rain with thunderbolts of plasma discharge. The planets were pummeled into new orbits around the sun. The Earth was scorched and knocked off its axis into a slow-moving wobble as she narrowly escaped death. The beautiful, comforting gods of the sky—the planets Saturn, Mars, and Venus—were gone forever, existing now as bright stars in a newly visible field of stars. Nothing would ever be the same. No longer would the even warmth of Saturn promote a lush landscape filled with fruit and vegetables, and with the planet decimated, as the days turned to months and years, many of those who survived died from starvation or simply lost the will to live. To survive, humankind had to become omnivorous, even carnivorous. Humankind would also have been affected psychologically. Such terror there would be watching the sky fall. Such horror there would be watching your fellow humans die. Fear and paranoia would settle in that a catastrophe of such magnitude could happen again.

Such a terrifying event did happen twelve thousand years ago, and we've been suffering from its psychological effects ever since. At first, humankind scavenged to survive, but as populations grew, fighting over resources existed in small bands of people, later in the form of armies of kingdoms, then in the form of larger armies of nations, which developed weapons and weapons systems to the point of insanity. By the end of the twentieth century, we became efficient enough at killing to annihilate two hundred million people in less than one hundred years of war. Now, with weapons development we've reached the ability to end all life on the planet—paranoia *must* have run its course by now.

Such a catastrophic event is also responsible for the mental condition the human species finds itself suffering from: *post-traumatic stress syndrome,* a disorder that has manifested itself from generation to generation through the development of a religious belief in divine kingship, then the formation of the modern institution of religion. We, with our Judeao Christian heritage, have maintained in our psyches the notion that we are an evil species that has somehow angered God and that we are in need of salvation. Such a notion instills fear and paranoia deep into culture and society, and perpetuates the need for authoritarian rule. Thus, the concept of original sin is also tied to this ancient catastrophic event.

Long before the biblical Genesis was written, before history was inscribed on stone, clay, bone, or bronze, the record of events was passed down orally, and the central story was the death of the gods, accompanied by humanity's eviction from paradise, the story of a celestial cataclysm that decimated the human species and destroyed our paradise planet. The perception was that the gods (or God) were angry and inflicted their wrath upon humankind. Originally, this "anger of the gods" story was told and retold to remember history, but as the generations passed, what was once a story explaining the events that created the world as we now know it became a literal truth. With the events of the cataclysm forgotten, humankind's fall from paradise took on new meaning in that all people were born of original sin, a legacy whose origins lay in a cataclysmic event. Original sin, however, never existed and doesn't exist. God was never angry. Religion, then, in its proper context, can be viewed as a traumatic reaction to calamity. In other words, the need to find a cause for a catastrophe that otherwise has no cause. The cause was that humanity must have done something wrong, which is captured in a single vague word—disobedience.

The truth of human nature, however, is quite the opposite of what dogmatic religious beliefs would suggest. As mammals, we are a species whose existence is genetically rooted in our ability to care and feel tenderness for the life we create, as well as our ability to continually nurture that life. Such a polarization between our feelings—our instinctive natures—and the beliefs that are imposed upon us through this artificial cultural institution of sin and authoritarianism creates misery, and it does so through the systems of economics and politics we have created for ourselves, embodied in the competition and labor we must endure to acquire life-sustaining resources, even to the point of stealing and killing.

Humanity, though, is resilient, and with the growing awareness of our own nature and how our nature is a part of a grander nature—even the cosmos—we have been healing ourselves all along. Reconciliation, however, to the new world that was thrust upon us twelve thousand years ago is a slow process.

HUMAN HISTORY AND ZODIAC AGES

During the Age of Leo (10,909–8640 BCE) a global catastrophe occurred that changed everything about our planet, particularly the climate and our view of the sky. Before the catastrophe Earth was a literal garden paradise able to support many species of large herbivorous animals. The view of the sky was dominated by the planets Saturn, Venus, and Mars. Saturn's exceptional luminosity, possibly a result of helium being discharged from its core,[37] created such a glow in space that it masked the field of stars we are accustomed to. Speculatively speaking, if Earth was a Saturn moon, Saturn's heat and lower levels of radiation (compared to the sun) could be responsible for the longevity of human life reported in Genesis, as well as the unusually long reigns of Sumerian kings before the Flood.

The catastrophic repositioning of the planets, including Earth, the attendant effect on Earth's climate, and the change in the human visual perception of the sky completely reoriented human thinking. No longer would the human experience be associated with a paradise lifestyle in a garden of the gods. The gods were gone and so was paradise. Human awareness became separated into gods and humans[38] thereby creating the theological foundation that humanity is somehow different and separate from nature.

As soon as the survivors—the ancient Followers of Horus—were certain the conflagration was over and the climate had stabilized, they embarked on rebuilding civilization, most likely just after 9420 BCE. The catastrophe itself, and its aftermath, likely covered several thousand years, beginning around 14,150 BCE, according to LaViolette, or 16,420 BCE, according to the history of the ancient Egyptians, the date the Followers of Horus began their rule. The latter, however, is probably an estimate based on the extrapolation of the newly visible nighttime sky.

Whatever the case may be, at Giza, the three pyramids were built, and their sister pyramids constructed along the Nile River as far south as Meidum shortly after 9420 BCE in an attempt to hasten food production by redirecting very low radio frequencies into the surrounding fields. We have only recently discovered that slow-moving, free electrons invigorate plant growth and inoculate plants from disease. Everything about the Giza Plateau and the other large pyramids suggests that these structures were designed to direct electrical currents that were naturally occurring in the ground from the pyramid's base to its peak, thereby creating in the upper chamber of the Great Pyramid resonance, which flowed into the atmosphere through two shafts in the north and south face of the pyramid. The result was a low energy "bubble," or force field, that deflected very low frequencies (VLF) and extremely low frequencies

(ELF) into the surrounding fields. At the base of the pyramid in the subterranean chamber, a ram style water pump existed that not only pumped water for irrigation, but also served to create a compression wave that resonated with the granite of the upper chamber. Although the concept behind this system involved an understanding of atmospheric and electromagnetic theory, the design and implementation are relatively simple, except, of course, for its construction, which would be considered a massive undertaking even by today's standards.[39]

According to Graham Hancock and Robert Bauval in *The Message of the Sphinx,* the structures on the Giza Plateau were erected in a certain position to mark a specific point in time, 10,500 BC. At that time, sunrise occurred within the background of the constellation of Leo on the spring equinox, the three pyramids just west of the Sphinx mirrored the belt stars of Orion, and the Nile River, the Milky Way.[40] Through their research, Hancock and Bauval were persuaded "that a scientific language of precessional time and allegorical astronomy was deliberately expressed in the principal monuments there and in the texts that relate to them."[41]

According to astrophysicist Dr. Thomas Brophy, who slightly disagrees with Hancock and Bauval, there's an even deeper astronomical meaning to the Giza Plateau structural layout. Orion's Belt stars align with Giza's three pyramids on 11,772 BCE as well as 9420 BCE, a time separation of 2,352 years and celestially 32 degrees of general precession. These two dates frame Earth's alignment with the Galactic Center as well as coincide with Orion's Belt culmination dates—culmination being the highest point above the observer's horizon. Thus, the Giza monuments mark the date and location in the sky of the Galactic Center's maximum culmination. According to Brophy, this means that the Giza layout functions as a clock marking the passage of the zodiac, where a zodiac period is 30 degrees of general precession. In other words, this alignment calibrates the "zero point" of the zodiac as it relates to the culmination of the Galactic Center. Moreover, there are other sequential alignments that mark calibration points of the Giza zodiac clock.[42]

Throughout the epoch of Galactic Center culmination, 11,772–

9420 BCE, Orion's Belt stars rose over or near the Sphinx as those stars were viewed from the Great Pyramid. And the Galactic Center rose over or near the Sphinx as it was seen from the third (smallest) pyramid. Furthermore, and perhaps an exclamation point from Giza's builders, these star risings directly pointed to the Age of Leo. They progressed from the Sphinx's rear forward to its paws as the sun, during the spring equinox, passed from the constellation of Leo's rear forward to its paws.[43] Furthermore, there was a simultaneous alignment of the Galactic Center, Sirius, Thuban, and Kochab, with the four shafts, two in the middle chamber and two in the upper chamber, of the Great Pyramid.[44]

For Brophy, "The complex of monuments at Giza can be seen as a ground-sky correspondence clock, calibrating the Zodiac Ages to the northern culmination of the Galactic Center in 10,909 BC at the start of the Age of Leo. The evidence for this is strong enough to warrant consideration of implications for understanding other very ancient human-created monuments and cultures."[45]

What happened to the knowledge, technology, and history of these builder gods of a primeval time—the Lords of Light, the ancestors who raised the seed for gods and men, the "Senior Ones" who came into being at "the beginning," these biblical "Sons of God, heroes of old and men of renown"—we may never know. The most reasonable answer is that as isolated groups of survivors emerged from a subsistence survival to build their civilizations, multiplied, and expanded into other territories, over the millennia, their culture and knowledge gradually faded into oblivion as new cultures migrated and mingled with theirs. By historical times, little was left of their legacy except a vague memory and the texts that served as the basis for dynastic Egypt's culture and philosophy.

It is reasonable to assume that those who rebuilt civilization in the Nile Valley during the tenth millennium BCE recognized the fate their sophisticated, technical tradition would eventually meet. And, like Gutzon Borglum, who carved the heads of the most influential U.S. presidents into the granite face of Mount Rushmore as a message to civilizations that exist thousands of years into the future, these ancient builders left us a message, an astrological cryptogram in architecture on the Giza Plateau in the universal language of the stars—a message embedded with its own cipher key, providing those who have gained the appropriate knowledge the ability to decipher.

With Earth now exposed to ultraviolet radiation from a new sun, by the end of the Age of Leo, human life was significantly shortened. The builders soon died. Their descendants, though, continued on and discovered during the Age of Cancer (8640–6480 BCE) that the nurturing feminine—the planet's life-giving force—still existed, giving birth to a renewed culture of the Great Mother Goddess.

During the Age of Gemini (6480–4320 BCE), astronomy developed into an ancient mystery school where the number and order of the stars now ruled in place of the former gods (the planets). Across the planet various cultures began to flourish, creating diverse societies and an assortment of languages, many of which from our point of view were archaic and technically simple.

Throughout the Age of Taurus (4320–2160 BCE), society became increasingly more organized and developed into city-states. With the birth of the Indo-European culture, kingship and its patriarchal view of society began to replace the old cultural ways of the Mother Goddess.

The Age of Aries (2160 BCE–0) brought war as kingdoms battled for control of land and resources. City-state fought city-state. Gradually, states that could maintain the political control of people and the physical control of resources expanded their armies, turning states into empires: the Akkadian, Babylonian, Persian, Greek, and Roman took turns ruling the Near East and the Mediterranean. Under Roman rule, pharaonic Egypt—the sole bastion of cultural sophistication and egalitarianism—ceased to exist during the first century BCE. Significantly, European cultures, first Greek then Roman, became the dominant and technical forces. However, their aggressive approach to society plunged humankind into an Age of Warfare, an attempt to seek peace through violence.

In Pisces (0–2160 CE), the age we are currently experiencing, humankind has become more self-reflective and seeks transcendent answers to social injustices under the imperial quest for wealth and power. Catholicism, in particular, initially folded the "pagan" Western beliefs into a single religious system based on the teachings Jesus Christ, for the sake of unity. From within this religious Christian movement, the search for truth escalated. Fifteen hundred years later, "modern" science was born, and in as little as five hundred years since its birth, it developed a means of uniting all peoples of the world (through technologies such as the Internet). Such is the history of the human species.

As each age passed to the next, new ideas and concepts were draped over the older, existing ideas and concepts. Society, as can be seen since the cataclysm, is gradually improving itself, evolving into something bigger and better. The destruction of the previous Golden Age plunged humankind into a twelve-thousand-year-long Age of Terror, pitting one culture against another, and with limited resources to sustain life, an economic system of resource control and specialization developed as a means of dominating nature—and life. Such specialization has enabled the leisure and freedom of humankind to pick up where our ancient ancestors left off more than ten thousand years ago. In an attempt to understand Pythagoras's harmony of the spheres, Kepler, who had already accepted Copernicus's heliocentric solar system, discovered the laws of planetary motion and in doing so claimed "I am stealing the golden vessels of the Egyptians to build a tabernacle to my God from them, far far away from the boundaries of Egypt."[46] The Scientific Age brought industry and technology and with them an understanding of the natural world. As science deepened its approach into the realm of the quanta, the door was opened to a whole new understanding of the universe, a philosophical return to a Golden Age, and the technology to make that Golden Age a reality, outpacing the long-held principles of economic and social control.

Science and technology have brought us today, like Brzezinski noted, into a world of political challenges for the establishment, particularly with the awareness movements started by Gamble, Joseph, Fresco, and other movements such as the Evolver Social Movement. Barbara Hand Clow believes "we are on the verge of a great spiritual and intellectual awakening."[47] With 43 percent of people in a CBS poll agreeing with the sentiments of the Occupy Wall Street demonstrators, there are most likely many others.[48]

We stand on the brink of a new age of humanity. With 148 years left before the Age of Aquarius (2160–4320 CE) begins, one would have to assume that the unification of all the world's societies into a single global civilization, which has already begun, will bring change. We already have the knowledge and technology to provide for the needs of each and every human being in the world. We already have the technology to provide food, fuel, and housing for every single person in the world. If history does repeat itself, one has to consider carefully the role of human experience and its effect upon the human state of mind, and how that state of mind shapes society, privately and politically. Today, with such heightened conscious awareness of ourselves, the planet, as well as the universe we live in, along with our seemingly limitless technical capabilities, there is no reason we *shouldn't* be entering a Golden Age. The only thing stopping us is the perception that there are not enough resources to go around, a perception that dates back twelve thousand years. A perception that we have used over many thousands of years to create a world based on resource hoarding and the domination of people, a system of violence that anthropologist Neil Whitehead refers to as the "cannibal war machine."

I find it fascinating that humankind, as a phenomenon and as an experience, has reached a state of unification similar to one reached long ago, according to the mythical Tower of Babel story. Today, a single language and a common speech are within our grasp. And, just as in the story of long ago, we find that today, "nothing restrained from them of that which they have purposed to do."[49] In more modern terms, "nothing they have imagined they can do will be impossible for them."[50] As the arrow of time continues to move forward, increasingly more people are imagining a world without poverty and war, without domination and control. History proves that totalitarian regimes, even those of a subtle nature, can never be sustained for long. Indeed, it is a mistake to think that a single person or a small group of people can control a population of billions. No one person or group of people, regardless of their cumulative wealth or power, will be able to halt the progression of humankind in expressing itself, socially, artistically, scientifically, or technically. Imagination, which every person has, can never be controlled.

ENVISIONING THE GLOBAL GOLDEN AGE

History demonstrates that from the beginning, scientific innovation has driven civilization forward, despite the existence of power mongers and empire builders. Capitalism has its place in history too, for without capital there is no vehicle to take the invention of one person and produce it on a large scale for the masses. Today, with the rapid progress of science and technology, along with venture capitalists that have propelled that technology into useful products, governments are always a step or two behind on creating laws and regulations to safely produce and distribute those products. With this in mind, some might argue that the coming global Golden Age will arrive only through capitalism—that world capitalism *is* the Golden Age. However, capitalism's shortcomings, in particular the principle of competition, which dictates that there always has to be a loser, and the sacrifice of humanity's well-being for the sake of profit, make a capitalistic system too inefficient to meet the needs of everyone. Socialism fairs no better, but even worse. Without incentives, nobody will work unless forced to work, even though innovation and creativity continue purely out of passion. A bureaucratic system is too slow and inefficient to manufacture new products, distribute them, and meet the needs of everyone. Competition has its place, but competition to the detriment of society is contrary to basic human nature.

Today, with such wealth concentrated in food, energy, and transportation—necessary resources for civilization—there is a *disincentive* to investigate alternative methods in providing to the people these necessities. Consider the economic principle that people always act in their own best interests, as opposed to society's best interests. This means that established industries will always move to prevent competition from being successful, even at the expense of social well-being, the most well-known example being the oil industry. If a hydrogen transportation industry was allowed to successfully produce a hydrogen-fueled automobile, oil-refining companies would suffer large losses. The same thing could be said for utility companies. What would happen to power companies if someone developed a stand-alone solar unit that produced a day's worth of electricity after being exposed to the sun for a few hours, regardless of the climate? Eventually, there would be no need for power companies.

The main difficulty with today's society, and the source of great anxiety that manifests in the use of mood-altering prescription medication as well as violent crimes, is money. But money is not really the problem. The problem is the control of resources, which is what money represents. According to the United States Census Bureau, in 2009, 82.66 percent of the population earned less than $90,000, and only 1.5 percent made over $250,000.[51] Anxiety exists because the vast majority of people labor all their lives simply to exist, not knowing whether their livelihood is secure. Corporations lay off workers to ensure the success of their businesses, regardless of the consequence to those they terminate. Thus, during severe economic recession, job loss can mean not only hardship but also the loss of a home from foreclosure. It's a rat race in a dog-eat-dog world.

Everyone needs resources to survive. The people who hold the mastery of extracting and refining resources for use and consumption and are willing to apply that knowledge to new and better ways of creating usable resources are the people who have the best interests of society at heart. They are educators and scientists, women and men who thirst for knowledge and are eager to spread that knowledge, as well as have a passion for people—philosophers, really. Such a statement is reminiscent of Plato's most famous and influential work, *The Republic*.

Plato's Philocracy

According to Plato, people come together in cooperation to share the great task of living. From this act of community, the state, or government, arises to meet the needs of people. Thus, individuals with diverse specific talents come together in communities to achieve common goals. This understanding of community produces a worthwhile society.

When human societies first developed, according to Plato, people formed a community based on honor. Over time, leaders in the "honor" society become torn between their philosophical ancestors—those who began the society—and contemporaries who praise the leader's ego. Such an ego-based society eventually leads to competition and greed. This type of social structure Plato refers to as a *timocracy,* and once established, the timocracy depends on the old, honorable ways of competition and greed. Later, as society matures, wealth becomes the standard measure of success, leading to the consolidation of power in an oligarchy, separating the state into two classes, the rich and the poor. Eventually, the continued polarization of society leads to revolution by the unhappy poor, who then form the most liberal state of all, the democracy.

At first, the relationship between the people and the government is amicable. However, representatives of the democracy eventually come to be ruled by their own interests, subordinating both reason and honor in favor of wealth and power. Under the rule of self-seeking representatives, the democracy gradually deteriorates, becoming the worst and most wicked form of government: the tyranny. The tyrant or dictator lacks morality and enjoys unlimited freedom while taxing the people. To ensure that his position is secure, the tyrant creates a police force whose mission is to destroy any and all threats to his power. At his height of power, the tyrant embodies prejudice and inequality, the opposite of what Plato defines as a wise leader.

Little has changed in 2,400 years, it seems, as people and societies of the world today struggle with these same issues and forms of government. Plato offers a solution to the problem of society and its governance by establishing three classes of people based on intelligence: a warrior class, a merchant class, and a class of "philosopher kings."

According to Plato, education is crucial to advance society as much as possible. Therefore, the leaders of the state reserve the right to raise children in order to mold their minds with uplifting tales of heroism and justice. In Plato's ideal state, education is more important than anything else because children of superior intelligence are destined to become the ruling class of the future. This is so regardless of their parents' social status. This way, society is always placing into leadership positions the most intelligent people society has to offer. Neither is there gender discrimination. Men and women together form the ruling class. Everyone else is separated into a working class of merchants and artisans or a warrior class of police officers and soldiers.

To prevent the ruling class of philosopher kings from becoming corrupted by wealth, they are denied the right of accumulating wealth even though everyone else retains that right. The nonruling class also retains the right to maintain the comforts of their own homes and families. However, nonrulers have no say in how the state is operated. Such a trade-off in Plato's logic appears simple and fair. Those "who have" can't rule, and those "who rule" can't have. Wisdom must rule, not power.

In the process of creating a class of philosopher kings, Plato calls for censorship in the primary education of children that extends in measure to the adult population. His concern is that the average citizen cannot tell the difference between reality and fantasy and that men and women might feel compelled to act out the plays they watch from their theater seats. Our eyes play tricks on us, in Plato's view, and in searching for a way to separate illusion from reality, he devised his theory of "forms" in an attempt to explain the varied and changing life we experience. Forms, in our understanding, are concepts or ideas.

Plato saw that there were two basic social problems: ethics and discontinuity in the human experience. Plato asks these questions: How can humans live a fulfilling and happy life in a world of continuous change where anything someone becomes attached to can at any time be taken away? How is it that the world appears to be both permanent and changing? The world perceived through the senses is always changing, while the world perceived with the mind appears to be permanent and unchanging. Which is most real and why does it appear both ways? Is there an absolute truth?

Plato's logic assumes that there are two realms of existence: the material realm and the transcendent realm of ideas. In Plato's concept of the human soul, people have access to the realm of ideas through reason, which allows conscious access to an unchanging world free from the changing and often painful realities of the material world. As a consequence, by detaching from the material world and embracing ideas, one can find value that not only never changes, but also can never be taken away. For Plato, this point of view solves the problem of ethics.

Separating the world into two realms also solves the problem of a permanent versus an always changing, temporary world. We perceive a different world of objects through our minds than we do through our senses, where the objective, material world is ever-changing. The mind, however, perceives a world that is permanent, and it is this unchanging world that is more real. In other words, the material, objective world is merely an imperfect image of a real, unchanging world.

Plato's definition of an idea (what he calls *form*) is that which is abstract as it is relates to an object. An orange, for example, can be separated into roundness, taste, texture, and color. If you consider its roundness only, you are thinking of the idea of roundness. Plato argues that this idea of roundness exists separately from the orange and exists whether or not someone thinks about it. So, everything that is round participates in the nonphysical realm of idea, which explains why ideas—such as the idea of geometric form—are unchanging. Even if all round objects at once were destroyed, the idea of roundness would still exist. In this way, ideas are pure and exist as properties separate from the object, which actually comprises any number of ideas.

Plato's forms, or ideas, are transcendent, pure, archetypes, real, and causal. Furthermore, they are all interconnected. An idea, such as color, has no location in space and time; therefore, it is transcendent. It exemplifies a single property, meaning it is pure. An idea is an archetype, meaning it is a perfect example of the property it exemplifies, and it is real in the sense that it is unchanging. All ideas are also systematically connected and move from the general to the more specific and from the objective to the more subjective. Such movement, general to specific and objective to subjective, is reflected in the structure of the dialectic process and is how we arrive at the knowledge of ideas. Ultimately, ideas are the cause and the origin of all things.

For Plato, the understanding of the relationship between the always-changing world of the physical and the never-changing world of idea defines wisdom. This understanding qualifies a person to be a member of the ruling class, a philosopher king or queen. The awareness that the world of material objects manifests through the world of ideas only comes through personal experience. One has to loosen the chains, stand up, and walk outside to see the real world for oneself, even though no one else back in the cave would ever believe you. Our modern cave is made up of culture, religion, and other institutions of civilization; as for the shadows on the cave wall, they are our television sets.

For Plato it was imperative that social leadership, and governance, come from men and women who were able to distinguish between what is eternal and real, and what is merely a human perspective based on the ego's attachment to the always-changing world of the physical.

There will be no real injustice in compelling our philosophers to watch over and care for the other citizens. . . . We have brought you into existence for your country's sake as well as for your own, to be like leaders and king-bees in a hive; you have been better and more thoroughly educated than those others and hence you are more capable of playing your part both as men of thought and men of action. You must go down, then, each in his turn, to live with the rest and let your eyes grow accustomed to the darkness. You will then see a thousand times better than those who live there always; you will recognize every image for what it is and know what it represents, because you have seen justice, beauty, and goodness in their reality; and so you and we shall find life in our commonwealth no mere dream, as it is in most existing states, where men live fighting one another about shadows and quarreling for power, as if it were a great prize; whereas in truth government can be at its best and free from dissention only where the destined rulers are least desirous of holding office.[52]

For Plato, only those who had gained wisdom—those who became aware of the events producing the shadows on the cave wall—were qualified to govern society. The experience of seeing reality as it really is provided them with the knowledge and awareness of life's source, which gave them an understanding of justice, beauty, and goodness and the ability to "recognize every image for what it is and know what it represents."[53] Then, in truth, government can be at its best, as opposed to men who "starved for lack of anything good in their own lives, turn to public affairs hoping to snatch from thence the happiness they hunger for."[54] They wind up "fighting one another about shadows and quarreling over power,"[55] which leads to an unjust system and ultimately poverty.

In effect, Plato is arguing that *imagination is real* and that from imagination our world of physical experience is created. In other words, for those who are able to free themselves from the confines of the cave and understand reality as it truly exists, they see, according to those still bound in the cave, their imagination. Only these "enlightened" people are fit to lead and govern society because their transcendental experience provides to them the deepest understanding of the human experience possible.

The intellect, in and of itself, is not wisdom. Intellect is the avenue that leads to questioning, which leads to seeking answers to those questions in a methodological way. Wisdom is the ability to experience intellect with a greater awareness of the human role in society, nature, and the cosmos, then apply that experienced knowledge within personal relations and society in general. Such a statement sounds outlandish to some, but the new science of quantum physics has experimentally demonstrated during the last century that what we call material reality is more of a hologram or virtual existence than something solid and permanent.

The Egyptian Legacy

Plato's realization that only through a philocracy can society avoid corruption of its leadership is a tribute to, and the legacy of, ancient Egypt. Although we have been taught that Greek philosophy was responsible for the first rational approach to nature and life—seen by historians as a miracle jump from ancient mythical ways—a much older civilization is responsible for the intellectual climate of the ancient world. That civilization is dynastic Egypt, which we now know based its philosophical approach to society on the beliefs of the survivors of a great civilization that existed in a timeless Golden Age of antiquity.

The success of dynastic Egypt is unparalleled in history. No civilization has lasted as long as dynastic Egypt. Despite two brief intermediate periods of social and political instability, from 3000 to 30 BCE Egypt flourished as the cultural and commercial center of the ancient world. So esteemed was ancient Egyptian culture and religious tradition that the ruling Greek Ptolemies embraced Egyptian fashions and participated in Egyptian religious life.

Greek philosophers contributed much to the Western world, and it is correct to consider their writings as the foundation of Western thought. Even so, they were inspired by and borrowed heavily from the Egyptians, who practiced a superior writing system representing ideas as opposed to sounds and developed a profound philosophy as well. Plato didn't deny it, and admitted as much in the *Timaeus*.[56] The most impressive aspect of Egyptian society is that it was ruled rationally by a group of men recruited for their morality and who underwent rigorous rites of initiation. Such was the inspiration of the Egyptian system of governance that Plato most certainly modeled his guardian philosopher kings after the Egyptian priesthood,[57] what René Schwaller de Lubicz refers to as the *pharaonic theocracy*.

In studying Eleusis, the historian Paul François Foucart (1836– 1926) became convinced that the Eleusinian Mysteries had their origins in ancient Egypt. The core of the Eleusinian Mysteries is the search for immortality and the belief that attaining knowledge of the mysteries could be achieved only by dying. Thus, the initiate goes through a symbolic death in order to be "born again" as an immortal. Although this concept was accepted throughout the ancient Near East, it was overwhelmingly strong in Egypt. Thus, Martin Bernall writes in *Black Athena* that "the consensus of ancient writers was that Pythagoras, Orpheus, Socrates, Plato and others concerned with the immortality of the soul learnt about it from Egypt."[58]

In *Bousiris,* a Greek tale about the mythical origins of the Egyptian civilization, Isocrates (436–338 BCE) portrays Egypt as the most blessed country in the world and eulogizes Bousiris as a mythical lawgiver responsible for creating Egypt's constitution. The Egyptian caste system with its division of labor allowed for leisure, whereby the philosopher-priests through education produced contemplative men of superior wisdom for the good of the state. More important, Isocrates insisted that not only was philosophy Egyptian, but that it *only* could have been an Egyptian product. According to Bernall, the word *philosophy* (Greek *philosophia*) appears to have been solely used by the Egyptianized Pythagoreans as long ago as the sixth century BCE. Its earliest use, however, comes from Isocrates' *Bousiris.*[59]

In *Bousiris,* Isocrates writes that the Spartans failed to apply the Egyptian division of labor principle, resulting in their constitution falling short of the perfect Egyptian model: "philosophers who undertake to discuss such topics and have won the greatest reputation prefer above all others the Egyptian form of government."[60] Although no one knows for sure what Isocrates was referring to, most likely he was referring to the Pythagoreans or possibly Egyptian politics itself. It has been argued that Pythagoras never existed as a person. However, there are strong ancient traditions that he did exist because his deeds were recorded by Herodotus and others. On this matter Isocrates is direct: "On a visit to Egypt he [Pythagoras] became a student of the religion of the people, and was the first to bring to the Greeks all philosophy."[61]

As for Plato's *Republic,* Bernall writes that "there are striking similarities between it [*Bousiris*] and Plato's *Republic.* In the latter, too, there was a division of labor based on castes ruled by enlightened Guardians produced by careful selection and rigorous education. Plato was sharply hostile to the turbulence of democratic politics in Athens, and this kind of model was clearly comforting."[62]

In fact, Plato spent some time in Egypt and in other parts of the Mediterranean prior to indulging in the extensive written works he is famous for. His affinity for Egypt is evident in his treatises. In *Phaedrus,* Plato has Socrates, whom he often uses as his main character, declare that Thoth, the Egyptian god of wisdom, invented numbers and geometry, and most important of all, letters. In *Philebus* and *Epinomis,* Plato goes into greater detail on Thoth as the creator of writing, and also credits him with the invention of language and science. In other works, Plato praises Egyptian art and music and calls for their Greek adoption. Indeed, Bernall writes, "the only reason for doubting that his *Republic* was based on Egypt is the fact that he does not say so in the text. This omission, however, has an ancient explanation."[63]

Within a few generations, the Greek philosopher Crantor (c. 250 BCE) explains Plato's ancient omission:

> Plato's contemporaries mocked him, saying that he was not the inventor of his republic, but that he had copied Egyptian institutions. He attached so much importance to the mockers that he attributed to the Egyptians the story of the Athenians and the Atlantines to make them say that the Athenians had really lived under this regime at a certain moment in the past.[64]

Early modern scholars also associated Plato's *Republic* with Egypt, such as the philosopher economist Karl Marx. In *Das Kapital,* he wrote, "Plato's *Republic,* in so far as division of labor is treated in it, as the formative principle of the state, is merely an Athenian idealization of the Egyptian system of castes."[65]

A caste system, however, is repulsive to the modern mind. So is censorship. So is state-sponsored molding of children's minds to fit a specific social role. Such state-sponsored child molding brings up images of the Hitler Youth. Indeed, Plato's thought experiment *The Republic* preaches fascism. But it also teaches us to think hard about how we move forward to a new Golden Age of humankind. Don't we already have a caste system based on wealth, although rarely addressed in the media? Don't we already have a type of censorship through corporate ownership of the media and state-sponsored education, whose goals seem to be the conditioning of new laborers and consumers more than anything else?

The Republic also suggests something unique and critically misunderstood by the vast majority of people today. It exists in almost all major religious traditions. In the Jewish tradition, it's referred to as Kabbalah. Buddhists call it Zen, or enlightenment. So does the spiritual movement commonly known as New Age, which really doesn't exist as a movement, but is a label created to demonize non-Christian beliefs. Christians calls it mysticism.

This enlightenment of human perception is best described as experiencing existence as it really is, a viewpoint derived not from the human mind but from outside the material world. This can be referred to as the viewpoint of "God" because the crucial phenomena that make us human are our self-awareness and conscious perception. In truth, we are one species whose origins are mystical and cosmic, because our planet, even our bodies, as Carl Sagan correctly stated, "are star stuff harvesting star light. Our lives, our past and our future are tied to the sun, the moon and the stars."[66]

Although today, Dr. Sagan's statement that we, physically speaking, are composed of the same substance as the stars appears to be a scientific breakthrough, such a concept was generally accepted in ancient Egypt more than four thousand years ago. In modern times, the ancient Egyptian use of animals as a means of describing natural principles has been misinterpreted as religious animism. Such thinking, however, is only a superficial assessment of ancient Egyptian culture. With a more in-depth approach to ancient Egyptian thinking, it becomes apparent that the two hundred or so Egyptian "gods" were merely aspects of a grand cosmic power that for all intents and purposes was unknown. In other words, the "gods" were principles of nature and formed a coherent thesis explaining that all of nature is, itself, the essence of "man." Thus, the royal principle on which the ancient Egyptian civilization was founded has little to do with the Western feudalistic concept of the king and his kingdom. Although there certainly was a person acting in a leadership capacity, the role of the pharaonic king was not based on a specific individual. Rather, the pharaoh, or more precisely "the House of Pharaoh," was a symbol, a pretext for embodying the mythical and the mystical nature of man—what the Greek philosophers referred to as the Logos and what Christians of the first century attributed to Christ.

The concept of the Logos is, at the same time, the human aspect of language as well as an irrational origin of all things experienced. The Logos resides in the language-oriented, creative capacity of the human experience and is identified with the source of inspiration we call imagination. From a philosophical perspective, it is the fragmentation of a homogeneous state of oneness into a physical state of individual uniqueness and experience. Logos refers to intellect and reason, but in its ancient, traditional sense, it is "weaving." Two threads by themselves amount to nothing, but woven together, they produce form. This weaving together to produce form is the heart of the metaphysical concept of divine creation, as well as the origin of the cross, which during the early times in the history of the Catholic Church became a representation of the divine Christ. Although the literal, and superficial, notion of the Christ is that he was crucified on a cross for humanity's sins, the deeper meaning is that God as an eternal, nonphysical being was crucified into form as the cosmos and ultimately the human experience of perception.

In Egyptian myth, Seth imprisons the Logos (the creative word) into physical form on Earth through the fall of man. The active principle of the abstract becoming form is Ptah, which represents the "fire in Earth." So Horus animates the king, but also must be delivered from his bodily prison in the same way the mortal's soul must be saved. In the end, Horus becomes the divine and perfect being, and represents all phases of creation, from the becoming to the resurrection and return. In this way, the universal Horus is the divine Logos in all that exists, just as Jesus was God incarnate.

Temple inscriptions in ancient Thebes explain this understanding of nature as a ritual in which the royal fulfillment of Horus goes through phases of death and rebirth as Horus becomes a glorified, eternal body. In the end, he becomes the "King of divine origin, almighty in things of created Nature," and is reflected in the mystic (godlike) names of the pharaohs, which represent the growth of the incarnate spirit that the king symbolizes. The temple does not humanize this principle; rather, it *anthropomorphizes* it. In the "theogamy" (marriage of the gods) chamber in the Temple of Amun, the spiritual birth of Amon-Ra is shown as the royal infant being baptized and named though celestial forces. The terrestrial father, the god, assumes the form of Thothmes IV, and Queen Mut-m-uia (Mut in the barque), the spiritual mother, becomes pregnant by him. Then Amon announces that the future child-king will be Amon-hotep heq-uas, the hotep of Amon, as leaven of the rising flux. Khnemu, the divine potter from Elephantine, then announces the child's conception and fashions his form to be more beautiful than that of all the neters. With the assistance of celestial principles, the child is brought into the world to be nourished with the milk of the "heavenly cow," from which all beings have life.[67]

Such a story is not primitive. Rather, the symbolism embedded in the story points to a coherent and highly refined cosmology, where Man is not destined by the fate of the cosmos, which is the physical fate of death. The story means that the human essence is eternal and that the fate of the cosmos is determined by humans—that is, humankind is the cosmos.

This story of "the becoming of the king" is that of the philosopher king Plato discusses in *The Republic,* a noble figure of governmental leadership. The pharaoh was not a dictator or a tyrant. Nor was he a god; he was a representation of humanity's aim, the resurrected Osiris—the true king—who has returned to the source. In other words, pharaoh (the Great House) is the living image of incarnation and of return to the source of the divine Word, or Logos. This cycle of birth, death, and rebirth is an ever-present idea that the king's persona makes tangible to the people. This is the only and true meaning of royalty.[68]

DNA AND THE HORIZON OF HUMAN EXPERIENCE

The world we experience is not what it seems, and our true nature is a mystery to behold. We find that the science of quantum physics describes the world we experience as the unified duality of waveform and particle. A mathematical equation of all the possible states that might exist is somehow collapsed into a single state we choose to experience. Psychologists and neuroscientists refer to this mystery as consciousness. The bigger mystery, however, is in the DNA molecule.

In 1953, when Francis Crick and James Watson first discovered the DNA molecule, it was thought to be a static blueprint of information expressed biologically as genes, meaning the DNA molecule was understood as the primary determinant of a person's biological character and, thus, a person's condition in life. Furthermore, experts thought heredity information flowed in only one direction, from the DNA to the proteins, and that it never flowed in the other direction, from the proteins to the DNA. Consequently, it was believed impossible for a person's DNA to change. However, in the late 1960s, while studying how tumor viruses infected a cell's genetic code, Howard Temin suspected, and then theorized, that DNA does change, in this case through the actions of a virus. Although Temin, at that time, was ostracized by his peers, since then he has been vindicated. In the fight against AIDS it was proven that the HIV virus uses the same genetic mechanism that Temin had earlier discovered. Other scientists, such as Duke biologist H. Frederik Nijhout, are discovering that genes are not self-emergent. In other words, genes can't turn themselves on or off and in fact are either being read or not.[69]

Even though much has been learned about DNA during the past thirty years, and its sequencing has been put into use by court systems to verify such things as paternity, biologists know very little about how genes communicate and cooperate in the growth and life of an organism. As much as 95 percent of DNA might be used within the organism in an integrative manner, and as long as science continues to view genetics in a mechanistic and reductionist way, we are likely to remain ignorant of DNA's true role in the diverse web of life that has driven Earth history.[70]

Given that all plants and animals are an expression of DNA, it is becoming clear that life on Earth is a system that is organizationally closed, although open to the flow of energy and matter. What can be theorized, then, is that Earth is a living system that is self-organizing "in the sense that its order and behavior are not imposed by the environment but are established by the system itself." In other words, living systems are autonomous. This does not mean they are isolated from their environment. On the contrary, they interact with the environment through a continuous exchange of energy and matter.[71]

The discovery of DNA initially gave scientists the impression that genes are some kind of biological software program executing the forms of life. Originally, it was believed that the random mutation of genes was a chance occurrence, and that these random mutations were the primary engine behind the evolution of life forms. However, the occurrence of such random mutations, which happen at a rate of once for every hundred million years, is too low to explain the great diversity of life that we observe, aside from the fact that most mutations are harmful and very few result in useful adaptations. Research, however, is now demonstrating that this approach is too simplistic and that the genes within all living organisms form a vast interconnected network involving feedback loops in which genes regulate other genes' activity. This genetic network at the heart of life is actually an "interwoven network of multiple reciprocal effects mediated through repressors and derepressors, exons and introns, jumping genes, and even structural proteins."[72]

Bacteria cells, experts have found, routinely transfer bits of genetic material to other individuals. According to biologists Lynn Margulis and Dorian Sagan, each bacterium has the use of accessory genes, sometimes very different strains of bacteria, which perform functions that its own DNA may not cover, and that each bacterium is able to combine some bits of that genetic information with the cell's native genes while passing others on. "As a result of this ability, all the world's bacteria essentially have access to a single gene pool and hence to the adaptive mechanisms of the entire bacterial kingdom."[73]

In light of her research, Margulis hypothesizes that the long-term symbiotic relationship between bacteria and other microorganisms living inside larger cells has led to, and continues to lead to, new forms of life. Symbiogenesis, Margulis claims, is responsible for the evolution of life through the permanent symbiotic relationship all life on the planet experiences.[74] When a living organism reaches a certain level of complexity, it couples structurally not only to its environment but also to itself, bringing forth not only its external existence but also an inner world. In human beings such an inner world most assuredly results in language, thought, and self-awareness. Thought, then, is not a representation of an independent, already existing world as is typically believed. Instead, thought, in fact, is the bringing forth of a world that is dependent upon an organism's structure. For the human species this means that we have brought forth an abstract world of symbol—language—as well as a technical world of physical structure.[75]

The interesting aspect of viewing the planet as a living symbiotic organism is that because DNA is responsible for all life forms on Earth, and we as self-aware humans have advanced from that DNA, what are the consequences of this continuing evolution as it relates to our future?

Viewing history as a totality, DNA has progressed life from bacteria to a great diversity of complex plant and animal life, including humans, who have extended DNA's "terraforming" of Earth through our self-awareness and by applying that self-awareness in imaginative ways, not only in invention and art, but also in altering the surface of the Earth to fit our needs. The expression of DNA as life forms has, over the eons, moved out of the physical and into the metaphysical with the human species. And, in the history of our species, we have become exceedingly more creative in thought, and as a result, are creating new things. That creativity somehow has to have a biological basis, because with each generation the overall level of knowledge and technology is increasing. Each and every generation has new ideas and ways of conducting society's affairs. It's just as clear in politics and commerce as it is in music and the arts, with science being the most obvious. It's as if something (DNA?) is pushing us, calling us, to a goal, whatever that goal might be.

Science has always struggled with its explanation of the subjective and the role of human consciousness within Earth history, and has yet to place a definition on consciousness, let alone the context in which it exists. However, in 1975, botanist and ethnopharmacologist Dennis McKenna and his brother Terence proposed a symbiotic relationship between plant life and human consciousness. According to the theory, early humans ingested psilocybin mushrooms and discovered that in low doses their effect was to increase visual awareness, which made humans better hunters, and because they were better hunters, they were generally healthier and produced more offspring. Over time, the DNA of the psilocybin-eating humans integrated the effects of the psilocybin into itself, producing an ever-increasing level of awareness, specifically, a link between the brain's metabolism of serotonin and harmine compounds and the advancement of human consciousness. Terence and Dennis McKenna hypothesized that serotonin and harmine allow information stored in DNA to be retrieved through the molecular intercalation (blending) of these compounds into neural acids. In other words, the energy (a waveform) stored in the neural cell's nucleus becomes a molecular broadcast of its electron spin resonance characteristics, meaning that information stored in the DNA is being "read" by the brain, thereby becoming a part of how we perceive ourselves and the world we experience.[76] In short, human DNA is changing the way it is expressed within the environment with the primary purpose of becoming more aware. It just so happens that we are the vehicles of its expression.

The way this change in expression of DNA might work is that certain amines, such as serotonin, might intercalate into RNA, thereby opening the molecule. Other neurotransmitters might penetrate into the nucleus through the opening and then intercalate into the DNA. This blending (intercalating) might then have two effects. The first is a separation of the nucleotide stands by charge transfer, which could function as inductors for RNA synthesis. Second, if this blending stabilized the helix form of the DNA, as opposed to separating it, then the portions of DNA involving in intercalation might not be open for transcription. The closed portions of the neural genome, then, could later be opened to synthesis:

> This suggests one possible mechanism by which the base sequence of neural DNA could be "altered" without necessitating an actual change in the structure; that is, given one situation in which amines are intercalated at particular sites on the DNA, then subsequently these amines could debond from some of these sites and bond into different sites, thus "coding" a memory or learned behavior and simultaneously rendering formerly "silent" areas of the genome available for transcription and "silencing" formerly active areas. This would amount to about the same effect as a restructuring of base sequences but has the advantage of not requiring an actual change in neural DNA.[77]

In the case of serotonin—the inhibition of which keeps our consciousness focused in our bodies—the electron spin resonance (an electrical signal) represents the electrochemical basis for consciousness as we experience it. Harmine, however, functions differently and seems to carry more information than do the electrical signals of normal serotonin metabolism. The quality of information flow that accompanies the shift from normal serotonin levels in favor of harmine suggests an adaptive advance of considerable significance. The levels of serotonin and beta-carbolines in human neural tissue may be undergoing a steady shift in the direction of increased beta-carboline secretion along with the increased inhibition of serotonin. This shift, according to the McKennas, is responsible for the advancement of consciousness, where consciousness is the self-perception that arises from the improving electrical signal between the holographic specie information of experience stored in DNA and the workings of the human brain. The conscious experience as a result of harmine blending in the brain is different from the normal conscious experience. Such a superimposition upon consciousness registers a higher cortical experience intellectually, understood as a continuously self-defining imagination, represented through time on any of an infinite number of possible symbolic levels. Furthermore, this harmine phenomenon can be stable through the permanent bonding of a harmine resonance unit into DNA being directly maintained through endogenous synthesis.[78]

What this all means is that, if true, the human brain will produce ever more complete analogical descriptions of the patterns stored in DNA. Terence McKenna explains:

> The subject feels these ideas [information stored in DNA] to be arising from a source outside the ego, but within her- or himself. The subject experiences the imminent presence of an agency, impersonal and without limitation, that produces these ideas. He or she not only feels this agency to be the more-than-cybernetic matrix of the DNA but also the nonego information "assures" the subject that this is the case. Further, it offers ever more elaborate models of itself, which are not only descriptions of a static goal that will represent complete concrescence but also; and inherently, these models act predictively relative to when this completion will be achieved. They offer a description of the shifting boundary conditions that will necessarily modify all the temporal moments that separate the present from this completion.[79]

During the past twenty years a new group of scientists seem to corroborate the McKennas' general idea that genes are not a static blueprint for life. During the 1990s, Marcus Pembrey, a clinical geneticist at the Institute of Child Health in London, discovered an anomaly in genetics as it applies to heredity. He saw two patients, a boy and a girl. Both inherited a syndrome that was caused by a missing DNA sequence in chromosome 15. Oddly, though, two different disorders were being expressed. The boy had a condition called Prader-Willi syndrome, and the girl was experiencing Angelman syndrome. In the former, children are characterized as having an insatiable appetite and grow to be extra-large people. The latter children experience jerkiness to their bodily movements as they walk, and although severely incapacitated, are unusually happy; they smile all the time. With more research, Dr. Pembrey and several other geneticists discovered a phenomenon they refer to as *epigenetics,* meaning "above" genetics. What mattered in the case of the two children was that the girl's missing chromosome 15 was from her mother, while the boy's missing chromosome 15 came from his father.[80]

Researchers also found that the townspeople of Overkalix near the Arctic Circle in Sweden are passing down through the generations the environmental effects of drought. Over the past twenty years of studying the townsfolk of Overkalix, Swedish public health expert Olov Bygren discovered that they were being affected by drought one hundred years in the past, even though they had not experienced drought themselves. They theorize that certain genes can be silenced as a result of hormones (stress in the case of the Overkalix townsfolk) present in the person, made during the creation of the female's eggs (while she is still in the womb) and in the male's sperm when he reaches puberty.[81]

A logical conclusion is that because environmental factors of a previous generation can affect the health in a subsequent generation, other things must be affected too. Intellect might very well be just as much a function of our ancestors as it is a result of good upbringing and good schooling. Dr. Pembrey thinks that today's more environmentally conscientious generation is a result of previous generations; specifically, this generation's realization that our world is a delicate living sphere, a closed system, sailing through space. This reality was enforced in the 1960s during the space race, when mankind first viewed Earth from outer space. Since then, people growing up have become increasingly more aware of the need to live life in a way that is less destructive to the environment.[82]

Such research has serious implications for society and particularly for civilization. If DNA is responsible for the biological terraforming of our planet from a lifeless, barren landscape into a dynamic living world, as evolutionary biologists claim, then what is the human species becoming?

What seems to be the case is that quantum physics' state vector of all possibilities—the energy wave existing behind all that we experience as physical reality—is actually the *imagination* that all human beings are endowed with! And it is our cumulative selection of a state that from which our reality emerges.

Put in a more conceptual way, humanity (or DNA) is our vehicle of experience and our perspective as a biological form. We are human, though, only in the sense that our experience of each other makes us human. Ultimately, we are eternal (in physics terms, nonlocal) beings of an unknown nature with an unknown origin, an abstraction of an abstraction, One Being juxtaposed through the principle of duality geometrically progressed into a multiplicity through bound states of consciousness between DNA and the form it is expressing. As a result, we exist as conscious individuals within an absolute entity, an omnipotent, omnipresent, omniscient entity we, in our Western tradition, commonly refer to as God. This "God," however, is not an entity that can be defined in any religious sense. Nor can it be defined by science, because science concerns itself only with what can be measured. Our experience, which is what defines our lives and makes us human, cannot be measured except through our own recollection of history.

Born into what we experience physically as a finite realm, we have no choice but to accept that the reality of our lives emanates from the eternal world of the conceptual, the abstract, the spiritual. In truth, we are thought forms built with layers of concepts and ideas, all imagined. In fact, we *are* imagination, because it is the only thing that is unchanging, the only thing that is real. Imagination is our character underneath all the cultural biases and beliefs. Even though we are conditioned to accept physical existence as the only reality, there are enough subtle hints evident in our experience that what is real lies in the world of the abstract—déjà vu, dreams, visions, coincidences, and things of the sixth sense. We've been taught to ignore these things and believe they are meaningless. But these are the very things we should never ignore, for they lead us directly into contact with life's essence. Experiences of the sixth sense hint that something deeper, something much greater links all of us into a commonwealth of life. And when we look inward to find that deeper thing, there is the Creator, who has been there all along, waiting for us to become aware of that fact. The Creator, the consciousness perception that everyone is at the core of their being, is a seventh sense. And, through this seventh sense we find peace, joy, and harmony.

As a species, humans experienced a Golden Age at a remote point before time existed as we understand it. Now that we have deciphered the mythical message left for us by our ancient ancestors, we know what happened to change society into a resource-hoarding competitive and destructive society. We also are coming to realize that we don't have to be like that anymore, that how we live is a matter of choice, a matter of will to stop watching the shadows on the cave wall and walk outside to embrace the sunshine and see our true identity.

On the horizon of human experience is a coming global Golden Age that has nothing to do with established patterns of belief or habits of life's affairs. Novelty, innovation, and creativity are increasing exponentially as each successive generation expresses new concepts and technologies, defying the existing habits of the previous generation. Such a state of human society, an unplanned and uncontrollable desire for DNA to continue expressing itself into the realm of the abstract, is reaching an "end point"—what McKenna refers to as the *eschaton,* the "final thing."

Twelve thousand years ago, human history began with an Age of Terror, as Earth ceased to be a garden paradise and became a planet of scarcity. With an intense desire to survive, we were forced to till the ground because the abundant fruit of the planet had disappeared. In desperation we were also forced to take the lives of other animals even though, over our lives, such a diet proved to be toxic. To rebuild the lives that we once enjoyed, we would have to do it ourselves, and we are rebuilding the paradise we lost through a process hidden behind the generational short-sightedness we naturally suffer from. Today, the technology we have developed over thousands of years, culminating within the last thirty years, has brought the world's people together through the freedom to share information and knowledge on an unlimited, uncensored basis. With such growing awareness of ourselves, resulting from DNA's desire to continue expressing itself in new ways, we are approaching a point in which our true nature will be revealed in its fullness, that is, to nurture and care not just for our lives, but for all life. Our nature as human beings is creative and peaceful, artistic and innovative, cooperative and nurturing.

We are intimately tied to a greater landscape, the ecosystem of the planet, where we exist within a diverse web of life. Our planet too is intimately tied to a greater landscape, the solar system, which is ultimately tied to a landscape we call the Milky Way galaxy. In the end, and in the beginning, we are tied to the landscape of the universe itself and to the strange, perplexing world of quantum physics, mind, consciousness, and experience. Knowing this seems, somehow, to be at least partially responsible for the change in awareness the planet is experiencing.

We are also intimately tied historically, spiritually, and subjectively to our mythical beginnings. Perhaps this memory of a Golden Age is sequenced in an unexplored area of DNA and is, along with our ability to tap into the realm of imagination, the engine behind the fast-changing world in which we live.

Even though political systems are attempting to manage and control that change, DNA, with its unceasing desire to continually recombine itself within the human species and produce new generations of people, seems to have an agenda of its own, and like Terence McKenna once stated in regard to this change, the most frightening aspect of all is that *there is no one in control.*

THE COMING GOLDEN AGE AND THE
NEW WORLD ORDER

No one knows exactly what this coming global Golden Age will be like. Our experiences and endeavors must first be imagined. We might eventually develop a new physics that takes us to the stars in some yet-to-be invented propulsion system providing energy far beyond the thrust technology we use in spacecraft today. Such a technology might even alter the fabric of space-time to get us there in an instant. Those things are best left to the men and women of tomorrow, our grandchildren and great-grandchildren. What is certain is that we will *not* be able to get there using our existing resource use and management systems, which brings up the most pressing issue for society: the need for a more effective method of distributing and allocating resources. A new system is needed in order to further develop civilization into what physicist Dr. Michio Kaku refers to as a Type I civilization—a civilization that has harnessed the power of the planet.

Consumer-driven capitalism has run its course, its character having become increasingly more monopolistic and gimmicky with the production and sale of a wide range of "stuff." Some corporations have become so powerful they control more resources than most of the countries of the world.

The time span from the dawn of the Industrial Age until now is only a little more than 250 years, and within that time, we as a society have moved from an agrarian way of life to a systematic scramble for market share and money, with the majority of people's lives swaying in the balance. They too are scrambling for jobs. Everyone wants and hopes for a Golden Age. After all, who wouldn't? The difficulty is that not everyone has the same vision for a Golden Age society.

Although a New World Order might be achieved at some point, the long-term success of any globalization requires the cooperation of the people, which means their consent and voice. More important, such globalization requires that society's problems be effectively addressed.

Crime, violence, abuse, disease, poverty—all these unwanted realities plague us today. Treating them with methods of punishment and rehabilitation as we have been is ineffective and costly.

One of the major hurdles to a New World Order is war, which is based as much on religious belief as it is on economics. The tensions existing between Islamic fundamentalists and Western nations must first be resolved. This, however, can occur only through the acceptance of a nonviolent and transcendent interpretation of the Bible and the Qur'an. And that depends on individual experiences of "Oneness" and teaching our children that all life is sacred.

The foundation of these social problems, however, is and has always been the need for money, whether gold, silver, or fiat currency. Money, however, is only an intermediary, a creation of human society. In fact, "money is a fiction—an abstract construction of the mind. . . . The concept of money is one of the great feats of man's imagination,"[83] states former British Under-Secretary of State for Economic Affairs and Financial Secretary to the Treasury Harold Lever (1914–1995). Money buys the things we need, which are resources to survive. For most people, the life this "need for money" creates is so demoralizing that alcoholism has become commonplace. Prozac or other mood-altering drugs are frequently prescribed to the anxious and stressed, or people resort to crime to get what they need. Taxing the people to create programs to deal with these social ills does little except to further burden society. New ways of conducting the affairs of life must be conceived, and to accomplish that, civilization needs visionary leaders who have obtained the truest form of wisdom, experienced knowledge. The intellect, in and of itself, is not wisdom. Intellect is the avenue that leads to questioning, which leads to seeking answers to those questions in a methodological way. Wisdom is the ability to utilize the intellect in conjunction with a greater awareness of the human role in society, nature, and the cosmos, and then to apply that experienced knowledge to personal relations and society in general. These new leaders must govern free from the temptations of power and wealth, acting in the most profitable way for society as a whole.

For that to occur, violence must cease being a primary and systemic trait of society. As Robert Kennedy once remarked,

> violence breeds violence, repression brings retaliation. . . . There is another kind of violence, slower but just as deadly, destructive as the shot or the bomb in the night. This is the violence of institutions; indifference and inaction and slow decay. This is the violence that afflicts the poor, that poisons relations between men because their skin has different colors. This is a slow destruction of a child by hunger, and schools without books and homes without heat in the winter.[84]

For a New World Order to be meaningful, for a New World Order to truly be a Golden Age, not that profitability should be forbidden, but the rights of people must take precedence over the rights to profit, and the management of resources must be efficient and effective for the long-term sustainability of the planet. The violence of our institutions that dictates our way of life—the cannibal war machine—must be laid to rest, and this tug of war between capitalism and socialism must give way to a new understanding of society. We have the knowledge, the infrastructure, the communications, and the technology to meet the basic needs of all people, and in doing so create paradise. We have a responsibility to ourselves to cultivate and promote a clear understanding that the least of us is just as important as those whom we shower with fame and fortune. We must change our ways of thinking from the paranoid view that there is not enough to a clear view of the world in which we live. There is more than enough, and it is socially destructive to continue with a system that forces people into monetary-based labor slavery simply to survive. Through the spread of clarity and shared purpose, we can change our minds and our habits. We also must realize that we can accomplish anything that we dream, because imagination is real. Therefore, we must imagine. Imagine peace.

9

A GOLDEN AGE OF
IMAGINATION

*The main source of all technological achievements is
the divine curiosity and playful drive of tinkering and
thoughtful researcher, as much as it is the creative
imagination of the inventor.*

ALBERT EINSTEIN, 1930

The Age of Science is drawing to a close, giving way to its source—
imagination. Science and scientific investigation, however, will not cease
to exist. On the contrary, the quest for scientific knowledge has led to
the unavoidable realization that DNA within the human species continues to evolve and express itself in new ways. Science will grow with
it. All of this takes place in a reality where solid matter is more a perception or a point of view than an enduring, permanent state. No scientist can deny that she or he is subjectively experiencing a "scientifically"
material and physical world. This phenomenon of consciousness we
experience every moment is a philosophical conundrum so devastating

that science can talk about only what "it" might be. Yet every person intuitively knows precisely that "it" is an experience predicated on an emotional reaction to the events we call life. Fundamentally, the phenomenon of consciousness is a state of existence, or "being," and an obvious result of continuing DNA expression. What else could it be? One might argue that through DNA's expression through the human mind into a world of the abstract, we are beginning to understand our true nature and at the same time remembering our past. The universe and our sentience within that universe can be effectively explained only through imagination, for there is no one true explanation of human origins. In the realm of conscious experience, there may not be a beginning. Even so, as the fully functional individuated consciousness that we were from the very beginning, our perception acclimatizes itself to the world we were birthed into through our first memories—with its wonders and joys, as well as its aches and pains.

While science is the engine behind today's technical civilization, its reductionist approach fails to grasp the deep significance that our experience is what matters most, a truth everyone shares, scientists and nonscientists alike. Science keeps finding smaller types of particles that interact (resonate) with other particles in such a way to form our physical world. And with an infinitesimally small probability (1 part in $10^{40,000}$) that the two thousand enzymes required for life somehow emerged through randomness,[1] there can be no other conclusion than the probability theory does not apply to Earth's diverse web of life or to evolution. Such an approach to science is a very abusive thought to the Western mind. Yet taking this viewpoint seems to be the only way to proceed, because all we are ever finding with a reductionist approach is smaller and smaller particles and vibrating strings. There is nowhere for science to venture except to accept the subjectivity of our nature, that DNA expression is, somehow, intelligent for a grander purpose. Because life is ultimately "one thing" that we each experience from a unique perspective, shouldn't we ask what quantum physics, chemistry, and biology have to do with psychology, sociology, and history?

Nobel physicist Erwin Schrödinger (1887–1961), one of the cofounders of the field of quantum physics who formulated an equation that describes the *wave function** of a quantum system, elucidated this point more than sixty years ago in *Mind and Matter:*

> Most painful is the absolute silence of all our scientific investigations towards our questions concerning the meaning and scope of the whole display. The more attentively we watch it, the more aimless and foolish it appears to be. The show that is going on obviously acquires a meaning only with regard to the mind that contemplates it. But what science tells us about this relationship is patently absurd: as if mind had only been produced by that very display that it is now watching and would pass away with it when the sun finally cools down and the earth has been turned into a desert of ice and snow.[2]

Nobel physicist Werner Heisenberg (1901–1976), another cofounder of quantum physics and creator of the *uncertainty principle,* agreed that life is something that exists beyond the reach of science:

> It is very difficult to see how concepts like perception, function of an organ, affection could be part of the coherent set of concepts of quantum theory combined with the concept of history. On the other hand, these concepts are necessary for an understanding of life to go beyond quantum theory and to construct a new coherent set of concepts, to which physics and chemistry may belong as "limiting cases"; History may be an essential part of it, and concepts like perception, adaptation, affection also will belong to it. If this view is correct, the combination of Darwin's theory with physics and chemistry would not be sufficient to explain organic life.[3]

---

*The *wave function* is a mathematical description of how a field of energy is perceived as a particle of matter with volume through the collapse of the wave.

Indeed, the father of the quantum physics revolution and the discoverer of the *energy quanta,* Nobel physicist Max Planck (1858–1947), understood that science can never solve the ultimate mystery of nature because in the final analysis, we ourselves are part of nature. As a result, we are a part of the mystery we are trying to solve. Planck also understood that music and art, to a degree, were also attempts to solve or at least to express the mystery of experiencing life. Thus, Planck stated the obvious:

> Science demands also the believing spirit. Anyone who has been seriously engaged in scientific work of any kind realizes that over the entrance to the gates of the temple of science are written the words: *Ye must have faith.* . . . If we did not have faith but could solve every puzzle in life by an application of human reason, what an unbearable burden life would be. We should have no art and no music and no wonderment. And we should have no science; not only because science would thereby lose its chief attraction for its own followers— namely, the pursuit of the unknowable—but also because science would lose the cornerstone of its own structure, which is the direct perception by consciousness of the existence of external reality.[4]

Viewing all the academic disciplines as a holistic description of nature—an academic approach to Schrödinger's "whole display," Heisenberg's "history," and Planck's "perception by consciousness"— the political "Over Mind" of science must come to grips with the fact that randomness does not exist in any meaningful way as it applies to the ever-increasing complexity of human history. This creates great difficulty for the current scientific paradigm because without randomness, cause and effect cease to exist as does a linear understanding of the world we experience. The physicists' a progression in thought leads to the conclusion that time doesn't exist. Not in the way we think it does, anyway, not as the electromagnetic radiation emitted or absorbed by the change in states of an atom or molecule of an atomic clock. Time makes more sense being tied to our perception in a manner similar to

Einstein's special theory of relativity, which indicates that time does not flow at a fixed rate.

If one observes the length and breadth of human history, an obvious feature is that the universe, the galaxy, solar system, planet, planetary ecosystem, and life forms, is self-organizing, each being a more complex state of the previous state of the universe. Using this approach the problem of astronomy's anthropic principle—explaining the universe requires explaining human existence—disappears. But a new problem appears. The universe can no longer be thought of as random, which automatically redefines cause and effect, leading to an even greater problem: What, then, is reality, and what is our perception of reality as an individual experience?

A genuine understanding of the answer, I believe, is the key to a global Golden Age. The answer lies in the realization that the subjective experience, immeasurable as it is, is the determining factor in how life should be lived and how we should be self-governing. Such an answer involves the philosophical investigation into human perception and the individual experience. Because there, in perception, is where life is truly lived—where life is experienced. That is where any real wisdom might be found.

THE INDIVIDUAL EXPERIENCE: REALITY AND PERCEPTION

In his Allegory of the Cave, Plato likens the human experience to prisoners chained in an underground cave sitting on a bench. Behind the bench puppets march across a walkway in front of a flickering fire, casting shadows on the cave wall. Chained and seated to the bench, the prisoners are unable to turn their heads and see the truth of their reality. They can only see the shadows on the cave wall. For them, only the shadows are real. Only when the chains are removed can an individual stand up and turn around to see that there is more to reality than shadows on the cave wall, that the deeper reality is unseen to those who are still shackled to the bench. Only when free from the chains can the individual turn to see the truth of his or her experience within the cave. Once free, the individual also notices light coming from the cave entrance. Only by going outside the cave can the individual escape the false reality played out in the cave and understand reality as it really is.

Plato also supposes that if someone were able to walk outside the cave and see reality for what it really is, he or she would feel sorry for those back in the cave who could only see the shadows on the wall. And upon returning to the inside of the cave, he or she would also be unable to covet any prize that those in the cave awarded for studying the shadows on the wall. For Plato, one returning to the cave after seeing reality for what it is would "feel like Homer's Achilles, that he would far sooner 'be on earth as a hired servant in the house of a landless man' or endure anything rather than go back to his old beliefs and live in the old way."[5] In other words, seeing reality as it really exists is life-changing.

Plato also writes that if a person did return to the cave and took his or her place among those who had never left the cave, it would take some time for that person to get used to the darkness again. Those who had not seen the reality of the shadows being created on the cave wall would laugh at the person who came back with his or her sight ruined and comment that it wasn't worth the effort to attempt such a thing as seeing reality for what it is. Indeed, they would even kill anyone who was trying to set them free and lead them out of the cave to see "truth."

Plato's conclusion in *The Republic* is that it is only through the knowledge of reality "as it really is"—outside the cave—that anyone gains wisdom. In other words, one must understand what Plato calls the essential Form (the concept or idea) of Goodness. In more modern terms, one must understand that the physical human experience is a virtual reality in existence for the sake of experiencing "life." "Without having had a vision of this Form," Plato wrote, "no one can act with wisdom, either in his own life or in matters of state."[6]

Plato also envisioned wisdom as an "upward journey of the soul into the region of the intelligible."[7] Dr. Martin Luther King Jr. expressed it simply as the "Promised Land." Plato was concerned with social justice in the governing of the state, as was Dr. King. Interestingly, the message of the Christ, which was established more than two thousand years ago, was the same. What does social justice have to do with being able to see reality for what it really is, and how does someone actually see reality as it really is? More important, perhaps, why would anyone want to?

In Plato's famous cave allegory, physical reality appears as shadows on the wall, and according to Plato, these shadows are merely an image, the casting of a much larger reality of which we know little, if anything. It's easy for us to mistake the cave wall and the shadows appearing on it to be physical reality, interpreted through our five senses. But, as Plato illustrates, this is not the case at all. Behind the physical world there is an abstract world of ideas and concepts, what he calls *Forms*. And from these concepts and ideas, the physical world emerges. What we might say today is that our physical reality, from our planet to the solar system and universe, does have an explanation. But that explanation has to be experienced by stripping away the belief systems we use to explain our existence. Plato's cave allegory is a colorful way of stating that we as human beings exist within a belief system of our own making. A belief system we are tied to.

This is not to claim that physical reality doesn't exist, but that it must be understood as a perception from within another existence we know little about. The shadows on Plato's cave wall are just as real as the fire behind those sitting on the bench, the puppeteers who carry objects in front of the fire, as well as the world that exists outside the cave. The cinema transpiring on the cave wall exists only if all the others things that produce it also exist. Believing that only the shadows on the wall are real is at the core of Plato's cave allegory. Plato is pointing out that our physical reality (the shadows on the cave wall) cannot exist separate from a larger reality we know little about (the fire, the puppeteers in front of the fire, and the upper world beyond the cave). We cannot explain our existence without referencing the concepts of something else producing the effects we experience, which in religion is the all-knowing, all-seeing entity called God. This is true whether the idea of a Creator is personally acceptable or not, because we are born into what we call the physical world to live out our lives, which we do without having a choice. Our finite existence in an unexplained universe demands that there be something else greater in some form, even though it is not comprehensible to us. As a young physicist I know put it, "Death is the best proof there is that we exist in a virtual reality."[8]

Why does it matter whether reality encompasses more than we physically perceive?

Because such knowledge brings understanding to life; everyone wants to be loved, wants a vocation that is personally meaningful, and wants justice in a corrupt and violent world. When we see reality as it really is, we also harbor a deep desire for social justice, because we understand that we are in an inescapable network together, tied in a single garment of destiny, as Dr. King put it. Social justice cannot be forced onto a population, but must first be cultivated within the hearts of the people, which is the reason why the biblical gospels depict Jesus of Nazareth traveling from town to town, spreading his message of love and truth. Plato, Dr. King, and those who first told the story of Jesus were all explaining very similar points of view.

The message of Christ is very powerful and dangerous: powerful because it provides a way of understanding "truth" in the esoteric manner, which is liberating; but it is also dangerous, as it can easily be used to control the way people think. With a culture devoted to the concept of attaining a true measure of Christianity—Christ Consciousness (giving to those in need and loaning money without the expectation of repayment, for example[9])—there would be little need for capitalism or large, aggressive governments. However, to the natural mind cultured by our social institutions—the mind that believes mere shadows on the wall depict reality—the sayings of Jesus make no sense. Those in need contribute nothing to the bottom line; they are a drain on society and a burden to the building of one's personal estate. To the natural mind, the condition of the less fortunate and the poor is their own fault, and they are to be shamed or at best pitied.

Science, the pursuit of knowledge, whose purpose is to explain the natural world around us, takes us to the edge of reality through physics. Religion does too in its purest nondogmatic and nonliteral form. Yet, to know what exists beyond our physical existence, to know what makes up our world, something more than scientific or theological knowledge is required, and as Plato stated more than 2,300 years ago, "every man does possess the power of learning the truth and the organ to see it with."[10] The organ Plato refers to is, of course, the brain. Learning the truth, according to Plato, requires, somehow, being freed from the chains in the cave; in other words, learning the truth requires being able to turn the focus away from the shadows on the cave wall to the forces that create those shadows from a different part of the cave. There's no way to accomplish this defocalization other than through the mind, through imagination, and when we sleep, dreams provide a natural avenue to accomplish that.

Dreams as Glimpses into Reality

Everyone dreams, even though most nighttime dreams are never remembered. People also dream during the day, as the mind wanders into an imagined land of happiness and personal pleasure. We call it "daydreaming." With daydreams, people conjure visions of a future life, of success, of being somebody special, or of achieving a personal goal. Such imagining over a long period of time is the motivating force behind the drive to achieve, whether in business, art, literature, entertainment, science, or invention.

Like being consciously aware of the environment as well as the self, nighttime dreams are a fundamental part of our mental state of existence. Certainly, dreams are an aspect of brain physiology. Our dreams are theorized to be a mix of memory creation, innate desires, and emotions that somehow bubble up from the subconscious mind. Dreams often include events of the day and people we know. There's no real cogency to them. They are just dreams and not part of our waking reality. Other dreams are disturbing, like the death of a loved one or being chased by a monster. Some dreams are whacky, like sitting in a circle with zombies eating ice cream cones. Still other dreams are very real, very vivid, and they create a permanent memory that sometimes last a lifetime. More mysteriously, some dreams bring back the memory of a previously forgotten dream. There are also recurring dreams and recurring themes from dream to dream. It's a fascinating aspect of the human experience. We have no control over the contents of the dream. Dreams just "happen."

Whatever dreams represent physiologically, one thing is certain. Dreams are conscious experiences apart from the body, apart from physical existence. So, in a sense, a dream can be viewed as a nonbody experience or an "out of body" experience. In relation to the three facts of existence—birth/death, love/sex, and conscious experience—dreams are a part of conscious experience as it applies to biological life. Most people take this fundamental "conscious" aspect of life for granted. We people are not only having a conscious experience, but a self-aware, conscious experience, and part of this self-aware, conscious experience is the dream, the daydream as well as the nighttime dream. Dreams are one of the most interesting aspects of our existence that is yet to be explained.

Much of the natural world is explainable by science. However, consciousness—our unique ability of being self-aware—is a mystery, as are dreams, which are directly related to conscious experience. At this time, science does not have the ability to study consciousness or dreams in a deep, meaningful way. The instrumentation to measure specific thoughts, or dreams, does not exist and may never exist. Therefore, from a scientific point of view, consciousness and dreams are beyond the bounds of research. Yet every scientist is a human being and is therefore aware that he or she is consciously experiencing his or her life. Furthermore, the scientist is also aware that he or she dreams at night.

No scientist would state that dreams are real in the sense that they are part of physical existence. Still, every scientist would state that dreams are real in the sense that they are experienced by the individual person, subjective certainly, but clearly an experience. We know that our waking consciousness is our perception of the physical world we live in—a statement of fact. If everyone dreams, and science tells us as much, then what would "dream consciousness" be a perception of?

It would have to be pure character: the inner you; the true you. And, as we exist with others in our physical reality, we also exist with everyone else in the dream environment. Furthermore, as we live our physical lives in circumstances beyond our control, the dream experience is also beyond our control. Materialist scientists would argue that the dream state is a reflection of the physical state, which at times certainly seems to be the case. However, the philosophy that has emerged from quantum physics during the past century suggests that there is more to dreaming than mere mental housekeeping, because what we perceive as physical reality is determined by probabilities; any event occurring in the physical world is related to the square of the amplitude of the wave function. In other words, the physical universe has a tendency to exist as we experience it. Such a philosophy from science blurs the distinction between the subjective and the objective, bringing about a more accurate description of the world we experience. Part of the time we live in an objective world while constantly moving in and out of the subjective world of perception, thoughts, and during the night when we sleep, dreams. The abstract self—the identity and character of who we are—exists somewhere in between these two states. In other words, subatomic matter does not exist independently from our observation of the physical realm.

Physicist and philosopher Fred Alan Wolf refers to this realm between the objective and the subjective as the "imaginal realm," or the realm of imagination, and from this realm, "dreaming develops and the self expresses."[11] For Wolf, from this abstract "imaginal" realm flow the probabilities that somehow produce a world of matter and energy, and this realm also gives rise to everything else that exists within our perception—"thoughts, feelings, sensations, physical space and time . . .

even the self."[12] He believes that the human subjective experience arises in the same manner as physical reality—when we observe. And this is why dreams play an important, universal role in the human experience. "These experiences [images, feelings, thoughts, etc., including such concepts as God and self] come from dreams and are hierarchical, rising through higher levels of self-reference that tend to change the boundaries that are envisioned to exist between the self and not-self."[13]

Where is this observing "self"? Wolf is convinced that the nature of self lies in the imaginal realm from which everything arises, objective as well as subjective. And the process by which we humans experience is the act of single nonphysical entity dreaming, with each of us sharing in a part of that dream.[14] When we dream at night, we cross the boundary between dream reality and the "big dreamer." Wolf wonders, are we "not only the dream of the Great Spirit, but with a single shift in the perspective view of this boundary, are we the dreamer?"[15]

Wolf also believes that archetypal images (symbols) make up the state of our unconscious minds and that these images are deeper than anyone's personal experiences, rising from a more fundamental reality that can be understood as the dream world. This, in a sense, makes the dream world more fundamental—more real—than what we call physical reality. So, when we sleep and dream, we return to that fundamental reality to retrieve information on how to navigate and survive in this "physical" reality. Ironically, Wolf writes, materialist scientists would agree with this, because the materialist philosopher believes that consciousness arises from matter. Indeed it does because "if consciousness exists in matter, then matter is consciousness. I am, therefore I think, or I think, therefore I am, becomes a tautology."[16]

Such scientific insights into reality turn the generally accepted worldview on its head. The dream world becomes the real world, and the real (physical) world becomes the dream. And in this is the power to explain the dichotomy between the quantum world of probabilities and the Newtonian world we observe in our waking state. The universe as it really is, at its most fundamental level, is an abstraction, a concept from which we are born into a virtual reality. The implications of this are crucial not only to understanding biological life, but all social and political systems we as a species construct for ourselves. Whatever we imagine, what we dream, eventually manifests in the physical world socially, economically, and politically.

Thus, life can be viewed more as a perpetual self-creating process that goes back many billions of years, perhaps even forever, than as a once-created physical machine that was set into motion. We are as much the product of the universe as it exists as a system as we are the system itself. How did this self-creating process begin? Why are we here experiencing, living life as biological beings? No one knows.

Such questions are left to the imagination, and finding those answers must be an individual quest. You have to imagine why you are here as a person, why you need purpose in your life, why you want to love and be loved. Imagine what love is. Imagine utopia. Just imagine. John Lennon did, and "Imagine" became one of his most popular songs.

Lennon was not only a musician, but also a peace activist, a philosopher, and a dreamer, and in his song "Imagine" he envisioned what life could be on the planet if everyone decided to stop focusing on the shadows floating across Plato's cave wall. There would be no heaven, no hell, no countries, no religion, and no possessions. These are all concepts and belief systems that we endlessly quarrel about. In "Imagine" Lennon considered that if belief systems did not exist, people would be living for today, in peace; there would be no greed or hunger.

Near-Death Experiences and the Light of the World

Other events in the phenomenology of consciousness support the notion that our individual perception is part of something greater. Hallucinogens can propel the wakened conscious mind into bizarre landscapes of the surreal. People who have suffered death and miraculously lived to tell about it speak of extraordinary peace and beauty in a place where dearly departed friends and family live on forever. Dr. Rick Strassman has clinically studied altered states of consciousness through the use of DMT, a naturally occurring molecule that catapults the mind into another reality. Drs. Raymond Moody, Melvin Morse, and Elizabeth Kubler-Ross have studied near-death experiences (NDEs) by interviewing patients who have undergone unusual experiences while they were dead. There is also the unusual case of Robert Monroe, a man who began having "out of body" experiences beginning in 1958 for no apparent reason and decided to hire his own team of scientific researchers to find out more about the possibility that "the imagined" landscapes of the mind are real.

These are just a few examples of the many men and women who have endeavored to understand what may exist beyond physical reality and whether there is life after death. Part of the difficulty in studying alternative states of consciousness—hallucinations, out of body experiences, dreams, and so forth—is that these experiences vary widely depending on the person, with the exception of one type of experience, the near-death experience. Even though all near-death experiences are not the same, nearly all people experience certain commonalities: being in another world, feeling peace and painlessness, and reviewing one's life are the most common. They also experience being out of body, encounter other entities, and witness the actual events surrounding their death and resuscitation. Some people also experience audible sounds or voices, an extraordinary light phenomenon, moving through a tunnel, and precognition.[17]

According to Dr. Melvin Morse, the father of neuroscience, Dr. Wilder Penfield, discovered the source of near-death experiences during the 1930s and '40s while "mapping" the brain. Although Penfield wasn't aware of the near-death experience at the time of his research, he discovered that stimulating an area of the brain called the Sylvian fissure, located in the right temporal lobe just above the ear, caused all features of the near-death experience to occur except for one, and that was the light that people often encounter, which they refer to as a "being of light" or a brilliant light of love and peace.[18]

With this medical data it could be concluded that near-death experiences are nothing more than the brain's last moments of life before fading into oblivion. However, such a conclusion does not take into account the effect the unusual experience has on those who glimpsed the afterlife. According to Dr. Raymond Moody, the father of NDE studies, having a near-death experience changes people. "The persons who died are never the same. They embrace life to its fullest and express the belief that love and knowledge are the only things that you can take with you."[19] People who have died and retained consciousness through their near-death experience no longer fear death, sense the importance of love, develop an appreciation for knowledge, gain a feeling of responsibility for their lives, and perceive a connection to all things.[20]

Nor does the conclusion that the near-death experience is the brain's last moments of life before fading into oblivion take into account the brilliant, loving light that people encounter upon death. From a medical or scientific standpoint, there is no explaining the light, nor is there a way of duplicating the light.

In *Closer to the Light,* Dr. Morse tells the story of a young boy named Mike who was dying of cystic fibrosis. As he approached death, his visions of other people, another land, and a bright light became more frequent, and near his death they occurred almost on a daily basis. His parents thought they were hallucinations that were terrifying him. However, what Mike thought was very different than what his parents believed. "He wasn't terrified, but confused since God and other people came into the room with him." According to Dr. Morse, "Mike looked forward to becoming 'One with God' in his visions."[21] And Mike understood that soon he would become one with God, then the dreams would be over and he would be dead.[22]

Another story of the afterlife comes from a fourteen-year-old boy who drowned:

As I reached the source of the Light, I could see in. I cannot begin to describe in human terms the feelings I had over what I saw. It was a giant world of infinite calm, and love, and energy, and beauty. It was as though human life was unimportant compared to this. And yet it urged the importance of life at the same time it solicited death as a means to a different and better life. It was all being, all beauty, all meaning for all existence. It was all the energy of the Universe forever in one place. As I reached my right hand into it, feelings of exhilarating anticipation overwhelmed me. I did not need my body anymore. I wanted to leave it behind, if I hadn't already, and go to my God in this new world.[23]

During the 1950s, while swimming in Washington's Cedar River, a woman named Sheila was sucked into a whirlpool. Unable to stay at the water's surface, she began to drown, but mysteriously, a brilliant rectangular light appeared to her in the water. She reached out to touch it, but before she could she found herself on the shore. Ever since that incident she has endeavored to understand humanity's purpose and states that, "The Light convinced me that there is more to life than most people experience."[24]

After her near-death experience, another young lady named Kathleen tried a number of religions only to find frustration. According to her, the God she sensed in the light was not the God put forth by the religions she had become familiar with. "The rules of religion are put there by people," she said. "From my brief encounter, I got the idea that being one with God is something that can be done without rule."[25]

What is this "light" that is so brilliant, this infinite source of love and energy that some people consciously experience during a near-death experience?

The science of quantum physics not only has a possible answer, but a very good answer, even though it may forever remain speculative, because an individual's experience of light would be impossible to substantiate with scientific data. Nonetheless, quantum physics deals with reality, that which makes up the physical world we perceive and experience.

It is our experience that life is made up of tangible objects that we can touch and see, things we can taste, smell, and hear. Nearly everyone is aware that biological forms can be broken down into smaller units: systems for respiration, digestion, reproduction, and so on, and these systems can be further reduced to subsystems, and then to the chemical compounds that make up the tissue of the organs of these systems. Finally, we arrive at the elements that make up the compounds. Most people are also aware that elements, which make up all that physically exists, are themselves made up of atoms, and atoms are composed of subatomic particles called protons, neutrons, and elections. These subatomic particles form an atom, with a nucleus composed of protons and neutrons and an electron shell. But what forms these subatomic particles?

According to quantum field theory, it is light; in physics terminology, photons.

Whether a liquid, solid, or gas, everything around us is matter. We can see, taste, touch, hear, and smell matter because that is our natural perception as human beings. For us, matter is actually all the objects around us, whether naturally occurring or manufactured. However, at the most fundamental physical level, matter is actually energy waves that can only be described mathematically. This is what matter truly is outside of our perception. We can't see it or feel it. Now, this "wave" is actually a mathematical probability that a photon will interact with it, and this wave creates, for us, the appearance of a particle.

When a photon (light) interacts with a wave, two things can happen. The photon can be absorbed by the wave and stay within the wave, or the photon can be absorbed by the wave and then be reemitted by the wave in a direction away from the point of interaction between the photon and the wave. If the photon is reemitted from the wave, then we perceive a particle, and all particles together form what we know as physical reality. In this manner, light (the original photon) and the photon being reemitted from the wave (the original photon's reflection, so to speak) create our perceivable reality.

In essence, the physical universe in its entirety is made of light, and we are beings of light. It is a mind-boggling concept to ponder: light and its reflection create the appearance of our physical reality, including our own physical bodies.

What are we then?

It is painfully obvious that we are flesh and blood, and that our lives are not an illusion. But the inner life we all live is what really matters, our perspective, which is a unique perspective provided by a dozen or more orders of magnitude, from the subatomic scale to the universal. Indeed, all the elements that bring life to our bodies were born in the interior of suns many times larger than our own sun, and then ejected into space as the lives of those suns ended with an explosion. How these elements came to Earth is speculative. Nonetheless, in a sense, we are the stars that have come to life, now living and breathing humans. Even though we know and understand relatively little of how consciousness arises, human or otherwise, or how it functions in our will to act, matter is consciousness.[26]

For Dr. Melvin Morse, the existence of the Sylvian fissure and its potential to produce the near-death experience has led him to include the concept of the soul in his medical thinking. The hypothesis that there is a soul existing independent of brain tissue is "the simplest, most logical way to explain our current knowledge of man's consciousness."[27]

Dr. Morse is far from alone in his belief that the soul animates the body. One day I asked twelve regular customers who frequent my coffee shop what they would ask their soul if they had the opportunity. Among those I questioned were a retired grade school teacher, an attorney, a part-time clerk at a local hardware store, a college student, two retirees, and a man who always stops by on his way to the Alcoholics Anonymous meeting. None of the twelve even questioned whether he or she had a soul or whether souls exist. Each of them spouted off anywhere from three to ten questions.

Perhaps science has lost touch with society in its quest to reduce and measure, thereby ignoring the very essence of life itself. What cannot be measured does not exist? So, any given scientist's imagination does not exist? The imagination that inspired him or her to invent that new device that saved thousands of lives is of no consequence? No scientist has ever gone to sleep faced with a problem only to awaken the next morning with the answer already in his or her head?

In truth, there are no dividing lines between science, society, philosophy, and religion. Each is a rationalization for what we are and why we are here. Each is a belief system. In truth, there is really only the experience of life, an experience where love and acceptance takes precedence, regardless of status, class, or occupation. Those are belief systems too. The person on the street needs no scientist to tell him or her there is a soul. The person on the street intuitively knows that he or she has a soul, that he or she *is* a soul.

What everyone wants to know is "why?" Why is life like this? Why is it so hard? Why is life a long series of failures with a few successes sprinkled in between the failures? What's the purpose of all this?

The answer does not lie externally, in a belief system, but in a place religion and science will likely tell you is not real. All the answers you want can be found in your imagination, your dreams. All you have to do is apply yourself to "yourself." Those who have died and lived to tell about it give us direction. There is no death. Life continues. Knowledge and love are the important things. Of course, for the profane public, experiencing life after death is only in the imagination, only a dream. Yes, it was. That's precisely the point, and it is entirely a matter of perception, which brings up another point. How do we know for sure that our perception in this life is not a dream and that the so-called afterlife isn't actually the "real world"?

We don't know for sure. But those who died and glimpsed the afterlife didn't want to come back. For them, it felt like home. Relatives who had already passed on were waiting and extended a warm welcome. Love and peace filled their being. Such a description of the afterlife makes our lives here feel like a biblical hell.

One young man Dr. Morse interviewed had his near-death experience when he was only five years old. While he was close to death, his consciousness left his body, and he looked on from above as the EMTs carried his dying body to the ambulance. Interestingly, his consciousness took the point of view of his sister, and he watched his father weep as he drove his family to the hospital. After leaving Earth through a long, dark tunnel, he emerged into brightness and was engulfed in a fog. There he stood and looked upon what seemed to be a border between himself and the true light, and he knew intuitively that if he went to the light, he would not return to his body. "The Light was all love, all knowing, and the sky was warm and friendly."[28] Twenty years later the young man confided in Dr. Morse that we are all born with the knowledge to solve life's problems. He said, "The answers are all inside . . . if we can just climb out of our egos."[29]

The picture painted by many a person who has experienced near death is that we continue to exist as we are except that our body in the eternal is not quite like it is in the ephemeral. We are whole, and we feel no pain because we have no flesh and blood to produce pain. The dark side of each of us doesn't exist. Only love and knowledge exist.

We categorize life into the subjective and the objective. But do we experience two separate worlds, one of the objective and one of the subjective? How can the objective exist without first the subjective existing? For example, how can an airplane (or anything) exist as an object without first existing within the realm of the subjective in someone's imagination? Everything we have ever invented, whether a tangible product or an applied concept, first must exist in the subjective as someone's idea. We don't want to apply that principle to our very lives, but how can it not be true, because it is the very thing that makes us what we are, and civilization is here in the manner it is to prove it?

God is a loaded word and means many things to many people. So I must define what I mean by *God*. At the foundation of what we call physical existence, something is responsible, the cause for all we experience. For the physicist, it is light (photons) and light's reflection combining to create the perception of matter. For the person who has experienced near death, it is also light, but light in its purity without the mirage of combining with its reflection. Everything that we see, taste, feel, hear, and smell is God's reflection. How this works is that everything, including your body and all that exists around you in the universe, is God's reflection, and the reflector is nothing other than your subjective experience, in other words, your consciousness. We, our lives, are God's imagination. And in that truth we see that imagination is the creator and that perception is the act of creating.

Sir James Jeans and the Ph.D. Within

Your soul is your consciousness. Your "self" is your consciousness. You are your soul, which has been mysteriously projected into a realm of existence that requires a physical body, and in this physical body an organ has emerged called the brain from which arises a mind specifically tuned to this world of the physical. We separate everything out—mind, soul, and body—for the sake of discussion and understanding as much as our minds can understand, but there really is no separation between them. That separation is a focused perception of a much larger reality. Your consciousness intuitively knows that and drops clues along the way that your mind picks up on, and this is the bait dangled in front of you. Intuition, hunches, déjà vu, synchronicity, and dreams— you have a choice: ignore them or seek their meaning.

As a society, we place so much importance on the words of the Ph.D., but fail to listen to the Ph.D. within. Neuroscience may very well someday find the link within the brain to the realm where consciousness exists, a larger existence of which we are but a part. Physics has already discovered that realm, but it exists in such a way that it is nondimensional or multidimensional or something else entirely. In the late 1920s, as the quantum revolution was shooting through the discipline of physics, British physicist Sir James Jeans (1877–1946) wrote in *The Mysterious Universe* that:

> The concepts which now prove to be fundamental to our understanding of nature—a space which is finite; a space which is empty,

so that one point differs from another solely in the properties of the space itself; four-dimensional, seven—and more dimensional spaces; a space which forever expands; as a sequence of events which follows the laws of probability instead of the law of causation—or, alternatively, a sequence of events which can only be fully and consistently described by going outside space and time—all these concepts seem to my mind to be structures of pure thought, incapable of realization in any sense which would properly be described as material.[30]

Jeans understood where quantum theory was leading physicists long before the Information Age. In the late 1920s Jeans viewed reality as a nonmechanical, nonmaterialist manifestation: "The universe begins to look more like a great thought than a great machine," he writes. "Mind no longer appears to be an accidental intruder into the realm of matter."[31]

To fully and consistently understand our universe, one must go outside space and time? The concepts of space and time and dimension are structures of pure thought? The universe is a great thought? We and everything that we experience are thoughts?

We are God's thought, God's imagination.

When did it all begin? That is not the right question. What about: How did it all begin? How did you get here? Did your parents create your conscious awareness?

They didn't.

My first moment of awareness of the life I am living took place a few months after my second birthday in the late spring of 1963. I discovered that rose bushes have thorns. I was already walking, talking, and grabbing things to experience the colorful world around me. My second memory a few months later is of the assassination of President John F. Kennedy. All I was concerned about, though, was my mother shrieking at the television. It seems trauma has a way of creating memory and bolstering awareness, as does elation. My point: *from each of our individual perspectives, we just appeared.* But it wasn't until sometime around my ninth birthday that I became aware of my mind. Suddenly, self-perception occurred as I stood in front of the bathroom mirror on a sunny summer day. *Who am I? Why am I me?* I gazed into the mirror as if, in the mirror, I could see the answer. But I couldn't, so I finished washing up and ran outside to play. Yet I never forgot that moment, even though I can't remember exactly what month or day it was.

How can God create a unique, diverse reality with nothing more than imagination?

Amazingly, the answer is simple. We do it all the time. The first men and women, whoever they were, imagined that they needed a shelter, and after contemplating it for a time, they imagined what to use and how to create the shelter from available resources. Maybe their first or second or even third try wasn't all that impressive, but as their knowledge grew so did their imagination. Finally, they built a shelter out of the existing natural resources. The same kind of process occurred with music and art. Many thousands of years later we are still using our imagination. We take rock, dirt, plants, and water and turn them into billions of objects, from houses to cars to musical instruments, and we do so first with our imagination and then with our hands.

From within a nonphysical realm we did the same thing to create our reality using only thought. God, which is defined as an absolute, undifferentiated, unlimited consciousness, imagined what it might be like to view and experience Godself. Why? Because in an absolute, undifferentiated state of existence, nothing exists except thought and imagination.

Imagine yourself in a small room with no windows and no light of any kind. The room is also soundproof and sealed, so there is nothing to hear and no odors to smell. Now, imagine that you are in a body cast. Not only can't you move, you can't feel anything either. This is what it would be like, using human terms, to be in an absolute state of undifferentiated existence. All you would have is your own consciousness and imagination. With that comes the birth of concepts, and with concepts comes the birth of something ingenious: the idea of exercising those concepts in order to experience.

Thought Exercise 1

> *I have said, "Gods you are, and sons of the Most High—*
>   *all of you,"*
> *But as man you die, and as one of the heads you fall,*
> *Rise, O God, judge the earth, For Thou has inheritance*
>   *among all the nations!*
>   PSALM 82:6–7 (YOUNG'S LITERAL TRANSLATION)

These verses from Psalms have special relevance as the epigraph of this thought exercise because the psalmist declares a unique relationship between God and humanity. It's one of the most unique passages of the Old Testament, for in it the boundary blurs between humans and God. On the one hand, we are all sons and daughters of God, meaning that there is a divine element in our existence. Yet, on the other hand, we are mortal. The psalmist struggles with what we today call the physical world in which we live, a world we are destined to exit from in death, as it relates to the world of our subjective experience. And it is there that we encounter the divine. Whether it's referred to as the divine or an abstract reality makes little difference. That's just language. The psalmist refers to an abstract reality that exists in each of us. The human experience seems to occur "out there," but in effect it actually occurs within our perception, drilling inward from emotion to thought to the very essence of being alive, consciousness. There, at the most fundamental level of consciousness, lies the mystery of life itself, a mystery that science cannot solve. We don't know where the anthropic universe came from or if it was even created at all.

With this is mind, there is only one assumption to make in explaining the universe and the human experience: something greater yet more fundamentally conscious exists. Whatever this entity might be from our perspective, it exists as an absolute, undifferentiated state of consciousness. However, in this absolute, undifferentiated state of consciousness, it's impossible to create in the same sense that human beings create because the only resource available is consciousness itself. Therefore, consciousness is the creative power to imagine. There is no point of reference and no meaning as to "where to create" except to state that within this absolute, undifferentiated consciousness because nothing else exists. In the English language this absolute, undifferentiated consciousness we call God. So "in the beginning," God had to imagine that another entity (another self) existed within Godself. This new entity within God can be viewed in human terms as a child, a son or daughter, but that is not what this new entity truly is. This new conscious entity is a *finite* image of God but still inherits all of God's nature and characteristics, which are consciousness and imagination. The only difference between God and the new entity existing within God is that God is infinite and the new entity is finite.

Using physics as an analogy, the manifestation of another entity within God can be viewed as the appearance of a wave, a wave being energy that is invisible and everywhere, energy that everything existing is composed of. From the human perspective, this wave simply exists and can only be described mathematically as an oscillation, the movement of a line with crests and troughs. In this manner the interaction between God and the new entity within Godself can be viewed, the first wave.

With the manifestation of another conscious entity within God two new concepts now exist: duality and relationship. The nature of this new abstract realm within God is of course consciousness and imaginative because that is the nature of God. However, the new abstract realm within God is also imbued with duality and relationship. Like God, this new abstract realm imagines within itself a new entity that inherits all of its characteristics—consciousness, imagination, duality, and relationship—and the new entity does the same. This sequence of imagining new entities within the next level of entities continues, but not for infinity, only to its limits. Although finite, an incredibly large number of new conscious entities exist within the original entity imagined. A googolplex of entities now exists within the first entity God imagined.

This type of growth is similar to the principle of the fractal that exists in our natural world, a mathematical equation that iterates, a form of feedback based on recursion. However, in an abstract world conscious entities are being produced through imagination, through thoughts, really, with each entity being a thought-space for consciousness to exist within in order to imagine.

However, with each new entity existing in a finite area, as more and more entities are imagined, each new entity becomes more limited in its view of the whole. Having nothing more than the ability of thought, each entity seeks a way of relating to the whole. Using the principle of duality, a new entity, a thought-space, is imaged within the original finite entity in order to understand the whole. The googolplex of entities relate to the new thought-space by interacting with it with their thoughts. Some thoughts are absorbed and others reflected in all ways possible, a process that creates dimension.

As the conscious entities within the googolplex react with the new thought-space, they begin to build an image of the whole through trial and error. However, the interactions of the googolplex of conscious entities with the new thought-space are unpredictable and represent a near infinite amount of possibilities. Which interaction would provide a proper view of the whole? A choice has to be made by each conscious entity within the googolplex of conscious entities. As a result, changes occur in the configuration of the new thought-space and create a moment of perception existing within dimension. We call it *time*.

With dimension and time now existing as the new thought-space, the googolplex of conscious entities imbued with the concept of duality and the ability to relate can attempt to envision the whole of their new "thought reality" through perception, one moment at a time. Within this thought-space called *space-time,* the conscious entities become a collective consciousness and start the imaginative process all over again, but this time with a new type of thought called perception, and through trial and error a complex thought-form with the ability to continuously perceive gradually emerges, capable of perceiving the whole.

Their perception of time-space begins with two simple notions, 1 and 2. We call them hydrogen and helium. Through this perceived duality, a multiplicity of other perceptions is possible through the continuous interaction of a self-creating system. Science calls it the cosmos. Religion calls it creation. In truth, it is the beginning of experience, the human experience.

For the conscious thought-forms that emerge in this new thought-space called space-time, their view of the replicated whole is complete with incredible sensations, but it is only a projection of a much deeper reality that is difficult to grasp because the experiences of sight, sound, taste, touch, and smell are so intense. These experiences are real. Just because imagination brought forth this perceived reality doesn't make experience a hallucination. In fact, this reality serves as a construct for experiencing whatever can be imagined. So, from continued interaction between conscious entities, forms develop in order to perceive this new realm of dimension and time. (Remember, matter is conscious.) The forms created, however, are weak and exist in a precarious equilibrium, which from their perspective is either to exist or not to exist. Not only are their forms weak, but the system of life they developed, the fuel they use to exist, gradually reduces their form to the point of nonexistence. Yet, through another system, a system of reproduction that they imagined from the beginning, their form continues, as does their quest to view the whole of reality. It's a brilliant concept.

The pleasure derived from the act of reproduction is so intense that it becomes the primary motivating force for their perceived existence, for hidden within the act of reproduction lies the secret to understanding the concepts of relationship and unity as they relate to all aspects of reality, even to the level of absoluteness and God's desire to experience Godself. Their existence based on duality, opposing genders become "one" in order to conceive a new form. This union, which appears to be purely physical, is actually transcendent. First, this union exists in the world of emotion, the sensations of form as it relates to the subjective experience within that form; then, with a greater awareness of "being," to the whole of reality. When both genders are consciously aware of their transcendent existence, no other experience is more magnificent. In truth, deep within the core of reality we find God experiencing Godself in the most intimate manner possible.

Such is the purpose of this googolplex of conscious entities, to imagine the whole. To experience what is real, however, first what is *not* real (what is imagined to be convincingly real) must be experienced, and with that there is perceived separation from the whole. Perceived separation is life as we experience it as humans. In truth, all life is a single entity. Perceiving separation is what we must do as souls in order to experience the life force that we actually are. Why we must perceive separation is to experience the lives that we live. Without separation there is no experience. This perceived separation is built into form, and like the conscious entities from which human beings are a projection, they too are conscious of themselves, left to their own imagination to understand where they came from and why. From this desire to understand come beliefs and belief systems, all of which are only an approximation of what's real, because perceiving the whole is impossible.

Remember the psalmist's struggle, which states that every man is a mortal God and that every God is an immortal man, which accurately describes the human experience. Every individual alive today, and anyone who has ever lived, has a unique concept of God. So how can God create a unique, diverse reality with nothing more than imagination?

God didn't. We did. At the core of our nature, our conscious perception, lies the multidimensional self, the same consciousness that imagined in the first place. We are God's imagination and at the same time our own imagination. It is a paradox, a paradox that has purpose, for we are in essence the cosmos perceiving itself, and God perceiving Godself. Yet the cosmos is distinctly *our* cosmos and a reflection of our own state of conscious existence, our own state of mind.

Astrologers have long believed that the stars affect the state of human consciousness. The opposite is actually true. Our consciousness is not a reflection of the stars. The stars are a reflection of our consciousness.

How long has this process of "reality creation" been going on?

If God is infinite, and creating experience is what God does, then it's been going on forever, because that is the nature of God, to experience Godself. It's only through our physical perspective that we can claim there was a beginning.

Thought Exercise 2

> *In the beginning was the Word, and the Word was with*
> *God, and the Word was God; this one was in the beginning*
> *with God; all things through him did happen, and without*
> *him happened not even one thing that hath happened.*
>
> JOHN 1:1–3 (YOUNG'S LITERAL TRANSLATION)

These verses from the New Testament have special relevance as the epigraph of this second thought exercise, because language—written words and vocal sounds acting as symbols—is abstract and represents not only objects but ideas and concepts as well. Presented in the introductory paragraph of John's Gospel, the concept of language as a creative force was an ancient philosophy long before the Christian era, dating to, at least, the seventh century BCE under the Egyptian pharaoh Shabaka. According to the stela Shabaka had inscribed, the principle of the Supreme Being, Ptah, created the world in Atum's image through words: "Through the heart and through the tongue something developed into Atum's image" and it did so through "Ptah, who gave life to all the gods . . . through this heart and this tongue."[32]

For anthropologist Henri Frankfort (1897–1954), the inscription on the Shabaka stela is the "true Egyptian equivalent of John's, 'In the beginning was the Word, and the Word was with God, and the Word was God.'"[33] Likewise, James Henry Breasted (1865–1835), founding director of the University of Chicago's Oriental Institute, believed that this Egyptian concept of creation through the Word was critical to a revised understanding of ancient history.[34]

Known as the Memphite Theology, this religious statement also blurs the distinction between God and humans, because humans communicate through spoken languages. God doesn't. This theology sets forth the concept that there is a connection between the subjective and objective—the objective emanates from the subjective through the spoken word—what the ancient Egyptians refer to as the principle of the Supreme Being, Ptah. In ancient Egypt, the heart referred to the mind and intellect—thought—whereas the tongue was the realization of thought. Creation, in other words, is as much intellectual and spiritual as it is physical and comes through thought, which is the divine heart, and through speech by the human tongue. What the Shabaka inscription is stating in an archaic way is that "being" or "existence" is "the image of Atum." Today, with materialistic science as the foundation of society, we wouldn't use such metaphors as the heart and the tongue to describe the human experience. But we do use the terms *subjective* and *objective.* Still, the subjectivity we experience as a perception becomes thought that we project into the physical world by speaking.

Thought Exercise 1 poses a question: How does a pure thought create a convincing, intense reality that we physically experience?

The answer is through *symbol,* which is the concept of something representing (or standing in place of) something else. In our experience, material objects represent something abstract, such as a book, which represents either a story or a thesis. Symbols can also be an abstraction that represents something physical, such as the word *automobile,* which represents a physical object, a device on wheels propelled by an internal combustion engine. In fact, human languages are symbolic systems. Any given word, which has no physical existence, in every language that has ever existed, represents the thoughts, images, and emotions of the speaker or writer. In the case of language, something abstract symbolizes something else abstract, and that concept is at the foundation of our physical reality, serving as a transition from the abstract to the physical.

Acting as a collective entity, the googolplex of conscious entities entered into this new thought-space through the selection of certain interactions (what we call subatomic particles), creating the existence of space-time. Each particle—every electron, proton, and neutron—is a perception at the subatomic level. In truth, particles are waves or oscillations of conscious entities, which have no physical substance to them and can only be described mathematically. However, within this new thought-space called space-time, waves can be selected to be interacted with (or not) by the googolplex of conscious entities. This creates a chaotic sea of perceived particles. It was discovered by this collective consciousness through trial and error that two very simple particles could be combined, and that their combination could be sustained. Hydrogen and helium emerged in space-time as a stable interaction between the collective consciousness of the googolplex of entities and the new thought-space called space-time: hydrogen with a single proton combined with a single electron and helium with a twin proton and twin electron.

Within this googolplex of consciousness—now perceived continuously in space-time and through continued interaction in space-time—a small portion of hydrogen and helium was transmuted into more than two hundred other stable combinations of elements. From the point of view of the conscious googolplex, these stable combinations are perceptions. We call these stable perceptions *naturally occurring elements,* and the interactions within space-time that create stable combinations, *the laws of physics.*

From the viewpoint of the googolplex of conscious entities, the elements now existing within time-space represent the consciousness of those entities and appear within space-time as a stream of consciousness. In fact, these stable combinations of particles are symbols of consciousness, an expression of consciousness in another realm of existence, another state of being.

From a perspective within space-time, these stable combinations of particles are called elements and serve as the building blocks for potentially anything that might exist within space-time. From the perspective of the googolplex of consciousness, they are perceptions of consciousness and are the building blocks that form a view of the whole, conscious thought being *symbolic* of the physical manifestation of that thought. The question is, what should that "whole" appear as?

Intelligence and consciousness are not just behind the formation of space-time, they are the formation of space-time, but there is no planned purpose except to seek out a relevant view of the whole. So, as is the case of creating perception in the new thought-space (space-time) in the first place, all interactions that lead to a greater view of the whole are discovered through trial and error, with the active ingredient being imagination.

LIFE'S MIRROR

Science has yet to fully understand how biological life forms appeared on our planet. All that can be said is that at some point in time life existed—a cell membrane, some type of digestive system, and a way to reproduce. According to Andrew Knoll, Harvard University Professor of Natural History and Earth and Planetary Sciences, "It's pretty clear that all the organisms living today, even the simplest ones, are removed from some initial life form by four billion years or so, so one has to imagine that the first forms of life would have been much, much simpler than anything that we see around us."[35]

One has to *imagine,* according to Dr. Knoll, because there is no other way to conceptualize in our minds the first biological life on Earth. How would there be a way to conceptualize the first biological life on Earth before that life existed? One has to *imagine.*

The googolplex of collective consciousness, as discussed in Thought Exercises 1 and 2, now perceiving space-time through the elements, continued to interact, attempting to view the whole. However, to accomplish this, the googolplex of collective consciousness needed a method to perceive itself from within space-time. Through trial and error, a combination of elements interacted with each other until a stable combination was found that was *aware* of the space-time environment and could reproduce itself in order to create a continuous stream of space-time environmental awareness. This simple single cell of consciousness most likely had a very limited awareness of its surrounding; nonetheless, the new thought-space called space-time became conscious.

How did these things occur, the emergence of a material realm from a nonmaterial realm as well as the development of awareness within the physical?

Although from within what we term the *material* there appear to be two realms, the tangible and the intangible, there is really only one realm; the material is actually a mirror or projected image of the nonmaterial, and what we call the objective is the subjective continued forward in time, moment by moment, through sustained awareness. This so-called "projection" occurs through *coherence* and *resonance*. Coherence occurs when individual waves or electromagnetic fields are in phase with every other one, in other words, synchronized, or working together as one. Resonance is oscillation induced into a system from another system that itself is oscillating at the same frequency. With resonance, one system (the nonmaterial) is able to store energy and transfer it to another system (the material), which is the animating force that brings life to the world, not to be confused with the energy (food) biological forms require to sustain life. That is another issue.

Remember that all matter is really light (a photon) combining with its reflection to create the appearance of matter. Coherence, or synchronization, that appears in the nonmaterial (quantum) world manifests in the material world through resonance with light and then serves as a means of communication, a feedback loop between the material world and the nonmaterial world with us, our consciousness, existing somewhere "in there" as the observer and ultimately, from our perspective, the actor. This is how we exist somewhere between the realms of the subjective and the objective.

Although biophysics and the use of photons by living organisms is a new field of study, much of the groundwork for light being a fundamental part of biology has already been laid by neurosurgeon Karl

Pribram; physicists Fritz-Albert Popp, Scott Hagan, and Kunio Yasue; and anesthesiologist Stuart Hameroff. In his research on consciousness, Dr. Hameroff theorized that microtubules found in dendrites and neurons might be pathways that act as waveguides for photons throughout the brain and possibly the body as a whole.[36] Dr. Popp theorized that consciousness exists not just in the brain but in the body as well and that consciousness at its most fundamental level is coherent light.[37]

Life is not what we think it is, because our view is through life's mirror. Thus, through the combination of a nonmaterial reality and a material reality, consciousness is creating its own experience. We are eternal beings of an unknown nature with an unknown origin, an abstraction of an abstraction, one being juxtaposed through imagination and the principle of duality, progressed into a multiplicity through bound states of consciousness. As a result, we exist as conscious individuals within an absolute entity, an omnipotent, omnipresent, omniscient entity we call God. God is living and experiencing, therefore, we are also experiencing and living. In truth, we are beings of light, and this light is at the source of life.

From a single instance of life—an individual cell aware of its environment through some process of development—here we are as a global civilization of people united in needs but divided in just about everything else. As self-aware biological forms, how did we become what we are?

We evolved. For some people, this is a fact. For others, *evolution* is a dirty word. There are so many diverse opinions and beliefs about evolution as well as religion and politics, how are we to make sense of them all? How can it be explained that there are billions of people existing along a continuum, from the simplistic human "animal" who cannot think beyond the immediate need to those who have found what they call enlightenment, with numerous degrees of existence in between? Why are some altruistic in their perspective, viewing humankind as a brother-sisterhood, while others couldn't care less, and still others, the majority most likely, fall somewhere in the middle? How is it that any given book can highly engage one reader yet fail miserably with someone else?

Individuals contemplating such concerns might ask the grand question: why? Why was I born? I didn't have a choice in the matter. Why is life filled with suffering? Some of it can be explained away by our own injustices toward each other, which stem, for the most part, from selfishness and greed. Yet disasters such as earthquakes, tsunamis, hurricanes, and famine have no explanation except to state "those events are acts of nature."

Self-reflection, depending upon one's mood and the particular memory being reflected, is a curse or a blessing—recalling the horrors of war, for example, as opposed to the sweet memories of someone loved. Self-reflection is so integral to our existence that we take it for granted and have a difficult time escaping its grip. We dwell on things, and we do it continually.

Have you ever wondered why you self-reflect? Perhaps more important, have you ever wondered how you self-reflect? Where does self-reflection come from? What are its mechanics?

Neuroscience, despite its wealth of knowledge about the brain, doesn't know, and may never be able to understand, the mechanisms behind self-reflection. Scientific investigation isn't necessary anyway. The enigmatic mechanism behind self-reflection, I have discovered, does not exist as a part of physical reality. Just as your mind isn't physical, self-reflection isn't physical either. Neither is your identity. The experience of life is about you, what is called the "self," and the self is not who you think you are but what you really are. Furthermore, belief has nothing to do with self-reflection, while perception and experience have everything to do with it. Regardless of culture or religion, political persuasion or economics, every person engages in the act of self-reflection, almost constantly.

The word *identity* is typically associated with a person's name, occupation, and physical description. Although this use of the word does serve a purpose, there is a deeper meaning to the term *identity*. Other than name, occupation, or physical description, how do you define yourself? It's a difficult question most people don't know how to respond to, and they answer with their name or occupation. The most fundamental answer is "I am me." Perhaps the best answer might be "I am that which perceives." In other words, the essence of my existence is based upon a unique perception, a subjective point of view on the objective world we experience.

What perceives is the important question. Several words can be used, such as self, spirit, or consciousness. However, the traditional word in the English language is *soul,* which generally refers to the nonphysical essence that animates and provides causality for an individual life. The human soul perceives, and this is the nature of our reality. More appropriately, the human soul is the action of perceiving. And perception with the additional ability to self-reflect translates to identity—the act of looking at the nature of you.

Interestingly, however, self-reflection requires the concept of two: the observer and the object being observed, both of which are the self. It's just that one self exists in the present moment (the observer), and the other self exists in the past (or future). Put another way, everyone talks to himself or herself about a lot of things, mostly mundane everyday things. Put yet another way, there is your conscious (awake) self and your unconscious (dream) self.

The skeptic might argue that this type of reasoning is all imagination. It is, and that is precisely the point. *We are our imagination come to life.* It is *because* of imagination that we are what we are. If we first imagined the light bulb before the light bulb was invented, and first imagined the use of timber to build a shelter before timber was ever used to build a shelter, why couldn't it be the case that from another realm we imagined our lives into a material and experiential existence?

The difficulty with imagining our lives into a material and experiential existence is that no one remembers. We are left with our own logic and reasoning to figure it out; the fact that our bodies are not only products of the material, but integral to the material realm in its entirety, leads us to believe that our nature is exclusively material. It's a very old argument based on reason. More than two thousand years ago, the Sadducees of ancient Judea were materialists believing that there was no such thing as life after death, meaning that there was no life other than the material life being lived now. Aristotle believed the same, viewing reality in material objects that are known through experience. Imagining our lives from a nonmaterial into a material and experiential existence makes no sense, or so we have been taught.

Materialist points of view, however, are too limiting and capture only half of reality—what we call the objective. One could be all-knowledgeable in the sciences but never be able to understand the essence of life and experience, the subjective, for such scientific knowledge is always an outward journey ending in theory after controversial theory. Science is always a measurement of something external to what we feel and experience internally, but that internal experience is what's real to us, which means that the true measure of nature is the subjective self. And for those who are on a journey to discover any type of meaning for their lives, the scientific outward journey has to become an inward journey of self-reflection. It's an age-old human practice that began with the first group of people but was somehow lost along the way in humanity's quest to rebuild civilization and regain our paradise lost. The latter is our history and humanity's cumulative experience.

HISTORY AS HUMANITY'S CUMULATIVE EXPERIENCE

History is our species' legacy. It is also what makes each of us uniquely "us." Each individual has a unique perception, and in the widescreen view of global events, every individual is important because individuals make up groups of people with common interests, and groups combine with other groups to make larger groups. Ultimately, people combine and make up society as a whole, with many varied interests. Even so, most people share a few basic common interests: the desires to love, raise a family, and simply enjoy life. Gaining the resources required to accomplish these desires, however, is another matter. The methods for acquiring resources are determined by humanity.

Throughout most of recorded history, society was led by a king placed in power by divine appointment. During the last several hundred years, societies across the world moved away from monarchies and developed various self-governing concepts, such as libertarianism and communism, seen in the current and ongoing tug of war between capitalism and socialism. The question now for society does not concern capitalism or socialism so much as the kind of resource distribution methods humanity will develop during the next hundred years. The most important factor determining our future will be history, not so much as a discipline to be learned, but as a repository of knowledge for guidance. History is the sum of all human experience as well as the expression of evolving life itself. History is predicated upon time, and time, as physicist Julian Barbour suggests, exists only as changes in the configuration in the universe.[38] We have our own time, which is built into the ecological climate as well as the spin and orbit of the planet.

If one observes the rate of change and creativity in humanity's expression over the course of history, it is clear that the human experience, which includes all things produced in that experience, is becoming more complex. What can be readily observed by this type of human evolution is that the universe prefers novelty. According to Terence McKenna's Timewave Zero theory, novelty is conserved in the universe rather than habit.

In the early 1970s, McKenna built a mathematical model around this concept of novelty by using the sixty-four characters of the King Wen sequence of the I Ching. These sixty-four symbols composed of six lines (a hexagram) occur in pairs in which the second hexagram is the inversion of the first. In all combinations of these hexagrams, there are eight cases where the natural structure of the hexagram effects no change. By translating these sixty-four characters of the I Ching into a mathematical software model, McKenna came up with a line graph matching significant events in history to the 64 character sequence of the I Ching. The result was a line graph shaped like a wave. McKenna's time-wave, with its dips and spikes, matches up with high and low levels of change and complexity in human civilization. Interestingly, parts of the graph correspond with future years, predicting the level and complexity of change to come. McKenna asks, "Why should this be the case?"[39]

He answers this question with the notion that whoever designed the sixty-four-character I Ching was able to peer deep inside the organization of matter itself and capture the fractal power of nature's creativity as it is expressed in the human experience. More interestingly, McKenna derived this theory in the early 1970s, unaware that the Mayan calendar ended on December 21, 2012. Ironically, McKenna's time-wave theory predicted that during December 2012, humanity would experience a totality of novelty, a singularity of sorts in experiencing something new. McKenna refers to this event as the eschaton, or "the final thing" that human history is building toward.

This eschaton, according to McKenna, is a universal, fractal morphogenetic field hypothesized to model the unfolding of space and time and to include all events of human history. This structure to history that McKenna decoded from the King Wen sequence of the I Ching is a complex three-level form utilizing the first order of difference as its primary unit. Six such structures in a linear arrangement compose the smallest level of the eschaton. Two make up the middle level, and a single layer is superimposed over these, becoming a third level that unifies the other two levels. Such an arrangement is similar to the structure of a hexagram, where six lines from two trigrams in turn compose a hexagram.

Humanity, it seems, is in a transition from a three-dimensional realm to a higher dimension that is entirely subjective. One can only imagine what this experience as a society might be, but by observing the cultural, economic, and political changes during the last few decades, one has to be hopeful of a future global Golden Age that rests in the young women and men of the millennium generation.

POSTSCRIPT

It's in the DNA

Ninety-nine percent of all life forms on our planet that have ever lived are now extinct, according to the American Museum of Natural History. Over the course of our planet's history, there have been seventeen minor extinctions, four intermediate extinctions, and a single major extinction. The first mass extinction occurred 550 million years ago, and the most recent transpired within human memory, around 12,000 years ago. The greatest mass extinction on Earth occurred 250 million years ago and eliminated 95 percent of the species living at the time.[1] On at least two occasions, mass extinction resulted from celestial forces.

Our planet was formed 4.5 billion years ago, lifeless and barren. The building blocks of life—amino acids—appeared in the oceans 500 million years later. After another 500 million years, a single-celled creature appeared, our universal common ancestor, giving rise to the web of life that eventually became all plants and animals that exist today.

For the first four billions years, life was limited to bacteria. Only recently, within the last 500 million years, did life blossom into great diversity. And only within the last 200,000 years did humanity take its current anatomical form. The engine behind the resiliency of life, of course, is DNA, with its ability to change and adapt to whatever is going in the environment while at the same time developing increasingly more complex life forms. At one time, the human genome was believed to be the most complex, with 100,000 genes. However, it was discovered by the Human Genome Project that human DNA has only 20,000 to 25,000 genes, about the same number of genes as in mice and fish.[2] In fact, according to Dr. Michael Skinner, the human genome is probably not as complex as the genome of many plants. Even more mysterious is the fact that the same key genes make a fruit fly, a worm, a mouse, and a human.[3]

Around twelve thousand years ago, humanity experienced mass extinction and drastic, sudden global climate change that brought about the Holocene epoch in which we live. Civilization was decimated, and those who survived carried forward under the mental stress of resource scarcity and a pervasive sense of guilt. Society has been slowly healing itself from this ancient trauma, and now we are on the cusp of a new Golden Age of humanity. Cultural mythology has always been believed to be fiction, yet ancient myth around the world, humankind's first known words, flamboyantly tells the tale of the "death of gods." Their story describes a highly traumatic event that is well documented by geology, archaeology, history, and religion. The survivors, who were afflicted by this trauma, rebuilt civilization and carried their affliction forward, generation after generation, throughout the millennia, all the while trying desperately to heal their wounded psyche.

Finally, we are in the position to fully heal that psychological wound and create a future where every one of us can thrive. Science, with its deep research into the laws of nature, not only has brought us together as a world society through its technical genius, but also has exposed the deepest secrets within the human experience, DNA. Regardless of whether a goal or purpose underlies DNA, its ability to create increasingly more complex plant and animal life forms in a dynamic geologic environment is clear. In a sense, our planet is not only alive with a grand diversity of simple and complex life forms, but is alive geologically as well, with a continually changing surface and oceans that regulate temperature and climate. One has to wonder whether DNA has an agenda of its own and, as a species, what we are evolving into.

In 2005, ABC News published a story about a new generation of children, stating that they are "highly accomplished, deeply spiritual and gifted with psychic abilities."[4] According to watchers of this phenomenon, these children began being born during the late 1970s and early '80s, and are called *Indigo children* because a blue aura can be seen at times glowing around them. Furthermore, the article states, "They often talk about speaking with God, angels or people who have died."[5] The article also says that Indigo children are not religious in the traditional sense, but experience a universal state of spirituality and a feeling of being connected to something infinite and divine.

In 2006, ABC News published another story about these Indigo children, highlighting the experience of a seventeen-year-old girl who claims to see spirits of the deceased and says she is on a spiritual path and has the psychic abilities to help people. According to this follow-up article, some say that 90 percent of all children today have Indigo traits. This phenomenon has gained enough of an audience that Diane Sawyer of ABC News interviewed the Glover family and their four Indigo children.[6] CNN's Anderson Cooper also hosted a ten-minute segment in 2010 reporting on the Indigo phenomenon. According to CNN reporter Gary Tuchman, despite the fact that "a lot of pediatricians and child psychologists basically say either they have never heard of it or don't really believe in it . . . there are an awful lot of people throughout the world who do believe this."[7]

With more than seven hundred books about these Indigo children now available on Amazon.com since Lee Carroll and Jan Tabor's *The Indigo Children: The New Kids Have Arrived* was released in 1999, there can be no question that a cultural phenomenon is occurring in our midst. *The Complete Idiot's Guide to Indigo Children* is even available from Alpha Books, an imprint of Penguin. Here's the important question for humanity: Are these Indigo children as mentally and spiritually gifted as their parents and others claim?

According to some psychologists and mental health experts, there is little evidence that so-called Indigo children exist. The definition itself is based on the notion that these children emit a blue aura, seen only by special cameras, from their bodies. It's possible that parents "embrace the Indigo label because they don't want to believe their children have behavior problems associated with ADHD, such as resistance to authority and trouble with school rules."[8] Even among those who embrace the idea of Indigo children, their sons and daughters display some unruly behaviors consistent with attention deficit hyperactivity disorder. According to Longwood University psychology professor David Stein, "The odds are that mixed in that group are a number of children who are very, very bright and astute and alert and very sensitive to picking up cues in other people. . . . I would not call them Indigo children. I would simply say it's a bright child who misbehaves."[9]

Until scientists change their approach to studying the human experience, they will likely never be able to corroborate the existence of Indigo children, because the main characteristics of these children are intuition, sensitivity, intelligence, and a desire to help—things that are subjective. Throughout history, societies have produced people who were intuitive, sensitive, and intelligent. Many of them offered a new way of looking at the world, such as Leonardo da Vinci, Nicolaus Copernicus, Johannes Kepler, Isaac Newton, and Giordano Bruno, just to name a few. Men such as Jesus of Nazareth (regardless of whether he existed), Meister Eckhart, and Martin Luther have had a profound impact on society. In modern times, Albert Einstein, Werner Heisenberg, Neils Bohr, and Erwin Schrödinger, Nobel Laureate physicists who pioneered the technology we enjoy today, also wrote esoteric commentaries on "the meaning of life." The psychologists Sigmund Freud and Carl Jung changed the way we approach the subjective world of psyche, thought, and mind. So, who's to know whether the so-called Indigo children are an evolutionary advancement of the human species?

Perhaps the Indigo children are the continuing expression of DNA, a new generation of humans that is experiencing difficulty fitting into an education system based on an outdated method of teaching. Perhaps these children are born with the understanding that there is no separation between humanity and nature, and when they come of age over the next thirty years, they will help usher in the educational, political, medical, and nutritional change that is so desperately needed.

I am not convinced that there are "Indigo children" who possess special powers. Every person is endowed with intuition, dreams, and creativity. The difference might lie in society itself—that we are willing to embrace the natural traits we see in our children with the hope that they will build us a future worth living. However, I am convinced that a new generation of children has inherited humanity's collective longing for peace, harmony, and goodwill to others, along with the intuitive sense that life is much more than a materialistic consumerist existence. Perhaps all of today's children are Indigo children, and humanity is taking a step forward.

Notes

INTRODUCTION

1. Gorbachev, *Perestroika,* 252.

CHAPTER I. A NEW WORLD ORDER

1. Sutton and Wood, *Trilaterals over Washington,* 1.
2. Shoup and Minter, *Imperial Brain Trust,* 3–4.
3. Stone, "'Civic Generation' Rolls Up Sleeves in Record Numbers."
4. Ibid.
5. Tan Sri Lin See-Yan, "'Occupy Wall Street' Goes Global," *Star Online,* October 22, 2011, biz.thestar.com.my/news/story.asp?file=/2011/10/22/business/9741558&sec=business (accessed October 22, 2011).
6. See occupywallst.org (accessed October 20, 2011).
7. "'Occupy': A Catalyst for Change?" Al Jazeera, *Inside Story,* October 16, 2011, english.aljazeera.net/programmes/insidestory/2011/10/2011101672419294658.html (accessed October 16, 2011).
8. "Is 'Occupy Wall Street' Really about Anti-capitalism?" *Fox Nation,* October 20, 2011, nation.foxnews.com/occupy-wall-street/2011/10/20/occupy-wall-street-big-con (accessed October 21, 2011).
9. "The Regime Concocted Occupy Wall Street to Target Mitt Romney," *The Rush Limbaugh Show,* October 6, 2011, www.rushlimbaugh.com/daily/2011/10/06/the_regime_concocted_occupy_wall_street_to_target_mitt_romney (accessed October 21, 2011).
10. "Geraldo Calls Beck Delusional and Paranoid about Occupy Wall Street

then Protesters Throw Powder at Him," *Glenn Beck,* October 17, 2011, www.glennbeck.com/2011/10/17/geraldo-calls-beck-delusional-and-paranoid-about-occupy-wall-street-then-protesters-throw-powder-at-him (accessed October 21, 2011).

11. "The Demand for 'Economic Justice,'" Al Jazeera, *Inside Story,* October 17, 2011, english.aljazeera.net/programmes/insidestory/2011/10/201110177526638328.html (accessed October 21, 2011).

12. Brian Montopoli, "Poll: 43 Percent Agree with Views of Occupy Wall Street," CBSNews.com, October 25, 2011, www.cbsnews.com/8301-503544_162-20125515-503544/poll-43-percent-agree-with-views-of-occupy-wall-street/ (accessed October 31, 2011).

13. "'Occupy': A Catalyst for Change?" Al Jazeera.

14. Sutton and Wood, *Trilaterals over Washington,* 5.

15. Butler, *War Is a Racket,* 1.

16. Ibid., 10.

17. "Ron Paul Says U.S. Has Military Personnel in 130 Nations and 900 Overseas Bases," *Tampa Bay Times* online, September 14, 2011, www.politifact.com/truth-o-meter/statements/2011/sep/14/ron-paul/ron-paul-says-us-has-military-personnel-130-nation (accessed November 5, 2011).

18. "Active Duty Military Personnel Strengths by Regional Area and by Country," Department of Defense, September 30, 2010, siadapp.dmdc.osd.mil/personnel/MILITARY/history/hst1009.pdf (accessed November 9, 2011).

19. "Military Ranking," *The Economist,* March 9, 2011, www.economist.com/blogs/dailychart/2011/03/defence_budgets (accessed November 9, 2011).

20. Dwight D. Eisenhower, "Eisenhower's Farewell Address to the Nation (January 17, 1961)," Information Clearing House, www.informationclearinghouse.info/article5407.htm (accessed November 9, 2011).

21. Ibid.

22. Ibid.

23. Ibid.

24. John F. Kennedy, "Speech at American University (June 10, 1963)," www.ratical.org/co-globalize/JFK061063.html (accessed November 11, 2011).

25. Ibid.

26. Ibid.

27. Georgina Prodhan, "Internet Firms Co-opted for Surveillance," Reuters,

September 30, 2011, www.reuters.com/article/2011/09/30/us-internet-security-idUSTRE78T2GY20110930 (accessed February 3, 2012).

28. Daniel J. DeNoon, "Chip Implants: Better Care or Privacy Scare?" Fox News, August 1, 2005, www.foxnews.com/story/0,2933,163983,00.html (accessed February 3, 2012).

29. Erik Kain, "The National Defense Authorization Act Is the Greatest Threat to Civil Liberties Americans Face," *Forbes,* December 5, 2011, www.forbes.com/sites/erikkain/2011/12/05/the-national-defense-authorization-act-is-the-greatest-threat-to-civil-liberties-americans-face (accessed February 1, 2012).

30. George H. W. Bush, "Toward a New World Order," A Transcript of Former President George Herbert Walker Bush's Address to a Joint Session of Congress and the Nation, www.sweetliberty.org/issues/war/bushsr.htm (accessed February 1, 2012).

31. Ibid.

32. Gorbachev, *Perestroika,* x.

33. Ibid.

34. Crozier, Huntington, and Watanuki, *The Crisis in Democracy,* 159–60.

35. Ibid., 161.

36. Ibid., 160.

37. Ibid., 169–70.

38. See www2.census.gov/econ/susb/data/2009/us_state_totals_2009.xls and www.census.gov/population/www/popclockus.html (accessed February 28, 2012).

CHAPTER 2. RESOURCES AND BELIEFS: THE SOCIAL EXPERIENCE

1. "The China Bubble: We're Counting on China's Growth to Save the World. Unless Its Economy Blows Up First," *Time,* October 31, 2011.

2. "I've Been to the Mountaintop," Martin Luther King Jr. Online, Dr. Martin Luther King's Last Sermon, Memphis, Tennessee, April 3, 1968, www.mlkonline.net/promised.html (accessed November 4, 2011).

3. Warren and Taylor, *King Came Preaching,* 174.

4. Ibid.

5. Joshua 6:21. New International Version.

6. Warren and Taylor, *King Came Preaching,* 174.

CHAPTER 3. ANCIENT SYMBOLISM AND
THE JOURNEY WITHIN

1. Gimbutas, *The Age of the Great Goddess.*
2. Kramer, *The Sumerians,* 112–13.
3. Maier and Kramer, *Myths of Enki, the Crafty God,* 28–30.
4. "The Exaltation of Inana (Inana B)," The Electronic Text Corpus of Sumerian Literature, etcsl.orinst.ox.ac.uk/section4/tr4072.htm (accessed March 6, 2012).
5. Wolkstein and Kramer, *Inanna—Queen of Heaven and Earth,* 8.
6. Schwaller de Lubicz, *Symbol and the Symbolic,* 77.
7. Gimbutas, *The Language of the Goddess,* 121.
8. "Middle Eastern Religion," Encyclopaedia Brittanica, www.britannica.com/EBchecked/topic/594804/Tiamat (accessed August 5, 2011).
9. Budge, *Egyptian Ideas of the Future Life,* 17–18.
10. Lamy, *Egyptian Mysteries,* 9.
11. McKenna, *Food of the Gods,* 70–73.
12. Ibid.
13. Ibid., 39.
14. Ibid., 120.
15. Ibid., 89.
16. Eliade, *Shamanism,* 399, 417.
17. Parrinder, *World Religions,* 179, 181.
18. Gimbutas, *Language of the Goddess,* 121.
19. Ibid., 137.
20. Ibid.
21. Narby, *The Cosmic Serpent,* 6.
22. Ibid., 7.
23. Ibid., 24.
24. Ibid., 38.
25. Ibid., 54.
26. Ibid., 55.
27. Ibid.
28. Ibid., 4.
29. Ibid., 38.
30. Ibid., 45.
31. Ibid., 58.

32. Ibid., 59.

33. Reichel-Dolmatoff, "Brain and Mind in Desana Shamanism," 81, 87.

34. Narby, *Cosmic Serpent,* 59.

35. Ibid., 63.

36. Genesis 28:12.

37. Narby, *Cosmic Serpent,* 157.

38. Ibid., 160.

39. Ibid., 157.

CHAPTER 4. SKY GOD:
ORIGINS OF THE WESTERN BELIEF SYSTEM

1. There are many examples. See, for instance, Ezra 7:23; Nehemiah 1:4; Psalm 2:4; 11:4; 2 Chronicles 7:1; Job 1:16; Psalm 113:6.

2. Acts 1:7–9.

3. Mallory, *In Search of the Indo-Europeans,* 14, 21.

4. Ibid., 185.

5. Gimbutas, *The Age of the Great Goddess.*

6. "Learning the Language of the Goddess," Lycaeum, interview with Dr. Marija Gimbutas, October 3, 1992, www.lycaeum.org/~maverick/gimbut. htm (accessed September 3, 2011).

7. Gimbutas, *Age of the Great Goddess.*

8. Ibid.

9. Ibid.

10. Ibid.

11. Ibid.

12. Ibid.

13. Ibid.

14. Akkermans and Miere, "The 1988 Excavations at Tell Sabi Abyad," 1–22.

15. Ibid.

16. Mellaart, *Earliest Civilizations of the Near East,* 68.

17. Roux, *Ancient Iraq,* 75–82.

18. Wilson, "Treasures from the Royal Tombs of Ur," 1–5.

19. Mallory, *In Search of the Indo-Europeans,* 139.

20. Roux, *Ancient Iraq,* 123.

21. Ibid., 135.

22. Ibid., 116.

23. Ibid., 116–17.

24. Ibid., 148.

25. Ibid., 146.

26. Ibid., 145–48.

27. Ibid., 149.

28. Ibid., 150–52.

29. Ibid., 154.

30. Ibid., 155–64.

31. Ibid., 168.

32. Emmanuel Anati, "The Time of Exodus in the Light of Archeological Testimony, Epigraphy and Palaeoclimate," Har Karkom, www.harkarkom.com/exodustimeVERS1.htm (accessed March 10, 2012).

33. Ibid.

34. Numbers 31:2. New International Version.

35. Numbers 31:7–12.

36. Deuteronomy 20:10–15.

37. Deuteronomy 20:17.

38. Deuteronomy 6:15–19.

39. Deuteronomy 6:10–12.

CHAPTER 5. CATASTROPHE AND ICE:
THE GREAT HISTORIC AND GEOLOGIC DIVIDE

1. Richard A. Muller, "A Brief Introduction to Ice Age Theories," Muller's Group, muller.lbl.gov/pages/IceAgeBook/IceAgeTheories.html (accessed February 22, 2012).

2. "Cracking the Ice Age," PBS, NOVA, September 30, 1997. For a full transcript, see www.pbs.org/wgbh/nova/transcripts/2320crac.html.

3. Kurt Sternlof, "Deep Ocean Current 'Seesaw' May Relate to Global Warming/Cooling Cycles," The Earth Institute, Columbia University, www.earthinstitute.columbia.edu/news/story2_1.html (accessed March 10, 2012).

4. Hapgood, Path of the Pole, xiv.

5. Ibid., 94–95.

6. MacDougall, Frozen Earth: The Once and Future Story of Ice Ages, 6–7.

7. Martin and Klein, Quarternary Extinctions, 466.

8. Ibid., 678.

9. Ibid., 553.

10. Ibid., 409.

11. Ibid., 447.

12. Lange, *Ice Age Mammals of North America,* 185.

13. Hibben, *The Lost Americans,* 157.

14. Ibid.

15. Ibid., 158.

16. Hibben, "Evidence of Early Man in Alaska," 254.

17. Ibid., 254–59.

18. Price, *The New Geology,* 579.

19. Velikovsky, *Earth in Upheaval,* 59.

20. Stewart, "Frozen Mammoths from Siberia Bring the Ice Ages to Vivid Life," 60–69.

21. "Raising the Mammoth," Discovery Channel, March 12, 2000. Available on DVD through Discovery Home Studios.

22. Firestone and Topping, "Terrestrial Evidence of a Nuclear Catastrophe in Paleoindian Times," 9.

23. Tiffany, "Was Ice Age America Victimized by a Massive Supernova?," 36.

24. Dalton, "Blast in the Past," 256–57.

25. Chandler, "Carbon, and Radiocarbon Dating," 8.

26. Firestone and Topping, "Terrestrial Evidence," 9.

27. Firestone, West, and Warwick-Smith, *The Cycle of Cosmic Catastrophes,* 174.

28. Ibid., 133.

29. Ibid., 147.

30. Ibid., 148.

31. Ibid.

32. Ibid., 293.

33. LaViolette, *Earth under Fire,* 161.

34. Allan and Delair, *Cataclysm!,* 209.

35. Ibid.

36. Aschenbach, Egger, and Trümper, "Discovery of Explosion Fragments outside the Vela Supernova Remnant Shock-wave Boundary," 587.

37. Ibid.

38. Ibid., 589.

39. Strom, Johnson, Verbunt, and Aschenbach, "A Radio-Emitting X-ray 'Bullet' Ejected by the Vela Supernova," 590.

40. Allan and Delair, *Cataclysm!*, 209.

41. Ibid.

42. Ibid., 204–5.

43. Ibid., 205.

44. Ibid.

CHAPTER 6. GOLDEN AGE MYTH AS EXPERIENTIAL HISTORY

1. Malkowski, *Ancient Egypt 39,000 BCE*, 117.

2. Dunn, "Mega Saws of the Pyramid Builders," 32–33, 64–65.

3. Schwaller de Lubicz, *Sacred Science*, 96.

4. Budge, *A History of Egypt*, 163.

5. Schwaller de Lubicz, *Sacred Science*, 87.

6. Herodotus, *The Histories*, 186.

7. Ibid.

8. Ibid.

9. Schwaller de Lubicz, *Sacred Science*, 87.

10. Herodotus, *Histories*, 187.

11. Wallbank and Taylor, *Civilization: Past and Present*, 56.

12. "Edfu Project," Göttingen Academy of Sciences and Humanities, www .edfu-projekt.gwdg.de/Project2.html (accessed March 15, 2012).

13. Hancock and Bauval, *The Message of the Sphinx*, 200.

14. Rundle Clark, *Myth and Symbol in Ancient Egypt*, 264.

15. Reymond, *Mythical Origin of the Egyptian Temple*, quoted in Hancock and Bauval, *Message of the Sphinx*, 106–7.

16. Hancock and Bauval, *Message of the Sphinx*, 201.

17. Ibid., 202.

18. Clark, *Myth and Symbol in Ancient Egypt*, 264.

19. Kramer, *Sumerian Mythology*, iv.

20. Ibid.

21. Genesis 11:1, Young's Literal Translation.

22. Genesis 11:6, New International Version. Young's Literal Translation uses the phrase "dream of."

23. Genesis 11:8–9. New International Version.

24. Giri, *The Holy Science,* xi.

25. Ibid., xiii–xiv.

26. Ibid.

27. Ibid., 103–4.

28. Genesis 1:29 and 3:17–19. New International Version.

29. Genesis 6. New International Version.

30. Ellis, *Imagining Atlantis,* 28.

31. Schoch, "The Mystery of Göbekli Tepe and Its Message to Us," 53.

32. Marinatos, "On the Legend of Atlantis," 195–213, quoted in Ellis, *Imagining Atlantis,* 233.

33. Ibid., 232.

34. Schoch, "The Mystery of Göbekli Tepe," 54.

35. Ibid., 55.

36. Ibid., 58.

37. Talbott, "The Lightning-Scarred Planet Mars."

38. Talbott, *The Saturn Myth,* 330.

39. Budge, *Legends of the Gods,* 14.

40. Ibid., 28.

41. Ibid., 29.

42. Ibid.

43. Ibid., 30.

44. Davidson, *Gods and Myths of Northern Europe,* 37.

45. Ibid., 38.

46. Talbott, *The Saturn Myth,* 331.

47. Hamilton, *Mythology,* 24–25.

48. Ibid., 45.

49. Frazer, *The Golden Bough.*

50. Ibid.

51. Immanuel Velikovsky, "Saturn's Golden Age," The Immanuel Velikovsky Archive, www.varchive.org/itb/goldage.htm (accessed April 13, 2012).

52. Ibid.

CHAPTER 7. GILGAMESH AND THE GREAT CELESTIAL FLOOD

1. Bierlein, *Parallel Myths,* 121–35.

2. Ibid., 134.

3. Sandars, *The Epic of Gilgamesh,* 9.

4. Ibid., 12.

5. Ibid.

6. Ibid., 19.

7. Maureen Gallery Kovacs, trans., "The Epic of Gilgamesh," Academy for Ancient Texts, www.ancienttexts.org/library/mesopotamian/gilgamesh/tab1.htm (accessed March 20, 2012).

8. Ibid.

9. Roux, *Ancient Iraq,* 120.

10. Thompson, *The Reports of the Magicians and Astrologers of Nineveh and Babylon in the British Museum,* xxv–xxvi.

11. Jastrow Jr., "Sun and Saturn."

12. Ibid.

13. Ibid.

14. de Santillana and von Dechend, *Hamlet's Mill,* 288–316.

15. Ibid., 57.

16. Sellers, *The Death of Gods in Ancient Egypt,* 5.

17. Ibid., 10.

18. Ibid., 93.

19. Ibid., 134.

20. Ibid., 185.

21. Ibid., 186.

22. Ibid., 203.

23. Ibid.

24. Ibid., 187.

25. Ibid., 21.

26. "Surface of Saturn Moon Titan 'Closely Resembles' Earth with an Assortment of Mountains, Lakes and Volcanoes," *Daily Mail,* August 7, 2009, www.dailymail.co.uk/sciencetech/article-1204786/Surface-Saturn-moon-Titan-closely-resembles-Earth-assortment-mountains-lakes-volcanoes.html (accessed March 22, 2012).

27. Victoria Jaggard, "Early Earth Turned Methane Haze On and Off?" *National Geographic News,* March 19, 2012, newswatch.nationalgeographic .com/2012/03/19/early-earth-turned-methane-haze-on-and-off (accessed March 20, 2012).

CHAPTER 8. THE COMING GLOBAL GOLDEN AGE

1. The United States Declaration of Independence.
2. Neil L. Whitehead, "Divine Hunger: The Cannibal War-Machine" (presentation at the Sacred Empowerment conference, University of Leeds, June 2011).
3. Marrs, *The Rise of the Fourth Reich*, 361.
4. Ibid.
5. Ibid., 362.
6. Ibid., 362–70.
7. Ibid., 370.
8. Ibid.
9. Ibid., 376.
10. Ibid., 375.
11. Ibid., 374.
12. "Brzezinski: For the First Time in History the World Is Now Consciously Awake," *Live Leak*, May 19, 2010, www.liveleak.com/view?i=42a_1274416173 (accessed March 24, 2012).
13. Ibid.
14. Ibid.
15. Ibid.
16. Marrs, *Rise of the Fourth Reich*, 374.
17. Foster Gamble, "Introduction," Thrive, www.thrivemovement.com/gdaintroduction (accessed February 11, 2012).
18. Ibid.
19. "What Is the Global Domination Agenda?" Thrive, www.thrivemovement.com/what-global-domination-agenda (accessed February 11, 2012).
20. "Mission Statement," The Zeitgeist Movement, www.thezeitgeistmovement.com/mission-statement (accessed February 12, 2012).
21. "Zeitgeist: The Movie Companion Source Guide," The Zeitgeist Movement, www.zeitgeistmovie.com/Zeitgeist,%20The%20Movie-%20Companion%20Guide%20PDF.pdf (accessed February 12, 2012), 94.
22. Harrit, Farrer, Jones, et al., "Active Thermitic Material Discovered in Dust from the 9/11 World Trade Center Catastrophe," 7–31.
23. Zeitgeist Movement, "Zeitgeist: The Movie Companion Source Guide," 142.
24. Ibid., 159.

25. Ibid., 170.

26. "Audit the Federal Reserve," RonPaul.com, www.ronpaul.com/congress/legislation/111th-congress-200910/audit-the-federal-reserve-hr-1207 (accessed February 13, 2012).

27. "Ron Paul Exposes the Federal Reserve and Explains Why It Doesn't Want to Be Audited," RonPaul.com, October 17, 2009, www.ronpaul.com/2009-10-21/ron-paul-exposes-the-federal-reserve-and-explains-why-it-doesnt-want-to-be-audited. Transcript from the radio show "Saturday Night with Dimitri," with host Dimitri Vassilaros, on NewsRadio 1020K.

28. Ibid.

29. Ibid.

30. Ibid.

31. Zeitgeist Movement, "Zeitgeist: The Movie Companion Source Guide," 171.

32. Interview in Zeitgeist: Moving Forward.

33. Ibid.

34. "What are Some of the Detrimental Effects of the Monetary System?" The Venus Project, www.thevenusproject.com/en/the-venus-project/faq (accessed February 17, 2012).

35. Clow, *Awakening the Planetary Mind,* 4.

36. Ibid.

37. "Saturn," National Geographic online, science.nationalgeographic.com/science/space/solar-system/saturn-article (accessed March 26, 2012).

38. Clow, *Awakening the Planetary Mind,* 25.

39. Malkowski, *Ancient Egypt 39,000 BCE,* 196–200.

40. Hancock and Bauval, *The Message of the Sphinx,* 247–67.

41. Ibid., 270.

42. Brophy, *The Origin Map,* 87.

43. Ibid.

44. Ibid., 90.

45. Ibid.

46. Johannes Kepler, cited in Schwaller de Lubicz, *The Temple of Man,* 273–74.

47. Clow, *Awakening the Planetary Mind,* 2.

48. "Poll: 43 Percent Agree with Views of 'Occupy Wall Street,'" CBSNews.com, www.cbsnews.com/8301-503544_162-20125515-503544/poll-43-percent-agree-with-views-of-occupy-wall-street (accessed August 6, 2013).

49. Genesis 11:6, Young's Literal Translation.

50. Genesis 11:6, The Amplified Bible.

51. "The 2012 Statistical Abstract: Income, Expenditures, Poverty, and Wealth," U.S. Census Bureau, www.census.gov/compendia/statab/cats/income_expenditures_poverty_wealth.html (accessed March 3, 2012).

52. Plato, *The Republic of Plato,* 234.

53. Ibid.

54. Ibid., 235.

55. Ibid., 234.

56. Bernall, *Black Athena,* 22, 25.

57. Ibid.

58. Ibid., 71.

59. Ibid., 104.

60. Ibid., 105.

61. Ibid.

62. Ibid.

63. Ibid., 106.

64. Proklos, *In Tim.* LXXVI (trans. Festugiere, 1966–68, vol. 1, p. 111), quoted in Bernall, *Black Athena,* 106.

65. Karl Marx, *Das Kapital,* vol. 1, part 4 (1983), p. 299, quoted in Bernall, *Black Athena,* 106.

66. Carl Sagan, "Who Speaks for Earth," episode 13, *Cosmos.*

67. Malkowski, *The Spiritual Technology of Ancient Egypt,* 302.

68. Ibid., 303.

69. Lipton, *Spontaneous Evolution,* 130–31.

70. Capra, *The Web of Life,* 78.

71. Ibid., 167.

72. Ibid., 204.

73. Margulis and Sagan, *Microcosmos,* 75.

74. Capra, *Web of Life,* 231.

75. Ibid., 270.

76. McKenna and McKenna, *The Invisible Landscape,* 203.

77. Ibid., 90–91.

78. Ibid., 203–4.

79. Ibid., 204.

80. "Ghost in Your Genes," PBS, NOVA, October 16, 2007. For a full transcript,

see www.pbs.org/wgbh/nova/transcripts/3413_genes.html (accessed June 14, 2012).

81. Ibid.

82. Ibid.

83. Heidensohn, *The Book of Money*, 6.

84. Robert F. Kennedy, "Robert F. Kennedy Speeches: Remarks to the Cleveland City Club, April 5, 1968," John F. Kennedy Presidential Library and Museum, www.jfklibrary.org/Research/Research-Aids/Ready-Reference/ RFK-Speeches/Remarks-of-Senator-Robert-F-Kennedy-to-the-Cleveland-City-Club-Cleveland-Ohio-April-5-1968.aspx (accessed April 26, 2012).

CHAPTER 9. A GOLDEN AGE OF IMAGINATION

1. Hoyle and Wickramasinghe, *Evolution from Space*, 24, 129.

2. Schrödinger, *What Is Life?* 138.

3. Heisenberg, *Physics and Philosophy*, 104.

4. Wilber, *Quantum Questions*, 162–64.

5. Plato, *The Republic of Plato*, 230.

6. Ibid., 231.

7. Ibid.

8. Conversation with physicist Thomas Malkowski. March 15, 2012.

9. Luke 6:27–35. New International Version.

10. Plato, *The Republic*, 232.

11. Wolf, *The Dreaming Universe*, 338.

12. Ibid.

13. Ibid., 339–40.

14. Ibid., 338–39.

15. Ibid., 343.

16. Ibid., 346–47.

17. Moody, *The Light Beyond*, 6.

18. Morse, *Closer to the Light*, 118.

19. Moody, *Light Beyond*, 2.

20. Ibid., 38–45.

21. Morse, *Closer to the Light*, 67.

22. Ibid.

23. Ibid., 137.

24. Ibid., 149.

25. Ibid., 169.

26. Libet, *Mind Time*, 221.

27. Morse, *Closer to the Light*, 198.

28. Ibid., 178.

29. Ibid., 179.

30. Jeans, *The Mysterious Universe*, 122.

31. Ibid., 137.

32. Bodine, "The Shabaka Stone," 19.

33. Frankfort, *Ancient Egyptian Religion*, 29.

34. Malkowski, *The Spiritual Technology of Ancient Egypt*, 182.

35. "How Did Life Begin?" PBS, NOVA, interview of Harvard biologist Andrew Knoll by Joe McMaster, July 1, 2004, www.pbs.org/wgbh/nova/evolution/how-did-life-begin.html (accessed August 2, 2011).

36. McTaggart, *The Field*, 93.

37. Ibid., 94.

38. Barbour, *The End of Time*, 70.

39. McKenna and McKenna, *The Invisible Landscape*, 135–66.

POSTSCRIPT: IT'S IN THE DNA

1. Benton, *When Life Nearly Died*, 17.

2. "From the Genome to the Proteome," Human Genome Project, www.ornl.gov/sci/techresources/Human_Genome/project/info.shtml (accessed June 13, 2012).

3. "Ghost in Your Genes," PBS, NOVA, October 16, 2007. For a full transcript, see www.pbs.org/wgbh/nova/transcripts/3413_genes.html (accessed June 14, 2012).

4. "Parents Claim Their Kids Have Psychic Powers," ABC *Good Morning America*, November 21, 2005, abcnews.go.com/GMA/AmericanFamily/story?id=1332961#.T3-3qtmCn10 (accessed April 6, 2012).

5. Ibid.

6. "So-Called Indigo Teen Says She Can Read People," ABC *Good Morning America*, July 24, 2006, abcnews.go.com/GMA/AmericanFamily/story?id=2224795&page=1#.T3_BjdmCn10 (accessed April 6, 2012).

7. "CNN—Anderson Cooper—Indigo Children," YouTube, September

22, 2010, www.youtube.com/watch?v=cxjdaEvyguY (accessed April 7, 2012).

8. Sharon Jayson, "Indigo Kids: Does the Science Fly?" *USA Today,* May 31, 2005, http://usatoday30.usatoday.com/news/religion/2005-05-31-indigo-kids_x.htm (accessed April 7, 2012).

9. Ibid.

BIBLIOGRAPHY

Akkermans, Peter M. M. G., and Marie Le Miere. "The 1988 Excavations at Tell Sabi Abyad, a Later Neolithic Village in Northern Syria." *American Journal of Archaeology* 96 (1992): 1–22.

Allan, D. S., and J. B. Delair. *Cataclysm!: Compelling Evidence of a Cosmic Catastrophe in 9500 B.C.* Rochester Vt.: Bear & Co., 1997.

Aschenbach, B., R. Egger, and J. Trumper. "Discovery of Explosion Fragments outside the Vela Supernova Remnant Shock-wave Boundary." *Nature* 373 (February 16, 1995): 587–89.

Barbour, Julian. *The End of Time: The Next Revolution in Physics.* New York: Oxford University Press, 1999.

Benton, Michael J. *When Life Nearly Died: The Greatest Mass Extinction of All Time.* London: Thames and Hudson, 2003.

Bernall, Martin. *Black Athena: The Afroasiatic Roots of Classical Civilization.* Vol. 1, *The Fabrication of Ancient Greece: 1785–1985.* New Brunswick N.J.: Rutgers University Press, 1987.

Bierlein, J. R. *Parallel Myths.* New York: Ballantine, 1994.

Bodine, Joshua J. "The Shabaka Stone: An Introduction." *Studia Antiqua* 7, no. 1 (Spring 2009): 1–21.

Brophy, Thomas. *The Origin Map: Discovery of a Prehistoric, Megalithic, Astrophysical Map and Sculpture of the Universe.* New York: Writers Club Press, 2002.

Budge, E. A. Wallis. *Egyptian Ideas of the Future Life.* London: Kegan Paul, Trench, and Trübner, 1900.

———. *A History of Egypt: From the End of the Neolithic Period to the Death of Cleopatra VII. B.C. 30.* Vol. 1, Egypt in the Neolithic and Archaic Periods. London: Adamant Media, 2005.

———. *Legends of the Gods: The Egyptian Texts, Edited with Translations.* London: Kegan Paul, Trench, and Trübner, 1912.

Butler, Smedley. *War Is a Racket.* Port Townsend, Wash.: Feral House, 2003.

Capra, Fritjof. *The Web of Life: A New Scientific Understanding of Living Systems.* New York: Anchor, 1997.

Chandler, James M. "Carbon, and Radiocarbon Dating: A Primer." *Mammoth Trumpet* 16, no. 2 (March 2001): 8.

Clark, R. T. Rundle. *Myth and Symbol in Ancient Egypt.* New York: Thames and Hudson, 1991.

Clow, Barbara Hand. *Awakening the Planetary Mind.* Rochester Vt.: Bear & Co., 2011.

Crozier, Michael J., Samuel P. Huntington, and Joji Watanuki. *The Crisis in Democracy: Report on the Governability of Democracies to the Trilateral Commission.* New York: New York University Press, 1975.

Dalton, Rex. "Blast in the Past." *Nature* 447 (May 17, 2007): 256–57.

Davidson, H. R. Ellis. *Gods and Myths of Northern Europe.* Baltimore, Md.: Penguin, 1975.

de Santillana, Giorgio, and Hertha von Dechend. *Hamlet's Mill: An Essay on Myth and the Frame of Time.* Boston: David R. Godine, 1977.

Dunn, Christopher. "Mega Saws of the Pyramid Builders." *Atlantis Rising* 70 (July–August 2008): 32–33, 64–65.

Eliade, Mircea. *Shamanism: Archaic Techniques of Ecstasy.* Princeton, N.J.: Princeton University Press, 1972.

Ellis, Richard. *Imagining Atlantis.* New York: First Vintage Books, 1999.

Firestone, Richard B., and William Topping. "Terrestrial Evidence of a Nuclear Catastrophe in Paleoindian Times." *Mammoth Trumpet* 16, no. 2 (March 2001): 9.

Firestone, Richard, Allen West, and Simon Warwick-Smith. *The Cycle of Cosmic Catastrophes.* Rochester, Vt.: Bear & Co., 2006.

Frankfort, Henri. *Ancient Egyptian Religion.* New York: Harper, 1948.

Gimbutas, Marija. *The Age of the Great Goddess: Ancient Roots of the Emerging Feminine Consciousness. An Interview with Kell Kearns.* Audiotape. Boulder, Colo.: Sounds True Recording, 1992.

———. *The Language of the Goddess.* San Francisco: Harper and Row, 1989.

Giri, Jnanavatar Swami Sri Yukeswar. *The Holy Science*. Los Angeles: Self-Realization Fellowship, 1977.

Gorbachev, Mikhail. *Perestroika: New Thinking for Our Country and the World*. New York: Harper and Row, 1987.

Hamilton, Edith. *Mythology: Timeless Tales of Gods and Heroes*. New York: Meridian, 1989.

Hancock, Graham, and Robert Bauval. *The Message of the Sphinx: A Quest for the Hidden Legacy of Mankind*. New York: Three Rivers Press, 1996.

Hapgood, Charles. *Path of the Pole*. Kempton, Ill.: Adventures Unlimited, 1999.

Harrit, Niels H., Jeffery Farrer, Steven E. Jones, et al. "Active Thermitic Material Discovered in Dust from the 9/11 World Trade Center Catastrophe." *The Open Chemical Physics Journal* 2 (2009): 7–31.

Heidensohn, Klaus. *The Book of Money*. New York: McGraw-Hill, 1979.

Heisenberg, Werner. *Physics and Philosophy: The Revolution in Modern Science*. Amherst, N.Y.: Prometheus Books, 1999.

Herodotus. *The Histories*. New York: Penguin, 1972.

Hibben, Frank C. "Evidence of Early Man in Alaska." *American Antiquity* 9 (1943): 254–59.

———. *The Lost Americans*. New York: Thomas Y. Crowell, 1968.

Hoyle, Sir Fred, and Chandra Wickramasinghe. *Evolution from Space: A Theory of Cosmic Creationism*. New York: Touchstone, 1981.

Jastrow, Morris, Jr. "Sun and Saturn." *Revue D'Assyriologie et d'Archéologie Orientale* (Paris) 7 (1910).

Jeans, Sir James Hopwood. *The Mysterious Universe*. Cambridge, U.K.: Cambridge University Press, 1930.

Kramer, Samuel Noah. *Sumerian Mythology: A Study of Spiritual and Literary Achievement in the Third Millennium B.C.* New York: Harper and Row, 1961.

———. *The Sumerians: Their History, Culture, and Character*. Chicago: University of Chicago Press, 1963.

Lamy, Lucie. *Egyptian Mysteries: New Light on Ancient Knowledge*. New York: Thames and Hudson, 1981.

Lange, Ian M. *Ice Age Mammals of North America*. Missoula, Mont.: Mountain Press, 2002.

LaViolette, Paul. *Earth under Fire*. Rochester, Vt.: Bear & Co., 2005.

Libet, Benjamin. *Mind Time*. Cambridge, Mass.: Harvard University Press, 2004.

Lipton, Bruce. *Spontaneous Evolution*. Carlsbad, Calif.: Hay House, 2009.

MacDougall, Doug. *Frozen Earth: The Once and Future Story of Ice Ages*. Berkeley: University of California Press, 2004.

Maier, John, and Samuel Kramer. *Myths of Enki, the Crafty God*. New York: Oxford University Press, 1989.

Malkowski, Edward F. *Ancient Egypt 39,000 BCE: The History, Technology, and Philosophy of Civilization X*. Rochester, Vt.: Bear & Co., 2010.

———. *The Spiritual Technology of Ancient Egypt*. Rochester, Vt.: Inner Traditions, 2007.

Mallory, J. P. *In Search of the Indo-Europeans*. New York: Thames and Hudson, 1989.

Margulis, Lynn, and Dorian Sagan. *Microcosmos*. New York: Summit, 1986.

Marinatos, Spyridon Nikolaou. "On the Legend of Atlantis." *Scientific Review Crelica Ghronica* (The Cretan Annals) 4 (1950): 195–213. Quoted in Richard Ellis, *Imagining Atlantis*, 232–33.

Marrs, Jim. *The Rise of the Fourth Reich*. New York: Harper, 2008.

Martin, Paul S., and Richard G. Klein. *Quarternary Extinctions: A Prehistoric Revolution*. Tucson, Ariz.: University of Arizona Press, 1989.

McKenna, Terence. *Food of the Gods: The Search for the Original Tree of Knowledge*. New York: Bantam Books, 1993.

McKenna, Terence, and Dennis McKenna. *The Invisible Landscape: Mind, Hallucinations, and the I Ching*. San Francisco: Harper Collins, 1993.

McTaggart, Lynn. *The Field*. New York: HarperCollins, 2002.

Mellaart, James. *Earliest Civilizations of the Near East*. New York: McGraw-Hill, 1965.

Michanowsky, George. *The Once and Future Star: The Mysterious Vela X Supernova and the Origin of Civilizations*. New York: Hawthorn Books, l977.

Moody, Raymond. *The Light Beyond*. New York: Bantam Books, 1988.

Morse, Melvin. *Closer to the Light*. New York: Ivy Books, 1990.

Narby, Jeremy. *The Cosmic Serpent: DNA and the Origins of Knowledge*. New York: Jeremy P. Tarcher/Putnam, 1998.

Parrinder, Geoffrey. *World Religions: From Ancient History to the Present*. New York: Facts on File, 1985.

Plato. *The Republic of Plato*. New York: Oxford University Press, 1973.

Price, George McCready. *The New Geology: A Textbook for Colleges, Normal Schools, and Training Schools; and for the General Reader*. Mountain View, Calif.: Pacific Press, 1923.

Reichel-Dolmatoff, Gerardo. "Brain and Mind in Desana Shamanism." *Journal of Latin American Lore* 7, no. 1 (1981): 81–87.

Reymond, E. A. E. *Mythical Origin of the Egyptian Temple*. Manchester, U.K.: Manchester University Press, 1969. Quoted in Hancock and Bauval, *The Message of the Sphinx*.

Roux, Georges. *Ancient Iraq*. New York: Penguin Books, 1980.

Sagan, Carl. "Who Speaks for Earth," episode 13, *Cosmos*.

Sandars, N. K., ed. *The Epic of Gilgamesh*. Harmondsworth, U.K.: Penguin Books, 1975.

Schoch, Robert. "The Mystery of Göbekli Tepe and Its Message to Us." *New Dawn Magazine,* September–October 2010, 53–60.

Schrödinger, Erwin. *What Is Life? With Mind and Matter and Autobiographical Sketches*. Cambridge, U.K.: Cambridge University Press, 2004.

Schwaller de Lubicz, René A. *Sacred Science: The King of Pharaonic Theocracy*. Rochester, Vt.: Inner Traditions, 1982.

———. *Symbol and the Symbolic: Ancient Egypt, Science, and the Evolution of Consciousness*. New York: Inner Traditions, 1981.

———. *The Temple of Man*. Rochester, Vt.: Inner Traditions, 1998.

Sellers, Jane B. *The Death of Gods in Ancient Egypt*. New York: Penguin, 1992.

Shoup, Laurence H., and William Minter. *Imperial Brain Trust*. New York: Monthly Review Press, 1977.

Stewart, John Massey. "Frozen Mammoths from Siberia Bring the Ice Ages to Vivid Life." *Smithsonian* 8 (1977): 60–69.

Strom, Richard, Helen M. Johnson, Frank Verbunt, et al. "A Radio-emitting X-ray 'Bullet' Ejected by the Vela Supernova." *Nature* 373 (February 16, 1995): 590–92.

Sutton, Anthony C., and Patrick M. Wood. *Trilaterals over Washington*. Scottsdale, Ariz.: August Corporation, 1978.

Talbott, David. "The Lightning-Scarred Planet Mars." *Symbols of an Alien Sky DVD Series*. Portland, Ore.: Mikamar, n.d.

———. *The Saturn Myth*. New York: Doubleday, 1980.

Thompson, R. Campbell. *The Reports of the Magicians and Astrologers of Nineveh and Babylon in the British Museum.* Vol. 2, *Luzac's Semitic Text and Translation.* London: Luzac, 1900.

Tiffany, John. "Was Ice Age America Victimized by a Massive Supernova?" *Barnes Review,* September–October 2006, 36.

Time, "The China Bubble: We're Counting on China's Growth to Save the World. Unless Its Economy Blows Up First," October 31, 2011.

Velikovsky, Immanuel. *Earth in Upheaval.* New York: Doubleday, 1955.

Wallbank, Walter, and Alastair M. Taylor. *Civilization: Past and Present.* Vol. 1. Chicago: Scott, Forsman, 1949.

Warren, Mervyn A., and Gardner C. Taylor. *King Came Preaching: The Pulpit Power of Dr. Martin Luther King Jr.* Downers Grove, Ill.: InterVarsity Press, 2008.

Whitehead, Neil L. "Divine Hunger: The Cannibal War-Machine." Presentation at the Sacred Empowerment conference, University of Leeds, June 2011.

Wilber, Ken. *Quantum Questions: Mystical Writings of the World's Greatest Physicists.* Boston: Shambhala, 2001.

Wilson, Karen L. "Treasures from the Royal Tombs of Ur." *The Oriental Institute News and Notes, Oriental Institute of the University of Chicago* 167 (Fall 2000): 1–5.

Wolf, Fred Alan. *The Dreaming Universe: A Mind-Expanding Journey into the Realm Where Psyche and Physics Meet.* New York: Simon and Schuster, 1994.

Wolkstein, Diane, and Samuel Kramer. *Inanna—Queen of Heaven and Earth: Her Stories and Hymns from Sumer.* New York: Harper and Row, 1983.

INDEX

BOOKS OF RELATED INTEREST

Ancient Egypt 39,000 BCE
The History, Technology, and Philosophy of Civilization X
by Edward F. Malkowski

Before the Pharaohs
Egypt's Mysterious Prehistory
by Edward F. Malkowski

The Spiritual Technology of Ancient Egypt
Sacred Science and the Mystery of Consciousness
by Edward F. Malkowski

Awakening the Planetary Mind
Beyond the Trauma of the Past to a New Era of Creativity
by Barbara Hand Clow

Time of the Quickening
Prophecies for the Coming Utopian Age
by Susan B. Martinez, Ph.D.

The Purposeful Universe
How Quantum Theory and Mayan Cosmology Explain
the Origin and Evolution of Life
by Carl Johan Calleman, Ph.D.

Atlantis beneath the Ice
The Fate of the Lost Continent
by Rand Flem-Ath and Rose Flem-Ath

Gobekli Tepe: Genesis of the Gods
The Temple of the Watchers and the Discovery of Eden
by Andrew Collins

INNER TRADITIONS • BEAR & COMPANY
P.O. Box 388
Rochester, VT 05767
1-800-246-8648
www.InnerTraditions.com

Or contact your local bookseller